Pass the 63™

A Training Guide for the NASAA Series 63 Exam

A comprehensive study guide for passing the
NASAA Series 63 "Uniform Securities Agent State Law Exam"

6th Edition

by

Robert Walker

FIRST BOOKS®
PORTLAND • OREGON
FIRSTBOOKS.COM

www.firstbooks.com

ISBN-13: 978-1-61007-044-7
ISBN-10: 1-61007-044-5

Publisher: First Books®

Printed in the U.S.A.
All paper is acid free and meets all ANSI standards for archival quality paper.

First Books is a signer of the Treatise on Responsible Paper Use, guided by the Green Press Initiative. Our printers have received certification through one or all of the following sustainable forest management organizations: the Forest Stewardship Council (FSC), the Sustainable Forestry Initiative (SFI) and the Program for the Endorsement of Forest Certification (PEFC). Certification through these organizations ensures that our company and our printers maintain a high standard of environmental responsibility by sourcing paper from sustainable forests and by providing long-term protection for the wildlife, plants and water quality within these forests and beyond.

Contents at a Glance

Detailed Table of Contents

The Big Picture

Most people studying for the Series 63 exam have no plans to harm investors. However, for a small and smarmy minority, harming investors is the name of the game. How do they do it? Usually, they gain referrals from friends, ministers, co-workers, book club members, etc. If Pastor Paulson introduces the nice, young man in the navy blue suit attending this Sunday's coffee hour, chances are the congregation will let the salesman into their homes when he starts following up on Monday morning. What happens next is often a long, drawn-out ordeal in which people who can least afford to lose money end up watching their life savings evaporate. Virtually every state has sickening examples of senior citizens who turn over their savings to some scam artist, who tells them the check is going into a stock, bond, or mutual fund when, in fact, the money goes straight into one of the swindler's many bank accounts.

The state regulators have one mission—to provide necessary protection to investors. Notice how they do not have a second mission of making sure that agents, investment advisers, and broker-dealers are protected—you are not protected under your state's securities law as an agent, broker-dealer, adviser, or adviser representative. Only the INVESTOR is protected. You simply mind your manners, file your paperwork, pay your fees on time, and maybe—just maybe—you'll be *allowed* to sell securities or provide investment advice within a particular state.

Before your state <u>allows</u> you to sell securities or provide investment advice, they want you to prove that you have some knowledge of the industry by passing certain exams. After passing your exams, you will submit a Form U4 or a Form ADV, on which you will disclose your residential and employment history and any disciplinary or criminal problems in your past. If you were convicted of counterfeiting or possession of stolen goods four years ago, your chance of getting licensed as a securities agent is equal to the chance of the Chicago Cubs facing the Chicago White Sox in the World Series this year—could happen, but I wouldn't bet on it.

Speaking of Chicago, the office of the Illinois Securities Administrator is located at 69 West Washington Street, about a 20-minute El ride from my office. I sometimes attend the public hearings held by the Illinois Securities Department when they're trying to officially determine that someone's license should be denied, suspended, or revoked after mistreating investors or filing false documents with the State. The hearings are held at a conference table in the Securities Administrator's office. The State hires an independent hearing officer, who is an attorney specializing in this area of the law. He doesn't wear a black robe or a powdered wig, and no one cries "Hear ye, hear ye" when he enters the room. Remember—it's not a court case. It's an Administrative hearing. The Securities Administrator sends one of their attorneys to the hearing, and the "respondent" to the allegations usually comes in with an attorney as well. The hearing officer listens to the State's arguments and also the arguments of the respondent's attorneys. He examines the evidence presented by both sides, listens to the testimony of witnesses on both sides of the issue, and then recommends appropriate enforcement action to the state.

A few years ago, I attended a hearing held after a 50-year-old woman cut a large check to the wrong person. The Securities Administrator's office was represented by one of their enforcement attorneys. The investor who cut the large check was there to give her testimony. The hearing officer was there. I was there. Regrettably, the only person who wasn't there was the guest of honor, the respondent.

Not a problem. The hearing officer determined that proper notice had been sent to the respondent, and that the hearing would go forward without him. So, the enforcement attorney for the State of Illinois Securities Department presented his case, complete with exhibits that included a copy of the check and a copy of the promissory note that was sold to the investor. The investor told the hearing officer her sad story, and after about 10 minutes, the hearing was over.

We're going to look at the official version momentarily, but since attorneys write in the same hard-to-read legalese used on the Series 63 exam, I'll give a brief summary first. This is what happened, as I understand it. The investor was referred by a friend to a man who was apparently quite the real estate wheeler-dealer. The guy said he was in the business of buying and rehabbing properties and talked the investor into cutting a check for $50,000 in order to finance construction of a house. He "secured" the investment of $50,000 with a "promissory note" that promised to pay interest monthly at an annual rate of 20%. Unfortunately, the investor never received the stated return *on* her money, and then couldn't seem to get a return *of* her money.

Not to worry. Even though she hadn't received any actual money yet, the guy told her she was listed as the owner on the house that was rehabbed with her $50,000. So, not surprisingly, she asked several times to see it. Unfortunately, the respondent repeatedly cancelled appointments and never actually showed her that an actual house was ever actually built with the money he actually took from her. In short, she cut this guy a check for $50,000, and that was the last she would ever see of that money.

The reason that the Securities Administrator had any authority over the real estate deal is that the respondent secured the loan with a "promissory note," which meets the definition of a *security*. And, with the word "promissory" right there in the name, the person who borrows money by issuing a "promissory note" *promises* to repay you. If he takes your money based on this promise, says nothing about a chance of default or risk, and then does *not* pay you, you have been defrauded. Securities fraud involves the wrongful taking of money or property through false pretenses when selling securities or providing investment advice. The Securities Administrator is primarily out to protect investors from fraudulent, deceptive offers and sales of securities, and this one provides a textbook example of exactly that.

Okay, so you have the background, but in order to prepare for the Series 63 you'll have to be able to translate legalese back to English. So, let's take a look at the actual notice of hearing to help you sharpen your skills. Don't be scared by the legalese. This book is written in Plain English, as you were told by your friend or your co-worker. But, we also have to show you the original legalistic version of various laws and securities regulations. Rest assured—we will always translate the legalese back into a language you are more familiar with—English.

STATE OF ILLINOIS
SECRETARY OF STATE
SECURITIES DEPARTMENT

)	
IN THE MATTER OF: MORTGAGE SPECIALISTS INC.>RILEY,)	Case No.
MICHAEL J., PRESIDENT)	0700376
)	

NOTICE OF HEARING

TO RESPONDENT: Michael J. Riley
3-a General Sheridan Ct.
Apple River, Illinois 61001

The Mortgage Specialists
1550 Spring Road #310
Oak Brook, IL 60523

Trust One Mortgage f/k/a The Mortgage Specialists
430 W. Erie St. Suite # 205
Chicago, Illinois 60610

You are hereby notified that pursuant to Section 11.F of the Illinois Securities Law of 1953 [815 ILCS 5] (the "Act") and 14 Ill. Adm. Code 130, Subpart K, a public hearing will be held at 69 West Washington Street, Suite 1220, Chicago, Illinois 60602, on the 25th day of January, 2008, at the hour of 10:00 a.m., or as soon as possible thereafter, before James L. Kopecky, Esq., or such other duly designated Hearing Officer of the Secretary of State.

Said hearing will be held to determine whether an Order shall be entered which would prohibit Michael J. Riley ("Respondent") from engaging in the business of selling or offering for sale securities in the State of Illinois, and/or granting such other relief as may be authorized under the Act including but not limited to the imposition of a monetary fine in the maximum amount pursuant to Section 11.E of the Act, payable within ten (10) business days of the entry of the Order.

The grounds for such proposed action are as follows:

1. That Michael J. Riley, ("Respondent") is an individual whose last known address is 3-a General Sheridan Ct., Apple River, Illinois 61001.

2. That The Mortgage Specialists ("Mortgage Specialists"), is a

business entity with the last known address of 1550 Spring Road, #310, Oak Brook, Illinois 60523.

3. That Trust One Mortgage f/k/a The Mortgage Specialists ("Trust One") is a business entity with the last known address of 430 W. Erie St., Suite #205, Chicago, Illinois 60610.

4. That in or around March 2004, Respondent met with Illinois Investor at the office of The Mortgage Specialists. At the meeting Respondent represented to Illinois Investor that he was the President of The Mortgage Specialists. Respondent also told Illinois Investor that he was in the business of buying and rehabilitating homes for people in financial distress, and that Illinois Investor could make a profit by providing Respondent with a loan of $50,000 to purchase a property located in Diamond Lake, Illinois. The loan was to be secured by a promissory note.

5. That on or around March 30, 2004, Respondent traveled to Illinois Investor's home and collected a $50,000 check from Illinois Investor. Respondent told Illinois Investor to make the check payable to Roscara Capital, Inc. ("Roscara"), stating that he was also the president of Roscara.

6. That in exchange of the $50,000 check, Respondent secured the loan with a promissory note, which was signed by Respondent and Illinois Investor on March 30, 2004,

7. That the promissory note states that Respondent promised to pay the principal of the loan plus interest to Illinois Investor by the "maturity date" of August 1, 2004. Respondent was to pay interest to Illinois Investor on a monthly basis at a yearly rate of 20% beginning April 1, 2004. Respondent was to make those payments every month until he had paid all of the principal and interest and any other charges that he owed under the note. The monthly payments were to be applied to interest before principal, and if he still owed amounts after the "maturity date", he would make monthly payments to Illinois Investor in the amount of $833.00.

Failure to Register

8. That the activities set forth in paragraphs 4 through 6 above constitute the offer and sale of a note, and therefore a security as those terms are defined at Sec. 2.1, 2.5, and 2.5a of the Illinois Securities Law of 1953 (815 ILCS 5) (the "Act").

9. That Section 5 of the Act states, inter alia, that all securities except those set forth under Section 2a of this Act,

or those exempt under Section 3 of this Act, or those offered or sold in transactions exempt under Section 4 of this Act, or face amount certificate contracts required to be registered under Section 6 of this Act, shall be registered as herein-after in this section provided, prior to their offer or sale in this State.

10. That Respondent failed to file with the Secretary of State an application for registration of the security described above as required by the Act and that as a result the security was not registered pursuant to Section 5 of the Act prior to its offer and sale in the State of Illinois.

11. That Section 12.A of the Act provides it shall be a violation of the provisions of this Act for any person to offer or sell any security except in accordance with the provisions of this Act.

12. That Section 12.D of the Act provides, *inter alia,* that it shall be a violation of the provisions of this Act for any person to fail to file with the Secretary of State any application, report or document required to be filed under the provisions of this Act or any rule or regulation made by the Secretary of State pursuant to this Act or to fail to comply with the terms of any order of the Secretary of State issued pursuant to Section 11 hereof.

<u>Fraud or Deceit/Misrepresentations or Omissions</u>

13. That Illinois Investor has not received the principal Respondent promised to pay on the note, nor has Illinois Investor received any of the promised interest payments Respondent was to begin paying on April 1, 2004, nor was she advised of any risk to repayment of principal or payment of interest. In addition, Respondent has persistently failed and refused to show Illinois Investor the property located in Diamond Lake, Illinois, despite numerous requests made by Illinois Investor to see it.

14. That Section 12.F of the Act provides that it shall be a violation of the provisions of this Act for any person to engage in any transaction, practice or course of business in connection with the sale or purchase of securities which works or tends to work a fraud or deceit upon the purchaser or seller thereof.

15. That Section 12.G of the Act provides that it shall be a violation of the provisions of this Act for any person to obtain money or property through the sale of securities by means of any untrue statement of a material fact or any omission to

state a material fact necessary in order to make the statements made, in the light of the circumstances under which they were made, not misleading.

16. That by virtue of the foregoing, Respondent has violated Sections 12.A, D, F, and G of the Act.

17. That Section 11.E(2) of the Act provides, *inter alia,* if the Secretary of State shall find that any person has violated sub-section A, D, F, or G of Section 12 of this Act, the Secretary of State may by written order permanently prohibit or suspend the person from offering or selling any securities, any mineral investment contract, or any mineral deferred delivery contract in this state, provided that any person who is the subject of an order of permanent prohibition may petition the Secretary of State for a hearing to present evidence of rehabilitation or change in circumstances justifying the amendment or termination of the order or permanent prohibition.

18. That by virtue of the foregoing violations of sub-sections 12.A, D, F, and G, Respondent is subject to an order of permanent prohibition from offering or selling any securities in the this state pursuant to Section 11.F(2) of the Act.

19. That Section 11.E(4) of the Act provides, inter alia, that in addition to any other sanction or remedy contained in this subsection E, the Secretary of State, after finding that any provision of this Act has been violated, may impose a fine as provided by rule, regulation or order not to exceed $10,000, for each violation of this Act, may issue an order of public censure against the violator, and may charge as costs of investigation all reasonable expenses, including attorney's fees and witness fees.

20. That by virtue of the foregoing, Respondent is subject to a fine, censure and costs of investigation pursuant to Section 11.E(4) of the Act.

You are further notified that you are required pursuant to Section 130.1104 of the Rules and Regulations (14 Ill. Adm. Code 130) (the "Rules"), to file an answer to the allegations outlined above within thirty (30) days of the receipt of this notice. A failure to file an answer within the prescribed time shall be construed as an admission of the allegations contained in the Notice of Hearing.

Furthermore, you may be represented by legal counsel; may present evidence; may crossexamine witnesses and otherwise participate. A failure to so appear shall constitute default, unless any Respondent has upon due notice moved for and obtained a continuance.

A copy of the Rules, promulgated under the Act and pertaining to Hearings held by the Office of the Secretary of State, Securities Department, is included with this Notice.

Delivery of notice to the designated representative of any Respondent constitutes service upon such Respondent.

Dated: This 7th day of December 2007.

JESSE WHITE
Secretary of State
State of Illinois

So, now what is this investor supposed to do about her $50,000? Unfortunately, not much. She can use the findings of the Securities Administrator to sue the guy, but if he's the sort who won't show up at his own administrative hearing, he's not likely to show up in civil court, and he's not likely to pay the default judgment that the court might or might not order him to pay.

How come the guy isn't in jail? First, the securities Administrator is not a criminal prosecutor—the office simply has the power to require financial services professionals and securities offerings to be registered with the state. If the activities are criminal in nature, the securities Administrator would have to refer the case to a criminal prosecutor and see if the attorney general's or district attorney's office wants to sweat somebody over $50,000. Turns out, it wasn't enough money to get the criminal prosecutor's attention in this instance. If that sounds shocking, remember that this is Chicago we're talking about—the criminal prosecutors of Cook County are already busy enough prosecuting violent crime without devoting a lot of resources to a case like this. Then again, I frequently see the District Attorney in Montgomery, Alabama—a town maybe 1/20th the size of Chicago—going after scam artists like the husband and wife who recently swindled investors by issuing worthless promissory notes totaling just $45,000. The DA in Montgomery was going after them on multiple counts of securities fraud, all of which are felonies,,so the guy who skipped his own hearing in Illinois got lucky, but if you plan on committing criminal violations of state securities law, you'd better watch where you do it. Sometimes you get lucky; sometimes you get a pair of prison scrubs and three squares a day.

If the state securities regulators catch anybody misleading people when offering/selling securities, they can take away their license. And, if you get in trouble with the Tennessee regulators, you're out of luck with the other states, too. If you got kicked out of Tennessee and tried to set up shop in Michigan, Michigan would use the revocation of your Tennessee license as a reason to deny you a Michigan license.

But how would the state be able to come down on somebody for offering and selling securities fraudulently unless they, first, defined exactly what they mean by the following terms:

- Offer
- Sale
- Security
- Fraud

Since those definitions are crucial to securities regulations, your Series 63 exam will require you to define such terms yourself. And, as frustrating as the process can be, it is not an exercise in futility. At another hearing I attended recently—one in which the respondent actually showed up—the attorney representing the guy in hot water continued to argue that the investment that his client had offered and sold did not even meet the definition of a "security," and, therefore his client did not, in fact, commit securities fraud and did not, in fact, have to register the investment in the first place. He actually had no luck whatsoever in convincing the hearing officer of this line of reasoning, but what are you going to do? A client pays you to provide some sort of defense; you work with whatever you have.

So, when the regulators try to come down on someone for offering and/or selling securities fraudulently, they have to carefully define all their terms. Did it really meet the definition of an "offer" or a "sale"? Was it a "security?" If not, the respondent and the investment are outside the scope of the securities Administrator's authority.

Helping your investors increase their wealth can be a lot of fun. Reading the rules surrounding the investment world—not as much. Similarly, playing or watching baseball can be exciting. Reading the rules and definitions—not so much. Most readers are probably familiar with the game of baseball and many have played it either recreationally or competitively. At the very least, most readers are confident that they know what a "strike" is. Let's see if your definition matches up with the official definition in the Major League Baseball rulebook:

```
A STRIKE is a legal pitch when so called by the umpire, which--

(a) Is struck at by the batter and is missed;

(b) Is not struck at, if any part of the ball passes through any
part of the strike zone;

(c) Is fouled by the batter when he has less than two strikes;

(d) Is bunted foul;

(e) Touches the batter as he strikes at it;

(f) Touches the batter in flight in the strike zone; or

(g) Becomes a foul tip.
```

In order to learn the baseball rulebook, you would have to learn the mind-numbing definitions of terms such as "strike," "strike zone," "batter's box," etc. In order to pass the Series 63, you'll have to learn the mind-numbing definitions of terms such as "offer," "sale," and "security." Definitions are hugely important to securities regulation and to the Series 63 exam. The most basic definition in securities law is the definition of "securities fraud," which the Uniform Securities Act defines like so:

```
It is unlawful for any person, in connection with the offer, sale,
or purchase of any security, directly or indirectly, to employ any
device scheme or artifice to defraud. To make any untrue statement
```

> of material fact or to omit to state a material fact necessary in order to make the statements made not misleading. To engage in any act, practice, or course of business which operates or would operate as a fraud or deceit upon any person.

Notice how the definition of "fraud" uses the phrase "any person" in connection with the offer, sale, or purchase of "any security." We'll see later that many securities don't have to be registered because of what they are or the way they're being sold. But regardless of whether the thing had to be registered, if the investment of money is a "security," it is subject to at least the anti-fraud statutes of the Uniform Securities Act.

So the "offer" is the attempt to sell. The sale happens when a security is disposed of or transferred to another party in exchange for value—usually money.

But, what is a security? An "investment contract" is an example of a security, and the US Supreme Court defined an "investment contract" through the Howey Decision. The Howey Decision said that an "investment contract"—which is a security—is "an investment of money in a common enterprise whereby the investor's fortunes are entwined with other investors and/or the promoter, and the investor hopes to benefit solely through the efforts of others."

Let's say an Iowa farmer needs to raise $500,000 to expand his soy bean and hog farming operation. He prints up 20 official-looking certificates on a color laser printer. Each piece of paper is offered for $25,000 and gives the investor a 2% ownership stake in the farming operation. That's an investment of money in a common enterprise whereby each investor's fortunes are bound together with other investors and the promoter, and whereby the investor hopes to benefit solely through the efforts of others—the farmer. The investors aren't getting up at 5 o'clock on a cold, February morning in Iowa to feed the friggin' livestock, right? They're just investors, and what they bought was an "investment contract," which is one example of a "security" as listed in the Uniform Securities Act and the federal Securities Act of 1933. So, if the farmer gives them all offering documents with inflated profits or forgets to mention the tractors he's been hiding in a neighbor's corn crib in case the repo man shows up, he has probably committed securities fraud. And, before he even *offers* these investment contracts, he needs to get them registered with the state, who will want to see the advertising, the prospectus, the underwriter agreements, etc.

But, not every investment of money meets the definition of a "security." And, if it's not a security, it's not covered by the Uniform *Securities* Act. The following investments are outside the scope of the Uniform Securities Act because they are *not* securities:
- Fixed annuities
- Whole life, term life, universal life insurance
- Commodities futures contracts

If those aren't *securities*, who regulates them to make sure investors don't get burned? Luckily, we already have insurance regulators for the insurance products and commodities regulators for the commodities futures. The securities regulators only regulate *securities*.

Some of this material might sound a bit fancy when you first read it, but it really all boils down to a simple concept. Regulators *hate* deception in the securities industry. Making you study for some exam called the Series 63 is their way of impressing upon you the importance of ethical sales practices before turning you loose with a license, a cell phone, and God knows what kind of intentions.

Let's get into some heavy details now, but no matter how difficult things get, just remember that it all really boils down to providing necessary protection to investors. Ready?

Let's get started, anyway.

CHAPTER 1

Administrative Provisions

(6 Questions)

THE ADMINISTRATOR

The Uniform Securities Act calls the official in charge of securities regulation the [**Administrator**] and puts the term in brackets, encouraging each state to insert the appropriate title. Often the Secretary of State is the Administrator, with a specific department enforcing the state's securities act. For example, in Illinois I would apply for a driver's license with the same office with which I would file Form ADV for my advisory firm. Is that office actually called "The Administrator?" No. But that office is an *administrative* authority with the power to grant, deny, suspend, or revoke licenses in order to protect residents of the state. We don't want dangerous, unlicensed drivers on the road making things unsafe for everyone else. Similarly, we don't want dangerous, unlicensed financial services professionals out there taking money from unsuspecting investors. So, in general, people have to get licensed before driving a car or working as a nurse, a dental hygienist, or an investment adviser representative. Whatever that office is actually called in a particular state, the Uniform Securities Act calls it "the Administrator." They are an administrative authority empowered by the state legislature to enforce the securities law of the state in order to provide necessary protection to securities investors.

ADMINISTRATIVE POWERS

Under the Uniform Securities Act, in order to "provide necessary protection to investors," the Administrator can:
- Issue rules and orders
- Issue subpoenas to obtain evidence and testimony
- Issue subpoenas at the request of other regulators
- Cooperate with other regulators
- Apply to a court of law to issue a court order to compel persons to comply with subpoenas
- Administer oaths, take testimony
- Investigate both in and outside the state
- Publish results of investigations, actions

An Administrative **rule** would include the requirement to file Form ADV with the state if you're an investment adviser. An **order** is issued if somebody breaks that *rule* by not bothering to register but going ahead with the investment advisory business, anyway. If somebody is violating the securities laws of the state, the Administrator can issue an order to suspend or revoke their license to sell securities or provide investment advice. Or, if the person is not currently registered/licensed, the Administrator can fire a formal warning shot, called a **cease and desist** order. Maybe the Administrator finds out that a local farmer is about to issue certificates that give 2% ownership stakes in his farm to investors. Wait—stop! Those securities must be registered before they are even *offered* (let alone sold) to investors. So, maybe the Administrator issues a "cease and desist" order, telling the farmer to cut it out until/unless the securities are registered and the folks offering/selling them are properly registered or properly excused from being registered.

How did the Administrator find out about it? Investors who lose a bunch of money tend to find out which office of the state they can talk to. State securities Administrators provide handy investor complaint forms, and they have investigators on staff who talk to investors and gather evidence.

What if a resident of, say, Louisiana is swindled by an agent with an office in, say, Nevada? No problem. The Louisiana Securities Administrator can investigate both in and outside his state in order to provide necessary protection to his investors. You mess with just one Louisiana investor, and the State of Louisiana has the authority to make life really difficult for you. Now, maybe you're thinking, "Big deal, so they'll lose their license in Louisiana—they can still sell in the other 49 states."

Au contraire! If you get your license suspended or revoked by one state, all other states can use that as a reason to suspend or revoke your license in their states. And, often, the states find out about an agent's or broker-dealer's activities when **FINRA** informs them of a disciplinary action they recently took.

A **subpoena** is a demand for information. If the Administrator issues a subpoena, and the affected party fails to respond or cooperate, that is known as **contumacy.** Which is bad. The Administrator would then have to apply to a court—or get the Attorney General's office to do it—and seek an injunction/restraining order from the court. If the affected party blows off a court order, he/they could be held in **contempt of court,** and that can lead to fines and even jail time. So, if some fast-talking entrepreneur is offering securities in one of his many ventures without bothering to register them, the Administrator might issue a cease & desist. If he fails to comply, the Administrator can seek an injunction/restraining order from the court.

What if the Administrator requires documents or testimony that somebody refuses to provide based on a criminal investigation that may be pending? In other words, the investment adviser says they can't testify at the Administrative hearing because the state is actually seeking criminal charges over what appears to be outright theft of client cash and securities? That's going to be a problem for the investment adviser. See, if the Administrator subpoenas records or demands your testimony, it's a violation of the act if you refuse to cooperate. As the Uniform Securities Act states:

> No person is excused from attending and testifying or from producing
> any document or record before the [Administrator], or in obedience
> to the subpoena of the [Administrator] or any officer designated by
> him, or in any proceeding instituted by the [Administrator], on the
> ground that the testimony or evidence (documentary or otherwise)
> required of him may tend to incriminate him or subject him to

a penalty or forfeiture; but no individual may be prosecuted or subjected to any penalty or forfeiture for or on account of any transaction, matter, or thing concerning which he is compelled, after claiming his privilege against self-incrimination, to testify or produce evidence (documentary or otherwise), except that the individual testifying is not exempt from prosecution and punishment for perjury or contempt committed in testifying.

So, you can plead the 5th, and the state will then grant you immunity from prosecution in exchange for your cooperation at the hearing. If, on the other hand, you don't talk to the Administrator, that's a violation of securities law that will cause your license to be revoked. So, if you're in the securities industry, you really, really ought to consider honoring every Administrative subpoena that crosses your desk.

In the bullet list above we saw that the Administrator of one state can issue a subpoena at the request of the Administrator of another state. The test might even go so far as to point out that this can happen, even if the violation leading to the subpoena did not happen in the Administrator's state, as long as it *would have been* a violation of that Administrator's state's securities law/regulations.

With so much power at their disposal, it's easier to talk about what the Administrator can't do. The Administrator cannot:

- Issue Judicial Injunctions
- Sentence people to prison or impose criminal penalties
- Make arrests

Why not? Because the Administrator is not a court of law. They can petition a court to issue a judicial injunction or have somebody fined and thrown in jail. But they have to ask first and convince the court to do what they're seeking. In other words, while an unruly agent can definitely have a court **injunction/restraining order** slapped on him or have himself fined and thrown in jail, it's not the Administrator who just snaps his fingers and makes it happen. It takes a court ruling, not just an **Administrative order**. Unfortunately, if the court/judge does issue an injunction, the Administrator can then use that as a reason to take away or deny the person's license, or prevent him from ever getting one.

ADMINISTRATIVE ORDERS

When the Administrator finds out that an agent or adviser is taking advantage of investors, he can issue an order against the person causing trouble. But, usually, he gives the person a heads-up and shows the reasons for the state's sudden hostility.

Punitive Orders

If it's an order to **deny, suspend,** or **revoke** a license, the Administrator will provide the affected parties with:

- Prior notice
- Opportunity for a hearing
- Written findings of fact, conclusions of law

They're usually nice enough to do that even before issuing a cease and desist order, but they don't have to be. It depends, of course, on what's going on. There are plenty of emergency cease and desist orders issued because what's happening or what's about to happen is so out of control that they need to take action right now. But your exam may ask you to say that before issuing a "stop" order (deny, suspend, revoke), the Administrator will provide the three bullet points above.

After receiving the notice of hearing from the Administrator, the **respondent** usually has to file an answer in writing by a certain deadline. If there is to be a hearing, it is open to the public, and the affected party can be represented by an attorney and can present evidence and witnesses in his favor. But this is not a trial. This is an Administrative hearing to determine if somebody's license should be suspended, revoked, denied, etc. The standard of proof is just "a preponderance of the evidence"—none of that fancy "beyond a reasonable doubt" stuff here. The Administrator's office sends one of their attorneys to present their findings to the hearing officer, and the respondent's attorney—if he can afford one—puts on a defense. The hearing officer is like an arbitrator, a disinterested third party who listens to the testimony, examines the evidence, and can recommend that the person have his license denied, suspended, or revoked. Let's hope that this whole experience I'm describing is only something you read about for your exam—you do not want to be referred to as the respondent in any documents or proceedings with the Administrator of your state, or any other state.

So, if the respondent has his hearing and doesn't like the decision, he can file an appeal of the Administrator's order in a court of law if he does so within 60 days. The Administrator's order to suspend or revoke the license is in effect until and unless the court is convinced and compelled to overturn the Administrative order. How often does an Administrative order get overturned by a court of law? Almost never. But, the possibility is there. Still, the courts consider the Administrator's findings and evidence to be conclusive, meaning, the appeal needs to be based on some new evidence, usually. As the Uniform Securities Act states: "The findings of the [Administrator] as to the facts, if supported by competent, material and substantial evidence, are conclusive." But, if there is new evidence, the courts could also ask the Administrator to reconsider the new evidence brought before it by the respondent's attorney, which might lead to the Administrator modifying the order. Maybe a revocation becomes a suspension that way.

The hearing, by the way, is open to the public, unless the Administrator in his discretion decides—and the respondents all agree—to keep it private. I have attended exactly three hearings at the Illinois Securities Department's Chicago office. At the first one, after a couple of hours, the hearing officer did exactly what I just wrote—decided to make it a private hearing. Apparently, the guy who'd ripped off the complaining investors had seen the light and was going to make it all go away with a series of nice cashable checks. I'm not saying the Administrator forced the respondent to do anything—the respondent and his attorney simply decided that maybe things would work out better that way. Once the investors had been made whole, the Administrator pretty much washed their hands of the whole affair, except to keep it all on record should the seller suddenly show up again on their radar screen.

Why would the Administrator want to issue a deny/suspend/revoke order, anyway? First, the order has to be "in the public interest, providing necessary protection to investors," and, then, somebody:
- has filed a false or misleading application
- has willfully violated or willfully failed to comply with any provision of this act

- was convicted within last 10 years of any securities-related misdemeanor or any felony
- is enjoined by any court from engaging in the securities business
- is the subject of an order of the Administrator denying, suspending, or revoking registration as a broker-dealer, agent, or investment adviser
- is the subject of an order entered within the past 5 years by the securities administrator of any other state or by the SEC denying or revoking registration as a broker-dealer, agent, or investment adviser
- is the subject of an order of the SEC suspending or expelling him from a national securities exchange or national securities association registered under the Securities Exchange Act of 1934
- has engaged in dishonest or unethical practices in the securities business
- is insolvent
- isn't qualified because they lack training, experience, and knowledge [Lack of experience isn't enough if the applicant does have training and knowledge]
- has failed reasonably to supervise his agents if he is a broker-dealer or his employees if he is an investment adviser
- has failed to pay the proper filing fee (denial only, and the order is vacated as soon as the fee is paid)

That might look like an intimidating list, but, really, it comes down to a few important concepts. Like, if any other regulator already has a problem with you, the Administrator may have a problem with you. If you're already misleading the regulators on your application, they don't want to see how much you'll try to mislead your investors. If you're a firm that isn't supervising a bunch of rowdy, cold-calling agents, the state can revoke your license. And—not surprisingly—if you're a convicted felon, or convicted of a misdemeanor concerning nonsense such as forgery, counterfeiting, embezzlement, perjury, fraud, etc., it could be a game-over for you. After letting you tell your side of the story, of course. And letting you spend a fortune on attorney fees.

Speaking of attorney fees, please don't be confused—an Administrative hearing over a license is not a trial in either a civil or criminal *court*, but you do generally pay a good attorney to present your case at the hearing and maybe convince the state to cut you some slack. Alternately, if you know your situation to be hopeless, you can be like many folks and just not show up for the hearing, which the state takes as an admission of all their findings of fact. It's called a **default decision** generally, in case the exam goes there. Again, the Administrator doesn't have any authority to hand down criminal convictions, but if you have been charged with or convicted of a felony or a securities-related misdemeanor, that would seem like a really good reason for the Administrator to deny, suspend, or revoke your license to sell securities or provide investment advice, right? In other words, the following line just doesn't work somehow: "So, Paul, I hear your financial planner was just paroled—is he taking on new clients?"

Notice how a felony is a felony, but the misdemeanors that will get you in trouble with the securities regulators have to do with mishandling money, forging signatures, lying under oath, counterfeiting, etc. See how those particular misdemeanors directly relate to the issue of whether you should be allowed to get investors' bank routing numbers, social security numbers, FEINs, etc.? Heck, I don't want a convicted felon even knowing the ages of my children or the name of my wife, let alone my sensitive financial information. What happens if his commissions dry up?

Is he going to start shaking me down, sending two of his buddies by the office to collect a little juice every Friday afternoon? Of course, I'm from Chicago, so maybe my perception is a little warped, but you get the idea. I'm just saying that extortion would—and should—be one of those misdemeanors that would tend to keep a guy out of the business.

You may be required to know that the Administrator can actually take two specific actions even without being nice enough to first give the respondent notice and an opportunity for a hearing. The "cease & desist" order can be issued without prior notice, because sometimes the thing that somebody is doing or is planning to do is so outrageous that the state has to at least try to stop him in his tracks. Also, the Administrator can "**summarily suspend** a registration pending final determination" of the matter. That means that until the hearing has been held and the decision has been reached, your license is "summarily suspended." Sorry about that. The exam could refer to this action as a **show cause** order. If a broker-dealer has five or six agents churning accounts and entering trades no customer actually ordered, a show cause or summary suspension order would likely be issued. The problem appears so severe that the state in this case is taking the rare step of temporarily shutting down your operations even before a hearing. If the respondent requests a hearing, a hearing must be granted within 15 days in this situation.

Let's see how the Uniform Securities Act explains it:

> Whenever it appears to the [Administrator] that any person has engaged or is about to engage in any act or practice constituting a violation of any provision of this act or any rule or order hereunder, he may in his discretion bring either or both of the following remedies:
>
> (a) issue a cease and desist order, with or without a prior hearing against the person or persons engaged in the prohibited activities, directing them to cease and desist from further illegal activity; or
>
> (b) bring an action in the [insert the name of appropriate court] to enjoin the acts or practices to enforce compliance with this act or any rule or order hereunder. Upon a proper showing a permanent or temporary injunction, restraining order, or writ of mandamus shall be granted and a receiver or conservator may be appointed for the defendant or the defendant's assets. In addition, upon a proper showing by the [Administrator] the court may enter an order of rescission, restitution or disgorgement directed to any person who has engaged in any act constituting a violation of any provision of this act or any rule or order hereunder. The court may not require the [Administrator] to post a bond.

So, in order to put this section to bed, remember that generally, the Administrator will not issue a disciplinary order without first giving the respondent prior notice, an opportunity for a hearing, and written findings of fact/conclusions of law. But, in some cases, the Administrator will issue a summary suspension or an emergency cease & desist order, even before a hearing has been held. And, if the cease & desist order gets blown off, the Administrator can then apply to a judge to issue an injunction/restraining order, see if that gets the dude's attention. The courts could even go so far as to appoint a conservator over the respondent and have his assets liquidated, or they could force the respondent to buy back the securities involved (rescission) or give back the money plus interest (disgorgement, restitution). So, I just said the Administrator can force people to give investors their money back, right?

No—as usual, it takes a court of law for something like that.

Non-punitive Orders

Cease & desist, denial, suspension, and revocation orders are all considered "punitive orders," because they provide a form of "punishment." There are two orders that are non-punitive, as well: **withdrawal** and **cancellation**. If the firm or agent decides they no longer want a license in, say, the State of Tennessee, they can withdraw rather than pay a renewal fee. Fine. Of course, if they think they can withdraw to avoid a suspension/revocation, I've got news for them. The Administrator can actually initiate a suspension or revocation proceeding for up to a year after their departure if he finds out that there was actually a reason they were in such a hurry to leave the state. And, as we said, that strike against them can knock the dominos over across all other states.

But a withdrawal in and of itself has nothing to do with punishment. The applicant or the registrant simply says thanks, but no thanks. As long as they haven't done anything wrong, the Administrator simply accepts the withdrawal. Or, as we'll see during our discussion of federal covered advisers, some years the investment advisory firm might send Form ADV to the SEC and, other years, they might go back to state-level registration. If you go from state-registered to federally registered, you would file a **Form ADV-W** with your state in order to withdraw your registration.

So that's a withdrawal.

A cancellation order happens because the party dies, goes out of business, is declared mentally incompetent, or simply can't be located. Canceled. The person, apparently, no longer needs the license, so it's canceled.

INSPECTIONS, ROUTINE & SPECIAL

So, clearly, if anyone is messing with investors in the state, the securities Administrator can take legal action to protect investors from any further harm. That doesn't mean the Administrator goes around inspecting all the broker-dealers and agents in the state. Routine inspections of broker-dealers are handled by FINRA, and we see a reference to this in the Uniform Securities Act, which states:

> e) All the records referred to in subsection (a) are subject at any time or from time to time to such reasonable periodic, special, or other examinations by representatives of the [Administrator], within or without this state, as the Administrator deems necessary or appropriate in the public interest or for the protection of investors. For the purpose of avoiding unnecessary duplication of examinations, the [Administrator], insofar as he deems it practicable in administering this subsection, may cooperate with the securities Administrators of other states, the Securities and Exchange Commission, and any national securities exchange or

> national securities association registered under the Securities
> Exchange Act of 1934.

What all that legalese means is that the Administrator has the authority to send representatives to any office for a special or periodic inspection, as long as it's deemed to be reasonable and necessary for the protection of investors. However, since FINRA is already all over their member broker-dealers, the routine inspections will be handled by FINRA, who handles such duties for the SEC. On the other hand, there is no self-regulatory organization (SRO) for investment advisers, so the state securities Administrator is in charge of overseeing all investment adviser representatives plus all the state-registered investment advisory firms. Inspections are up to the rulemaking authority of the Administrator, and if the investment adviser has custody of client assets (explored in more detail elsewhere) they will have to pay a CPA firm to do an unannounced annual inspection and then file a report with the Administrator.

CRIMINAL PENALTIES

Your exam may ask what the criminal penalties are for **willful violations** under the Uniform Securities Act. The penalties are three years in prison, a $5,000 fine, or both, per violation. It would have to be real clear that you knew what you were doing was a total scam and you showed reckless disregard for investors. You weren't registered as an agent, and the so-called "stock" you offered and sold was just a fancy thing you printed up on a color laser printer with a nonexistent company's name across it. You basically stole money with the point of a pen rather than the point of a gun.

Try not to do that. As the exam might say, "criminal liability attaches" when the person knew what he was doing—was aware of his actions and not mentally incompetent—and did it anyway. Doesn't mean the guy had to know that what he was doing was against the law—he just had to be aware of what he was doing. For example, he knew that his firm had custody of client assets but refused to indicate that on Form ADV. Did he or the firm actually read the particular rule prohibiting that? Doesn't matter. He knew the truth, and he put down a different answer, anyway. That's a willful violation. It's not as serious as printing up bogus stock certificates or a family of little pretend mutual funds, but it could still lead to criminal prosecution. According to the Uniform Securities Act, there is only one situation where the state would have to prove the person knew he was making a false statement, and that's when filing an allegedly false document/application with the state. Not that too many folks are going to get prison time for fudging on Form U4, but if the criminal case centers on an application or a false document filed with the Administrator, the state would have to first prove the person knew the statement to be false. Notice that this is not required to take away somebody's license for misleading clients, or for a civil court to award monetary damages to the other side. If the buyer was given bogus or false information, the buyer was defrauded, period, and probably entitled to her money back.

Because of the **statute of limitations**, the criminal prosecutors at the district attorney or attorney general's office have to come after a violator within 5 years of the alleged misdeed. Otherwise, the statute of limitations runs out in his favor. Not that he's ever going to work in the securities industry again, but at least he won't be spending any time in prison, which is something.

Normally, you'd think ignorance of the law is no excuse. However, under the Uniform Securities

Act, in the case of a false/misleading document being filed with the Administrator, if the respondent can prove that they did not mean to make a misleading filing, they cannot be imprisoned. They can be fined in this case, but not imprisoned. In a criminal case, the burden of proof is almost always on the prosecutors representing the state, but in this weird situation, the burden of proof would shift to the respondent who's claiming ignorance or invoking some version of the big-oops-theory.

Not that it really matters, but we're talking about the criminal penalties under the Uniform Securities Act only. There are other state and federal laws that somebody can be tried under. I mean, if you break into one of your investing clients' homes and steal $500,000 from the wall safe, I think we can place all issues concerning your securities license at the bottom of your priority list. You're going to prison for breaking and entering, burglary/home invasion, maybe getting a mandatory minimum sentence of 20 years if you were also crazy enough to be carrying a loaded gun, etc. The fact that you'll lose your license as an agent is a foregone conclusion once you get convicted of a felony. The fact that it involved "misappropriation" of large sums of cash means that even if you plead it down to a misdemeanor, it's the type of misdemeanor that regulators use to revoke licenses.

The Uniform Securities Act makes this all pretty clear when it states:

> The Administrator may refer such evidence as is available concerning violations of this act or of any rule or order hereunder to the attorney general or the proper district attorney, who may institute the appropriate criminal proceedings under this act.
>
> Nothing in this act limits the power of the state to punish any person for any conduct which constitutes a crime by statute or at common law.

Visiting the Texas regulatory website recently, I saw that an investment adviser had gotten himself into a bit of hot water for telling an investor in another state to go ahead and wire $55,000 for a new investment opportunity he was putting together. Unfortunately, the investor was unknowingly instructed to wire the money to the guy's personal checking account in order to cover a major overdraft of, coincidentally, just under $55,000.

Oops! That's not just a securities violation. That's a laundry list of federal crimes that could send a so-called "investment adviser" to a federal penitentiary for a long sabbatical. So, remember that the securities Administrator does not prosecute criminal cases or hand down criminal penalties; however, there are criminal penalties under the Uniform Securities Act that the state's district attorneys or attorney general's office could seek if someone is defrauding investors or pulling other such shenanigans. In other words, there tends to be a lot of hair-splitting on the Series 63 exam, so, please, pay close attention to the meaning of the words we're using.

CIVIL LIABILITIES

Almost nothing scares me more than prison, but the **civil liabilities** under the Uniform Securities Act are pretty scary, as well. If I sold you securities for $50,000 in violation of the securities law and rules of the state, you could sue to make me return your $50,000 plus interest, plus court costs/attorneys' fees.

Under the Uniform Securities Act the plaintiff (victim) can sue for and recover:

- Price paid for the security and/or advice
- Plus interest
- Plus court costs/attorneys' fees
- Minus any income received on the security

That last item is a little jarring—but if the agent or the security wasn't registered, or if the investment advice was tainted or incompetent, the plaintiff can still deduct any dividend or interest payment the security provided before the whole thing went sour. And, we're not talking about "pain and suffering" here. Just give the investor her money back, plus interest, basically. And try not to screw up again if you can help it.

If it's discovered that the security sold wasn't registered, or that the agent wasn't registered, or some type of deception took place, the buyer can sue if he initiates action within two years. That's actually "two years from discovery, or three years, whichever comes first." So, if he knew about it longer than two years, or if it happened more than three years ago, it is too late to file a lawsuit. If the investor still holds the security, he will "tender it" or present it to the other side. If he no longer holds the security, he will still receive damages as if he had it in his hands. Notice that the seller of a security or the provider of investment advice can be sued. In the case of investment advice, the client could receive the amount paid for the advice and any loss due to the advice. So, if the test sweats you on that fine detail, notice that the adviser could be forced by a civil court to return the money the client paid for the advice *and* make him whole on any securities purchased or sold pursuant to that advice. So, if the investment adviser took money from clients and deceptively funneled it to one of his other businesses, he could be sued and made to return the price paid for the advice plus the money he took—plus interest, attorney fees, etc.

Sometimes the seller will realize that the security sold was unregistered. If so, he screwed up, but he can make the buyer a formal offer of **rescission**. This is a legal "do-over," where he offers to buy back the security plus interest. The buyer now has 30 days to accept the offer. If they just sit on it for more than 30 days, it's too late. Also—in case the test gets this technical—if the investor receives the offer of rescission after he's already sold it, the only way he'll be able to sue is if he rejects the offer of rescission within those 30 days. Why on earth securities regulators expect folks like you to know something like—no idea.

Some people seem to think that any time the seller of a security misleads the investor, all he has to do is claim a big "oopsie" and the whole problem goes away. Actually, no. In a criminal trial, the defendant can prove he had no way of knowing what he did was a crime to stay out of jail. In a civil case, the defendant would have to prove he had no way of knowing that what he said or did was misleading to avoid liability. And as we see from this passage of the Uniform Securities Act, meeting that burden of proof would be tough for any agent or advisory professional worth his salt. The "Act" states that the seller of the security will be liable to the buyer if the seller "does not sustain the burden of proof that he did not know, and in the exercise of reasonable care could not have known, of the untruth or omission." Again, claiming you *did not* know would be pretty easy. Proving you *could not* have known—with a little bit of digging—could be tough. Of course, if the agent who sold you the stock was relying on the assertions of lawyers and accountants any reasonable person would believe, then—rightfully—it's not the agent who owes you money. Right?

What if an investor unwittingly signed some waiver that signed away his rights to sue over violations of the securities laws? As the Uniform Securities Act states: "any condition, stipulation, or provision binding any person acquiring any security or receiving any investment advice to waive compliance with any provision of this act or any rule or order hereunder is void." So, it's a violation for the adviser or broker-dealer to get clients to sign such nonsense, but even if they go to the trouble of doing so, the agreements will not be worth the paper they're printed on in a court of law.

If an issuer of securities has civil liability because their prospectus was misleading or incomplete, exactly who could be held liable to the investors who lost money on the deal? As the Uniform Securities Act makes clear, the net is cast far and wide:

> (c) Every person who directly or indirectly controls a person
> liable under subsections (a) and (b), including every partner,
> officer, or director of such a person, every person occupying a
> similar status or performing similar functions, every employee of
> such a person who materially aids in the conduct giving rise to
> the liability, and every broker-dealer or agent who materially aids
> in such conduct is also liable jointly and severally with and to
> the same extent as such person, unless able to sustain the burden
> of proof that he did not know, and in exercise of reasonable care
> could not have known, of the existence of the facts by reason of
> which the liability is alleged to exist.

So, if it looked like you were in on the deception, you would have the burden of proof "that [you] did not know, and in exercise of reasonable care could not have known." If you were the CFO or CEO, the presumption is that you know EVERYTHING that goes on at the company—and, chances are, you've made public or written statements boasting exactly that. So, if investors lose millions through a fraudulent offer of securities, there is really no telling how many individuals and business entities will end up being sued. The lawyers start at the top, and who knows how far down they'll go from there?

And, as long as we're going overboard, you *might* need to know that if anyone knows about the violation of securities regulations involved through the signing or performing of a particular contract or activity, that person would not be able to sue. The Uniform Securities Act puts it like this:

> No person who has made or engaged in the performance of any contract
> in violation of any provision of this act or any rule or order
> hereunder, or who has acquired any purported right under any such
> contract with knowledge of the facts by reason of which its making
> or performance was in violation, may base any suit on the contract.

One of my favorite orders found at various state regulatory websites shows that even though the person who defrauded the heck out of people over some oil-drilling "opportunities" has died, his estate can—and will—be sued by those affected. Similarly, if the investor has passed away, her children or grandchildren could still file suit on an agent who defrauded her. The Uniform Securities Act, in its proverbially punchy prose, points out that:

> Every cause of action under this statute survives the death of any person who might have been a plaintiff or defendant.

NO ABUSE OF OFFICE

The Administrator may not use the office to his own personal benefit. As the Uniform Securities Act states:

> It is unlawful for the [Administrator] or any of his officers or employees to use for personal benefit any information which is filed with or obtained by the [Administrator] and which is not made public. No provision of this act authorizes the [Administrator] or any of his officers or employees to disclose any such information except among themselves or when necessary or appropriate in a proceeding or investigation under this act. No provision of this act either creates or derogates from any privilege which exists at common law or otherwise when documentary or other evidence is sought under a subpoena directed to the Administrator or any of his officers or employees.

Basically, that passage means that the Administrator cannot use information obtained through registration records or investigations for his own benefit. For example, if I could get myself appointed the securities Administrator, I could maybe find out which firms need help with compliance and then point them toward my wife's compliance consulting firm. Or, if my brother is a hedge fund trader, maybe my office could help him find out exactly which positions a particular adviser or broker-dealer is sitting on by sending out a few subpoenas. The last statement about subpoenas above means that if the Administrator subpoenas records from, say, an investment adviser, the adviser doesn't lose any privileges or protections afforded it in a court proceeding. So, yeah, an employee of the securities department putting the information up on Facebook would be a problem if the documents are confidential.

CHAPTER 1 REVIEW QUIZ

1. **Punitive orders include all of the following except**
    A. Suspension
    B. Cancellation
    C. Denial
    D. Revocation

2. **The state securities Administrator may not**
    A. Issue subpoenas to investment advisers in other states
    B. Issue subpoenas to investment advisers in the state
    C. Issue injunctions to investment advisers in the state
    D. Issue subpoenas at the request of another state securities Administrator

3. **Which statement best explains criminal liability under the Uniform Securities Act?**
    A. Willful violations are subject to prison time and monetary penalties
    B. There is no criminal liability for professionals who are properly registered
    C. In all criminal cases the state must prove the offender knew of the specific statute he was violating
    D. The Administrator prosecutes all criminal violations of the Uniform Securities Act

4. **You are the executor of your grandmother's estate. Your grandmother, you discover, was sold an interest in a natural gas exploration program that appears to be a fraud. Therefore,**
    A. There is a cause of action only if the defendant is still alive
    B. There is no cause of action, as the investor is now deceased
    C. Your grandmother's estate may file action within two years of discovery provided three years have not passed since the sale of the investment
    D. Your grandmother's estate may file action within five years of discovery provided ten years have not passed since the sale of the investment

5. **The Administrator is not required under the Uniform Securities Act to provide prior notice and an opportunity for a hearing**

   A. Under any circumstances

   B. When issuing a suspension order only

   C. When issuing a default decision only

   D. When issuing a cease & desist

6. **When a securities agent is accused by a client of churning the account, the Administrator would most likely**

   A. Issue an order of summary suspension

   B. Contact the agent and demand a written response

   C. Initiate criminal action

   D. Initiate a civil suit

CHAPTER 1 REVIEW QUIZ ANSWERS

1. **ANSWER:** B

   WHY: the Administrator cancels a license for reasons that have nothing to do with violations of the Uniform Securities Act.

2. **ANSWER:** C

   WHY: the Administrator has subpoena power but is not a court of law and cannot issue a judicial injunction.

3. **ANSWER:** A

   WHY: being registered won't protect anyone from criminal prosecution, and a "willful violation" occurs when the person was aware of what he was doing—not that he had knowledge of the statutes he was violating. Criminal cases are passed off to a District Attorney or Attorney General for prosecution.

4. **ANSWER:** C

   WHY: the cause of civil action goes on for the usual two years from discovery/three years from the event even after the plaintiff or defendant has died.

5. **ANSWER:** D

WHY: emergency cease & desist orders are quite common. A default decision can only happen after the state has provided all the time and notice they're required to and the respondent still has not cooperated.

6. **ANSWER:** B

    WHY: the Administrator doesn't prosecute criminal cases and doesn't go around suing people on the exam. It's too soon for a summary suspension, but the Administrator will likely want to hear/see the agent's side of the story.

CHAPTER 2

Registration of Persons

(24 Questions)

INVESTMENT ADVISERS

Imagine how the typical investor feels when trying to deal with the intimidating task of saving for retirement. Many of them know the importance of investing, but maybe they lack the time, skill, or interest to do it on their own. Maybe they'd rather pay a professional to manage their investments for them. Turns out, there are plenty of **investment advisers** out there who would be happy to manage client investments in exchange for, say, 1% of assets. If the client puts $1 million under the adviser's management, 1% would work out to be $10,000 a year to the adviser.

That's a big difference from how the traditional **stockbroker** working for a **broker-dealer** gets paid. A stockbroker gets paid a commission when the customer buys a stock and then gets paid a commission when he sells the stock—regardless of whether the customer makes money or loses his shirt. But an investment adviser acting as a portfolio manager gets paid a percentage of the assets in the account. The client's $1 million account balance will pay the adviser $10,000 a year if they bill 1% of assets. But, if that account grows to $1.3 million, the adviser's fee rises to $13,000, and so on. On the other hand, if the adviser puts the client into a bunch of dogs and the account drops to $400,000, their paycheck drops right along with it, to $4,000. That's why many investors prefer to work with a **fee-based investment adviser**, knowing that their compensation is linked to the value of the investor's account rather than the number of trades they can talk the client into.

But, before we get all high and mighty about investment advisers, understand that to some clients, the whole percentage-of-assets billing model is crazy. In fact, I had to laugh out loud when a Series 63 tutoring client the other night told me his story of "some effin' guy trying to sell me some fee-based account bulls*** the other day." I'd tell you the rest, but he's from Brooklyn, and this is a family-friendly book. Long story short, my client did not like the idea of paying somebody a fee even when the account goes nowhere or goes down. Made more sense to him to just pay a commission when and if he decides to buy or sell some stock.

Which model is better for the investor? Depends. Most of the full-service financial firms can either sign up clients as brokerage customers or as advisory (fee-based) clients. If the client has, say, a $10 million account and only likes to buy and sell a few times a year, she would almost certainly save money paying commissions in a brokerage account the few times she traded compared to 1% of $10 million every year...since that works out to $100,000. But, if the client believes in active portfolio management anyway, the advisory side could set him up with a **wrap account,** which bills a flat fee as a percentage of the account value for a professional to trade/manage the account, and that might make more sense.

We'll dig deeper into these issues later. For now just understand that broker-dealers and the stockbrokers who work for them make money by executing buy and sell orders for securities. Investment advisers, on the other hand, don't get paid for executing securities transactions, and they don't sell securities to clients. Investment advisers are compensated for advising investors. It might seem strange that somebody actively trading the client's account is "advising" the client; I mean, isn't he doing a little more than just giving advice? Yes, but "investment advice" is a legal definition that covers a few different types of business models, all of which have one thing in common—the professional's compensation comes from telling investors how to invest in securities or investing on their behalf.

So far, we've considered the advisers who manage client portfolios for a percentage of assets. Another type of investment adviser is the **financial planner.** A financial planner doesn't trade the investor's securities portfolio; rather, the planner puts together detailed financial plans that may concern insurance needs, reducing taxes, estate planning, education funding, retirement planning—the whole financial picture. With this business model, the adviser would usually meet with the client once or maybe a few times per year, charging an hourly rate or a flat fee. $200 an hour would not be unheard of for a financial planner. Or maybe $3,000 for a complete financial plan updated semiannually.

The definition of *investment adviser* also includes professionals who issue reports/analyses on securities for compensation. Maybe you sell reports on technology stocks to investors that help them determine which ones to buy or when to buy and sell them. If so, you're an investment adviser.

For extra credit, go to the SEC website at http://www.adviserinfo.sec.gov/(S(1b1q3up21ihbmxw dt0q05n0a))/IAPD/Content/Search/iapd_Search.aspx.

Type in the name of an investment adviser and click through key sections of their ADV. Very educational stuff. You will see dozens of testable points illustrated for you in a real-world format, especially if you read carefully. That URL—like all quoted in this book—could change without warning, but you should be able to find it regardless at www.sec.gov under "funds & advisers."

INVESTMENT ADVISER REPRESENTATIVES

In order to register with a particular state, the folks setting up an investment advisory business typically have to pass the Series 65 or the Series 66-plus-Series 7 combination. That means a sole proprietor setting up his or her own **RIA,** or **registered investment adviser,** would pass the Series 65 exam, and then register the firm with the state where they have a place of business. If the adviser is a partnership, LLC, or corporation, the folks who run the business have to pass the exam and get registered.

When the firm then hires individuals to manage money or solicit clients, those individuals must register as investment adviser representatives (IARs). I almost went that route myself a while back. I was working for one of the big companies in the test prep business and a few floors above us was a registered investment adviser who happened to be looking to hire a few **investment adviser representatives (IARs).** I got an interview and was told that the firm charged 1.5% of client assets and gave 1/3 of that (50 **basis points**) to the representative. Well, I'm pretty good at crunching numbers, and when I realized I'd have to pull in about $12 million in new account assets just to make ends meet, I decided to keep teaching and writing my little books instead.

In any case, you can probably guess that an investment adviser representative is an individual who represents an investment adviser. If he's a heads-down portfolio manager, or a guy out wining and dining clients, he's probably an investment adviser representative (**IAR**) who needs to pass the exam and get registered. Do all individuals working for an investment adviser have to register as investment adviser representatives? Not necessarily. But, if the individual working for an investment adviser helps to make recommendations to clients or sells the services of the firm, she has to register as an investment adviser representative. Or, if she supervises people who do that stuff, she has to be a registered investment adviser representative. On the other hand, the employees performing clerical work, what the law usually calls "ministerial" work, are not defined as "investment adviser representatives." So, the individual who makes the coffee, replaces the toner, and tells callers that Mr. Williams-is-at-lunch-would-you-like-to-go-to-voice-mail…that employee probably does not have to register.

Investment Adviser Representatives are registered employees of investment advisers who:
- manage accounts
- make recommendations
- determine recommendations
- sell services of firm
- supervise those who do any of the above

So, the investment adviser is the business that provides investment advisory services to its clients. The individuals who <u>represent</u> investment advisers to those clients are called "investment adviser representatives." See, this stuff is hard, but it isn't rocket science. I mean, come on, think of some of the people you know who have already passed. Just sayin'.

BROKER-DEALER VS. INVESTMENT ADVISER

Broker-dealers are in the transaction business. Besides helping people trade securities on the secondary market, broker-dealers also bring securities to market for the first time and raise money for their clients as **investment bankers/underwriters.** You have probably heard the term "IPO" or "initial public offering." This is when investment bankers (Morgan, Merrill, Goldman Sachs, etc.) take a privately owned company and sell its shares to the public for the first time in order to raise millions or even billions of dollars for the issuer, and a few percentage points for the investment bankers as well. Once those shares trade among investors, broker-dealers act as **market makers** for over-the-counter stocks not listed for trading on the NYSE. A "market maker" stands ready to buy a security at one price and sell it for a slightly higher price at all times during trading hours. If a market maker publishes a quote of "BID - $10, ASK - $10.05," a market has been made for that security—customers can buy the stock for the ask price of $10.05, and customers holding the stock can sell it for the bid price of $10.

Whether they're helping investors trade securities on the secondary market or raising capital for their clients on the primary market, broker-dealers are in the transaction business. They get paid because somebody wants to buy or sell securities. Their conduct is covered by the Securities Exchange Act of 1934, with its "know your customer" rule. Basically, as long as you are making suitable recommendations based on the information you have from the client, you are probably well within the rules of the brokerage business. Unlike investment advisers, broker-dealers don't have the **fiduciary** duty of loyalty spelled out in the Investment Advisers Act of 1940 and, therefore, don't have to provide as much disclosure of potential **conflicts of interest**. In fact, if you get down to it, a salesperson trying to sell you something is *the very definition of* a conflict of interest. You want to hang onto your money and get the best possible deal—he wants you to give up your money, whether it's the best deal or not. As long as he tells the truth and follows suitability requirements, he's fine.

I'm not bashing broker-dealers here. I'm just trying to point out the subtle and very confusing differences between broker-dealers/agents on one hand, and investment advisers/investment adviser representatives on the other. I've taught classes recently where people who have been working with their Series 6 and 63 for years figured that they *are* **fiduciaries** because they're good people who always think of their clients first. That's all well and good, but a "fiduciary" is determined to be a fiduciary by the relationship between the professional and the client, not the purity of the professional's heart. Is the professional selling something to the client and taking a percentage of what the client pays to buy it? Not a fiduciary relationship. Or, is that professional managing the client's money on *behalf of* the client? Now *that* is a fiduciary/trustee relationship. If you're selling somebody a security, you're a salesperson/agent. If you're giving advice including financial planning services, or managing portfolios, you aren't selling products—you're investing the client's money on the client's behalf. And you therefore have a fiduciary/trustee relationship with that client, since, basically, they have opened up their purse to you. How many people would you entrust with your life savings—here, you invest these assets for me? Well, an investment adviser needs to be one of the few people to whom you would give that responsibility.

Broker-dealers can also help you invest, of course. You just need to understand that their motivation is to get you to buy and/or sell securities. Period. An investment adviser has to put the clients' needs ahead of their own, since they're essentially spending the client's money in a way that is supposed to benefit only the client.

Another way to separate the broker-dealer on one hand and the investment adviser on the other is to consider the mutual fund industry. The firm who sponsors/markets the fund shares to investors is a broker-dealer. They get paid because investors are buying shares of the mutual funds. What happens when investors put money into the fund? That money is then managed, for a "management fee," by an investment adviser. Usually, the investment adviser and the broker-dealer are affiliated companies, but even if they are, they get paid in completely different ways. Janus Distributors LLC, for example, is the broker-dealer who markets the Janus mutual funds to investors. Janus Capital Management LLC, on the other hand, is the investment adviser managing the mutual fund portfolios for a % of assets.

The large full-service firms often have a broker-dealer and an investment advisory business set up under the same parent company. That's fine, but the two entities are still separate from each other, with separate names, as well. Of course, whether the firm is an investment adviser or a broker-dealer, the securities regulators have the authority to crack down on those who violate securities laws and regulations.

INVESTMENT ADVISER REGISTRATION PROCESS

The first thing an investment adviser about to apply with a Form ADV notices is that the same form can be used to accomplish four different things. Actually, the first thing they notice is this:

> WARNING! Complete this form truthfully. False statements or omissions may result in denial of your application, revocation of your registration, or criminal prosecution.

Then, right after that, we see the four different ways that an adviser could use the same Form ADV:

- Submit an initial application to register as an investment adviser with the SEC.

- Submit an initial application to register as an investment adviser with one or more states.

- Submit an annual updating amendment to your registration for your fiscal year ended _____.

- Submit an other-than-annual amendment to your registration.

Whether the adviser registers with the SEC or with one or more state regulators, Form ADV is now filed electronically through a system called the **Investment Adviser Registration Depository (IARD).** Setting up an IARD account is the first step in the registration process. Once an adviser establishes an IARD account, the adviser can access Form ADV (Part 1) on IARD, complete this part of Form ADV, and submit it electronically to the SEC.

To register with the SEC, the adviser has to check at least one box showing the SEC why they're eligible. For example, if the assets under management are at least $100 million, or if the adviser manages registered investment company portfolios, they are eligible for federal registration. Within 45 days, the SEC will either grant the registration or—in rare, unfortunate cases—start proceedings to determine if maybe the registration should be denied. Maybe there are regulatory histories that give the regulators pause, or maybe the balance sheet looks about as reliable as an Enron balance sheet. In most cases, assuming the form is filled out correctly and the payment clears, the adviser will be granted a registration.

So, one use of Form ADV is to file an initial application with the SEC. Another use is to update the registration on an annual basis. Within 90 days after the end of each fiscal year, the adviser must file what the SEC calls an "annual updating amendment" in order to renew the registration. They must update their responses to all items on Form ADV Part 1 when they do this. And—as always—they must pay a fee. You're dealing with the federal government; they like fees.

A third use of Form ADV would be the "other-than-annual updating amendment" mentioned on Page 1 of the form. That means that if something major changes at the firm—they move to a different state, their business structure changes, or management changes hands—they must file a new Form ADV to inform the SEC of the change promptly (within 30 days of the change). See the difference? You update your ADV Part 1 every year, period, with the annual updating amendment.

And, if something major changes at your firm, you go ahead and update promptly, whenever this change occurs. Since the latter is used for a purpose other than the purpose of updating annually, it is called, very cleverly, an "other-than-annual updating amendment."

Form ADV contains two parts. Part 1 contains the following information:

- the name and form of organization under which the investment adviser engages or intends to engage in business; the name of the state or other sovereign power under which such investment adviser is organized; the location of his or its principal business office and branch offices, if any; the names and addresses of his or its partners, officers, directors, and persons performing similar functions or, if such an investment adviser be an individual, of such individual; and the number of his or its employees;

- the education, the business affiliations for the past ten years, and the present business affiliations of such investment adviser and of his or its partners, officers, directors, and persons performing similar functions and of any controlling person thereof;

- the nature of the business of such investment adviser, including the manner of giving advice and rendering analyses or reports;

- the nature and scope of the authority of such investment adviser with respect to clients' funds and accounts;

- the basis or bases upon which such investment adviser is compensated;

- whether such investment adviser, or any person associated with such investment adviser, is subject to any disqualification which would be a basis for denial, suspension, or revocation of registration of such investment adviser under the provisions of subsection (e) of this section; and

- a statement as to whether the principal business of such investment adviser consists or is to consist of acting as investment adviser and a statement as to whether a substantial part of the business of such investment adviser consists or is to consist of rendering investment supervisory services

All the list is really saying is that the SEC would like to know some basic information about your investment advisory firm. What's the address? Is this a business address or a makeshift office above your garage? Yes, an adviser could be a sole proprietor. He could also work from home in his pajamas all day long. I would assume he would shower, shave, and dress for any SEC staff inspections, but I'll leave that to the individual. In any case, the regulators want to know if this advisory business is a sole proprietorship, a partnership, a corporation, an LLC, etc. If it's a corporation, where is it incorporated? Tell us a little bit about the partners, officers, and directors of the firm—who knows, maybe some of their mug shots will pop up when we do a criminal background search, and won't that be fun? What is the education and business background of these big shots at the firm? How many employees do you have? What kind of services do you offer your clients? How many and what types of clients do you serve? How are you compensated? Do you have discretion over the accounts, or custody over client assets? Do you act as a principal in client transactions? Do you get compensated from broker-dealers that have custody of your client accounts? Et cetera, et cetera. Basically, it's the information you would expect the regulators to want to know in order to protect investors from advisers who have no business being in the business.

FEDERAL COVERED ADVISERS

Okay, so which advisers are eligible to register with the SEC? Here we go with the bullet points:
- Adviser with at least $100 million of assets under management
- Adviser to a registered investment company
- NRSROs (Nationally Recognized Statistical Rating Organizations, e.g., Moody's and S&P)
- Pension consultants
- Internet investment advisers
- Multi-state investment advisers (15+ states)
- Affiliates of federally registered adviser if the principal office and place of business of the affiliate is the same as that of the SEC-registered adviser
- Newly formed advisers that reasonably believe that they will become eligible for federal registration within 120 days
- Adviser with their principal place of business in the US Virgin Islands or Wyoming
- Adviser with their principal place of business outside the United States

Remember that an adviser with over $100 million of assets under management *must* register with the SEC, as must an adviser managing investment company assets. The others are *eligible* to register with the SEC. Why would they even want to register with the SEC? Well, if you were an internet adviser in Colorado with clients in Montana, California, Oregon, and Washington, you might get tired of dealing with five different regulators; therefore, it would be easier to just register with the SEC.

NOTICE FILINGS

On Form ADV the SEC asks which states need to receive a copy of the form. See, even though the investment advisory firm is registering with the SEC, they also need to make a notice filing with a state if they have a place of business in the state. Since the federal covered adviser would be filing notice with various states, the regulators go ahead and call this process a **notice filing**. For the privilege of having the SEC file a duplicate of the form with various state regulators, the adviser pays a notice-filing fee. So, even though the firm is federal covered, they still would perform a notice filing in the state(s) where they maintain an office. And, they would still be subject to the state's anti-fraud authority. It was NSMIA (National Securities Markets Improvement Act) that created this concept of "federal covered advisers," but NSMIA made it clear that the state regulators still have the authority to require and collect a fee for a notice filing, and still have the authority to legally pursue even a federal covered adviser if they're misleading and defrauding the heck out of investors in the state. Not that the SEC wouldn't jump right on the pile once the state regulators got things rolling.

WITHDRAWAL FROM FEDERAL REGISTRATION

If the adviser wants to **withdraw** their registration, they file a **Form ADV-W**. They don't just stop showing up at the office, in other words. I suppose the IA might just be getting out of the business. More likely, they're switching from federal to state-level registration. Why? Maybe they're lousy stock pickers, who just turned $105 million of assets to just $75 million. Hate it when that happens. Or, maybe they're just a bunch of rude, arrogant jerks and all of their big customers have left. In any case, the IA would file their annual updating amendment reporting that they are no longer registering with the big dogs because of the level of assets under management. They would then file an ADV-W ("w" for "withdrawal") within 180 days after the close of their fiscal year. During this period while they are registered with both the Commission and one or more state securities authorities, the Investment Advisers Act of 1940 and applicable state laws will apply to their advisory activities. And that is precisely the type of weird, trivial question I would expect on the exam. "What happens if Dilrod Investment Advisers has filed a withdrawal from SEC registration? Is Dilrod subject to the Investment Advisers Act of 1940 only? Subject to the applicable state law only? Subject to both the Investment Advisers Act of 1940 *and* applicable state law? Subject to no authority at this time?"

Don't worry—it will all be over soon.

Although this next scenario is not a withdrawal, it makes sense to talk about the opposite case here, where the IA is moving up from state-level registration to federal (SEC) registration. Why? Maybe their assets under management have grown to over $100 million, or they now advise registered investment companies. In this case, the IA must apply for SEC registration within 90 days of filing an annual updating amendment to Form ADV that showed why they're suddenly eligible to play with the big kids.

Also know that even if a firm has withdrawn its registration with the SEC, they can still end up getting in trouble with the feds. In fact, although the ADV-W is considered effective when it's filed, the registration actually continues for 60 days just in case the SEC finds out they need to take regulatory action against a firm that is suddenly in a big hurry to flee from their watchful eyes.

STATE REGISTRATION

In general, the large firms register with the SEC (federal), while the smaller firms register with the states. If the firm has not been excluded from the definition of *investment adviser* and has not been granted an exemption (excuse) from state registration, they'll have to register in the states where they have a place of business. The investment adviser would file an application with the state securities Administrator, and this is usually the same Form ADV used for SEC registration. The state securities Administrator might also require the applicant to publish an announcement in one or more specified newspapers published in the state. The initial application is accompanied by a **consent to service of process**, which you can see at www.nasaa.org under "uniform forms."

Finally, fees must also be paid to the state when the applicant registers. No big surprise there. Until the fees are paid, the application/license will keep being denied, as we'll see elsewhere. We'll also see how quickly everything becomes okay once the check clears.

DISCLOSURE BROCHURE

Whether the adviser is registered with the SEC or with one or more states, most prospects and customers must also be given a **disclosure brochure,** which is usually a copy of **Form ADV Part 2**. The test might ask you when the brochure must be delivered to a prospect. The answer is within 48 hours (before) of signing the contract, or at the time of signing the contract if the client has five days to cancel without penalty. If an investment adviser provides substantially different types of advisory services to different clients, any information required in the disclosure brochure may be omitted for a particular client if that information does not apply to that particular client. For example, if a particular client is not being charged performance bonuses, there would be no need to provide a detailed explanation of how performance bonuses are calculated.

The adviser's disclosure brochure must either contain substantially the same information as—or be an actual copy of—ADV Part 2. This part of the form tells customers the essential information on their investment adviser, such as:

- Types of securities about which advice is rendered and the types of analyses used to make such recommendations
- Services provided, fees charged
- Education and business background of all officers of the firm and any employee that determines advice
- Any compensation incentives to the adviser for placing trades through particular broker-dealers/affiliations with other securities professionals
- A balance sheet if the adviser has custody or requires prepayment of fees of >$500 six or more months in advance
- Criminal and regulatory disclosure (if any is required) over previous 10 years

But, of course, not ALL Investment Advisers have to deliver this brochure. If the client is an investment company, we don't need to deliver a brochure. Investment companies are big boys and girls. If the advice is considered "impersonal," meaning it isn't tailored to specific client situations and costs less than $200 per year, we don't need a brochure. The opposite of "impersonal" advice would be "supervisory services," where the IA purports to tailor advice to each client, rather than directing advice to a whole group of clients—retirees, teachers, day traders, small-cap value investors, etc.

Now, things are always changing in this industry, and just in case your exam wants to bring up some recent changes to Form ADV Part 2, let's be ready for it. In the past Form ADV 2 has been presented in a check-box format. Now the SEC requires advisers to drop the check-box format and use a narrative, "Plain English" style when creating the disclosure brochure. As the SEC explains, advisers must now:

- Use Plain English.
- Use a narrative form as opposed to the former check-box approach.
- Add a table of contents with the disclosure items listed in the same order as the items in the form.

- Provide a supplement (ADV Part 2B) about advisory personnel on whom clients rely for investment advice.
- Provide a copy of the current (updated) brochure annually to existing clients that includes or is accompanied by the summary of material changes; or provide existing clients a summary of material changes that includes an *offer* to provide a copy of the current brochure.
- Attach a cover page to the adviser's brochure (ADV Part 2) that states that the brochure has not been approved by the Commission or any state securities authority. Also, if an adviser refers to itself as a "registered investment adviser," it also must include a disclaimer that registration does not imply a certain level of skill or training.

Concerning the New ADV Part 2B, let's just let the SEC tell us what's what in their own words:

> Rule 204-3 also requires that each firm brochure be accompanied by brochure supplements providing information about the advisory personnel on whom the particular client receiving the brochure relies for investment advice. Among other things, the brochure supplements will contain information about the educational background, business experience, and disciplinary history (if any) of the supervised persons who provide advisory services to the client. The brochure supplement thus includes information that would not necessarily be included in the firm brochure about supervised persons of the adviser who actually provide the investment advice and interact with the client. We are requiring as proposed that a client be given a brochure supplement for each supervised person who: (i) formulates investment advice for that client and has direct client contact; or (ii) makes discretionary investment decisions for that client's assets, even if the supervised person has no direct client contact. We believe that clients are most interested in learning about the background and experience of these individuals from whom they receive investment advice. We are adopting as proposed, the requirement that advisers deliver an updated supplement to clients only when there is new disclosure of a disciplinary event, or a material change to disciplinary information already disclosed.

Finally, advisers will now File ADV Part 2A (not the supplement) electronically with the SEC. They will create it in Adobe PDF format, and then upload it electronically.

WRAP-FEE PROGRAMS

We've discussed the differences between broker-dealers and investment advisers. One of the inherent problems with a brokerage account is that the client always wonders if the broker-dealer is executing trades simply to make commissions. Some clients would really prefer to pay a portfolio manager whose compensation is tied to the value of the account, while also knowing that there are no extra charges for large numbers of trades. The solution for these clients is the **wrap account.** A wrap account is an advisory account where portfolio management services, custody, and brokerage transactions are "wrapped" together into one flat fee called a **wrap fee**. Investment advisers sponsor these programs by getting custodial broker-dealers on board to charge a flat fee for all trades entered by the adviser's portfolio managers. This way the client receives portfolio management and pays nothing extra even if a large number of trades are executed on his behalf. This eliminates the concern for **churning.** If the adviser sponsors a **wrap fee program**, the adviser must deliver a written disclosure statement (**wrap fee brochure**) of how these wrap fees work, pointing out that the client may pay more this way than if the services were purchased separately. Generally, clients who are comfortable with frequent trading do better under wrap-fee programs, while those who are more buy-and-hold types would probably save money paying for each transaction if/when it occurs. Also note that if one adviser refers the client to another adviser who will provide the client with a wrap-fee brochure, the first adviser does not need to do so. Believe it or not, *that* is a testable point—yes, the exam is *precisely* that trivial. But, again, it will all be over soon.

RECORD KEEPING

Investment advisers have to keep all kinds of **books and records** on their business, such as:
- Receipts and Disbursements Journals (money and/or securities)
- General Ledger
- Order Memoranda
- Bank Records (for the firm)
- Bills and Statements (for the firm)
- Financial Statements (for the firm)
- Originals of all written communications received and copies of all written communications sent by the investment adviser relating to (A) recommendations/advice, (B) any receipt, disbursement or delivery of funds or securities, or (C) the placing or execution of any securities transaction
- List of Discretionary Accounts
- Advertising
- Personal Transactions of Representatives and Principals
- Powers Granted by Clients
- Disclosure Statements
- Solicitors' Disclosure Statements
- Performance Claims
- Customer Information Forms and Suitability Information
- Written Supervisory Procedures

If the adviser has custody of client funds or securities, the IA must keep the following records:

- Journals of Securities Transactions and Movements
- Separate Client Ledgers

- Copies of Confirmations
- Record by Security Showing Each Client's Interest and Location Thereof

Notice above that the adviser needs two separate and related lists: one is a list of each client and which securities he holds in his account, another list is by each security, e.g., MSFT common stock, and how many shares each advisory client owns of that total. You can imagine how those cross-referenced lists could help spot any discrepancies.

If the IA actively manages client assets, the firm must maintain the following records:

- Client Purchases and Sales History
- Current Client Securities Positions

These records (the two above bullet points) are required to be maintained in an easily accessible place for a period of five years from the end of the fiscal year during which the last entry was made and, for the first two years, the records must be maintained in the adviser's principal office. Electronic records are okay, as long as the firm can verify that the records are accurate and complete and could not have been easily altered. Maybe a test question will want you to say that a "read-only" file would work, since it would not allow anyone to make alterations to the records. In other words, electronic records have to give the regulators confidence that certain transactions have not been accidentally deleted or altered to conceal some sort of violations. Remember that record-keeping is a big responsibility and that deficient records lead to fines and sanctions by the state regulators all the time. Every year NASAA publishes data on the results of state securities regulatory examinations of advisers, and every year the main problem is a lack of record keeping. If the adviser has discretion but doesn't keep sufficient records on the transactions made using that discretion, it's a problem. If the adviser puts out advertising touting their stock picks, but can't seem to back it up with trade confirmations and account statements, it's a problem. If the adviser seems to have five or six more investment adviser reps working at the firm than they've indicated on Form ADV, well, you get the idea.

Finally, if a firm is deemed to have custody of client funds and securities, what sort of questions would the state regulators be trying to answer? Luckily, NASAA saw fit to tell us. As NASAA states on their website (www.nasaa.org):

> If an adviser has direct or indirect access to client funds or securities, it is considered to have custody of client funds and is subject to additional scrutiny. State regulators will want to see how you handle those assets by asking the following:
>
> - Has the adviser complied with the rules relating to safeguarding client assets in the adviser's custody?
>
> - Does the Form ADV reflect that the adviser has custody?
>
> - Are these assets maintained in segregated accounts?
>
> - Does the adviser maintain the required records of client assets in its custody?
>
> - Does the client get an itemized statement at least every three

months showing the assets in the adviser's custody and the activity in the account?

- Has a surprise audit of client assets been conducted at least annually by an independent accountant?

- If the adviser has discretionary authority over the client's account, is there any evidence of excessive trading, self-dealing, preferential treatment, unsuitable recommendations, unauthorized transactions, or incomplete disclosure?

BROKER-DEALER AND AGENT REGISTRATION

As we've mentioned, broker-dealers are in the business of completing securities transactions. They are compensated for "effecting transactions in securities for the account of others or for their own account." That's just a legalistic way of saying that they can help somebody buy or sell securities and charge a **commission**, or they can take the other side of the trade with somebody and make a **markup** or a **markdown**. In the first case, they act as a broker for the account of others; in the second case, they act as a dealer for their own account. Also, broker-dealers bring securities to the public markets for the first time when acting as investment banker. Notice that either way the broker-dealer business model involves getting paid to help complete transactions in securities.

We saw that investment advisers register with Form ADV. Not surprisingly, broker-dealers register with **Form BD**. On this form, the regulators request information on owners and executive officers of the firm, so if any of those individuals also wants to act as a securities agent, no separate registration is required. These individuals include the board of directors, the CEO, CFO, Chief Compliance Officer, and other executive officers, and also anyone who has a certain level of ownership in the firm.

A broker-dealer hires principals to supervise the firm's operations: the registered representatives, the communications, the written customer complaints, etc. It's important to know that if you're a registered representative/securities agent, you must consult with your principal on just about everything. Still, the principal doesn't have a magic pen that can make prohibited activities suddenly okay. If you get a test question that implies that violating the rules is somehow okay as long as you receive "prior principal approval," that could be a trick. Yes, you do need prior principal approval to do many things in the industry, but getting a principal to sign off on something also doesn't make it automatically okay to do. Written customer complaints have to be forwarded immediately to a compliance principal, of course. A principal has to review and accept each new customer account. A principal has to review all the trade/order tickets placed by the firm that day. Sales literature, advertising, and public appearances all first have to be cleared by a compliance principal, as well.

While the broker-dealer (the firm) registers with Form BD, principals and agents are registered as "associated persons" of the firm through a Form U4. Depending on who's filling it out, Form U4 can be more painful and embarrassing than an annual physical. Right at the beginning, Item #2 is talking about FINGERPRINT information, for crying out loud. Pretty soon, it wants my residential history over the previous five years. Then, a detailed employment history over the previous 10 years. And then—bam—it wants to know about all those embarrassing felonies and misdemeanor charges and/or convictions. And, unlike with the 5-year residential and 10-year employment history, the form asks if I have *ever* been charged with any felony or any misdemeanor involving "investments or an investment-related business or any fraud, false statements or omissions, wrongful taking of property, bribery, perjury, forgery, counterfeiting, extortion, or a conspiracy to commit any of these offenses?"

I mean, do we really have to go through all that again? No. Only if I want to get registered as an agent or principal of a broker-dealer. BTW, this U4 criminal disclosure section is a big deal. If you get a chance Google something like "can I get registered as an agent if I have a felony?" and you'll see that thousands of people are currently awaiting that answer very nervously even as we speak.

Even if the applicant has never been charged with, convicted of, or pled guilty to a crime, there are still annoying sections asking about any regulatory actions by any state or federal regulator of virtually any financially based industry, any civil actions in which a court handed down a penalty, or even arbitration awards to customers over a certain amount. U4 asks if the applicant has ever voluntarily resigned, been discharged or permitted to resign after allegations were made that accused [him] of:

(1) violating investment-related statutes, regulations, rules, or industry standards of conduct?

(2) fraud or the wrongful taking of property?

(3) failure to supervise in connection with investment-related statutes, regulations, rules or industry standards of conduct?

And, in case that wasn't enough probing, the form then asks about creditors and bankruptcies over the previous 10 years. The regulators aren't going to prevent someone from associating with a firm just because of a bankruptcy, but they still want the information disclosed.

So, as you can see, there's the license exam phase of the registration process that takes out a certain percentage of applicants, but even after many applicants pass their exams, the U4 phase of the process can delay the registration and in many cases end it outright. For example, you could get a 90% on your exam, but if you also have a recent conviction for shoplifting, the regulators can prevent you from getting licensed. And a common problem is that the young, drunk, and stupid crowd frequently gets young, drunk and stupid enough one fateful weekend to get a felony charge that is then pled down to a misdemeanor. If the conviction/guilty plea were connected to theft of a barstool or a really cool beer light, for example, suddenly the applicant has *real* problems on his hands. If it was more than 10 years ago, and there is no other nonsense on the applicant's record, he (it's usually a he) will probably get in the business. But if it happened recently, and/or there's a history of having a total lack of respect for things like honesty and other people's stuff, good luck getting registered in this industry.

Now before some readers panic, a misdemeanor involving the following would not be considered investment-related:

- Possession of a controlled substance
- Public intoxication
- DUI
- Assault, battery

If those charges were felonies, it could be a game-over situation, but if they were misdemeanors they would not even have to be disclosed on Form U4. Would the regulators even find out or hassle the applicant about them? Definitely, but the true game-over situations involve *any* felony at all, or any misdemeanor that happens to involve money or dishonesty. Remember, working in the financial services industry is not a birthright, it's a privilege. You have to earn it, first by passing a test of competency and then by passing the smell test that the regulators use before putting you out there for public consumption.

Later on we'll look at all the people who escape having to register. We won't go there right now. First, let's talk about the folks who do have to register and how they go about getting registered. As the Uniform Securities Act says:

> It is unlawful for any person to transact business in this state as a broker-dealer or agent unless he is registered under this act.

The next sentence of the Uniform Securities Act says:

> It is unlawful for any broker-dealer or issuer to employ an agent unless the agent is registered. The registration of an agent is not effective during any period when he is not associated with a particular broker-dealer registered under this act or a particular issuer. When an agent begins or terminates a connection with a broker-dealer or issuer, the agent as well as the broker-dealer or issuer shall promptly notify the [Administrator].

I can picture at least a handful of test questions based on these concepts. For example, if a broker-dealer's license is suspended/revoked by the Administrator, what's the deal with their agents' licenses?

Well, they're not currently in effect, since they are no longer "associated with a particular broker-dealer registered under this act," right? I'm not saying the agents' licenses are suspended/ revoked because the folks in charge of the firm screwed up. I'm saying that it's time for the agents to find a new job. Another concept is that if a broker-dealer employs somebody to help clients buy or sell securities, that somebody had better be registered as an agent. Otherwise, the firm is in big trouble. A pretty common test question asks what needs to happen when an agent terminates employment with one broker-dealer and signs up with another broker-dealer. Answer: both broker-dealers and the agent must notify the Administrator promptly. In practical terms, that means that the one firm completes the U5 to terminate the agent's employment, and the other firm completes the U4 to hire the agent. The agent is also filling out the information, so "both broker-dealers and the agent" are informing the Administrator. One of the Administrative orders at www.nasaa.org mentions that a firm had moved without informing the Administrator, which the Administrator felt was rather impolite. See, the Administrator wants "persons" to register and to keep all their registration information current with the Administrator. The Administrator will do unannounced inspections from time to time, and if they come in for an inspection and find a hair & nail salon at the address they have for a broker-dealer, well, that's not cool, no matter what the current condition of their cuticles may, in fact, be.

RECORD-KEEPING REQUIREMENTS

The Uniform Securities Act's "Post-Registration Provisions" state that:

> Every registered broker-dealer and investment adviser shall make and keep such accounts, correspondence, memoranda, papers, books, and other records as the Administrator by rule prescribes.

Remember that there is no SRO (Self-Regulatory Organization) for investment advisers the way that FINRA exists for the broker-dealer side. Therefore, NASAA has a lot more specifics on record keeping for investment advisers than they do for broker-dealers, who are simply required to comply with FINRA/SEC record-keeping requirements. For investment advisers, the Administrator follows with this next statement in the Uniform Securities Act:

> With respect to investment advisers, the [Administrator] may require that certain information be furnished or disseminated as necessary or appropriate in the public interest or for the protection of investors and advisory clients. To the extent determined by the [Administrator] in his discretion, information furnished to clients or prospective clients of an investment adviser that would be in compliance with the Investment Advisers Act of 1940 and the rules thereunder may be used in whole or partial satisfaction of this requirement.

And that's why the state securities regulators typically write rules that require investment advisers to do X, Y, and Z in compliance with SEC rules made under the Investment Advisers Act of 1940. Those federal regulators in Washington, DC, do a fine job churning out rules for advisers, so why should the states waste time reinventing the wheel? Whether the Administrator writes his/their own requirements or just requires the firms to comply with the federal regulations, the Administrator not only wants the **books and records** preserved; he may want to have himself a look someday. If you poke around the state regulatory websites long enough, you'll probably find instances where some hard-nosed broker-dealer or investment adviser told the state they couldn't see client communications that were "protected by attorney-client privilege." And, once they've finished wiping the tears of laughter away, the Administrator and his or her staff will then prepare a notice of an opportunity for a hearing to determine why they shouldn't, in fact, just go ahead and revoke the firm's registration at their earliest convenience. For the hard-nosed firms who thought they could deny access to records, y'all must have forgot to read the following section of the Uniform Securities Act:

> All the records referred to are subject at any time or from time to time to such reasonable periodic, special, or other examinations by representatives of the Administrator, within or without the state, as the Administrator deems necessary or appropriate in the public interest or for the protection of investors.

The word "books" still conjures an image of paper, but the "books and records" required by broker-dealers and investment advisers are typically kept electronically these days. Of course, that immediately brings up concerns about the ability to alter the records, lose them, or give access to them to people who shouldn't have it. NASAA published a model rule on record-keeping requirements, which made the following major points:

> In the case of records created or maintained on electronic storage media, the investment adviser must establish and maintain procedures:
>
> (A) To maintain and preserve the records, so as to reasonably safeguard them from loss, alteration, ordestruction;
>
> (B) To limit access to the records to properly authorized personnel and the [Administrator] (including its examiners and other representatives); and
>
> (C) To reasonably ensure that any reproduction of a non-electronic original record on electronic storage media is complete, true, and legible when retrieved.

MINIMUM FINANCIAL REQUIREMENTS

When a broker-dealer or investment adviser registers or renews their license, the Administrator may by rule require a **minimum net capital**. That means that, depending on their activities, the Administrator can rule that the firm's balance sheet must show a net worth of at least this amount. Remember here that agents/IARs don't have minimum net capital requirements. We don't expect you to have a net worth of $10 million just to be an agent. In fact, we're sort of hip to the fact that you're just about broke at this point after buying study materials and paying testing fees.

But broker-dealers and investment advisers have to file financial reports as required by the Administrator (balance sheets, trial balance sheets, etc.) to show that they're meeting the net capital requirements. "If the information contained in any document filed with the Administrator becomes inaccurate or incomplete in any material respect, the registrant shall promptly file a correcting amendment," says the Uniform Securities Act. Seems reasonable enough. If the firm's net capital drops from, say, $5 million to $5,000, the Administrator might just want to know about that. Broker-dealer net capital requirements would be based on the types of activities the firm is involved with—the riskier the activities, the greater the minimum net capital requirement. NASAA has a model rule that declares the minimum net capital for an adviser based on certain activities:

- Adviser with custody: $35,000
- Adviser with discretion but not custody: $10,000
- Adviser accepting prepayment > $500 six + months in advance: positive net worth

Because maintaining custody leads to higher net capital requirements and the responsibility to have the books audited, most advisers try to avoid maintaining custody and use a qualified custodian instead. Also note that if the adviser has custody or accepts prepayment as indicated above, the adviser must submit an audited balance sheet to both the Administrator and the client. And, of course, an accounting firm has to be paid to audit that balance sheet and sign off on it.

State regulators may not require an adviser properly registered in its home state and meeting that state's net capital requirements to maintain a higher requirement. Federal covered advisers who provide notice filings in the state, though, will be subject to the SEC net capital requirements. The states could not make the adviser comply with a higher requirement than what's covered under the Investment Advisers Act of 1940, should the exam decide to go there. Similarly, the Administrator can't require a higher net capital for broker-dealers than what is required under the Securities Exchange Act of 1934.

RENEWALS

Not only must persons in the securities industry file an initial registration, but also they must renew their license every year. When do registrations/licenses of persons expire? On December 31st, unless properly renewed. How do you renew your license? Same way you renew your vehicle registration—by paying the required fee.

So, the Uniform Securities Act and the exam want you to understand that broker-dealers, agents, investment advisers, and investment adviser representatives need to apply for a license, need to renew that license every year, and need to keep whatever records the Administrator requires. The Administrator has the power to take a look at the required records whenever it's necessary or appropriate in the public interest or for the protection of investors. And, if you try to prevent the Administrator from inspecting the required records, you just violated the Act right there and will soon be signing for some registered mail.

MORE SPECIFICS ON REGISTRATION, GENERALLY

The Uniform Securities Act gives the Administrator the power to decide by rulemaking what is required of a broker-dealer, agent, investment adviser, and investment adviser representative for purposes of registration. The Act says:

> The application shall contain whatever information the Administrator by rule requires concerning such matters as:
>
> - Applicant's form and place of organization
>
> - Applicant's proposed method of doing business
>
> - Qualifications and business history of the applicant
>
> - For broker-dealers and investment advisers—qualifications and business history of any partner, officer, or director
>
> - Any injunction or administrative order or conviction of a misdemeanor involving a security or any aspect of the securities business, and any conviction of a felony

- **Applicant's financial condition and history**

Even if that seems like dense legalese, all it's really saying is that before you start doing business in the securities industry within a state, you need to apply for a license, on which you tell the state about your background and how you propose to do business. Is the broker-dealer a partnership or a corporation? If a corporation, where is it incorporated and can we please see a copy of the articles of incorporation and the bylaws? Does a court or another state Administrator sort of have a problem with you? Are you financially sound, or teetering on the verge of bankruptcy? That sort of thing. Since the SEC has done such a fine job of developing Form ADV and FINRA Form BD and U4, the state securities Administrator uses these same forms with minor alterations as he/they see fit.

After you register, assuming the state sees no problem with the information provided, your license will be granted no later than noon of the 30th day after filing. Of course, if you indicated that the State of Alabama recently revoked your license, it's probably going to take more than 30 days to grant your registration in this state if, against all odds, they decide to grant one at all. If while reviewing your application they see that you indicated an arbitration award you had to pay to a client in New Jersey, they may need you to file an amendment to your application, which could slow things down a bit. Nevertheless, your registration will be granted by noon of the 30th day, except in the rare cases when it isn't.

When filing your initial application as a broker-dealer, agent, IA, or IAR, you need to attach a form called a **consent to service of process**. This document gives the Administrator the authority to receive "service of process" in any non-criminal suit against the applicant. In other words, should another state need to serve papers on an out-of-control investment adviser, they don't have to chase them around and around. Instead, they can just serve the papers on the Administrator, which is the same thing as serving them on the person who has already signed his consent to let the Administrator receive the process on his behalf.

This means that a regulator or a plaintiff in a civil suit would not have to chase down a suddenly hard-to-locate adviser; instead, they could just serve process on the Administrator, which would have the same validity of serving them on the party who doesn't seem to be returning voice mails all of a sudden. But, in case the test gets highly detailed here, know that the plaintiff in a civil suit or a regulator in a proceeding would serve process on the Administrator, but would also have to send a copy by registered mail to the respondent/defendant. As the Uniform Securities Act states:

> **but it is not effective unless (1) the plaintiff, who may be the [Administrator] in a suit, action, or proceeding instituted by him, forthwith sends notice of the service and a copy of the process by registered mail to the defendant or respondent at his last address on file with the [Administrator].**

Oh, and what if somebody sort of forgot to ever file the consent to service of process? Basically, the law just treats him as if he did, in fact, file it and keeps moving. Remember this consent to service of process thing—it is filed with the initial application for advisers, adviser reps, broker-dealers, agents, and securities subject to state registration. The consent to service of process is filed only initially; it does not have to be filed with every renewal application.

Firms and individuals may both be required to maintain **bonds** in amounts up to $10,000.

The test question may point out that this bond can be obtained by a cash deposit or a deposit of securities. You probably don't let carpet cleaners into your home unless they're "bonded and insured." Same idea here. From the Uniform Securities Act we see:

> the [Administrator] may…require registered broker-dealers, agents, and investment advisers who have custody of or discretionary authority over client funds or securities to post bonds in amounts as the Administrator may prescribe, subject to the limitations of section 15 of the Securities Exchange Act of 1934 (for broker-dealers) and section 222 of the Investment Advisers Act of 1940 (for investment advisers) and may determine their conditions. Any appropriate deposit of cash or securities shall be accepted in lieu of any bond so required. No bond may be required of any registrant whose net capital, or, in the case of an investment adviser whose minimum financial requirements, which may be defined by rule, exceeds the amounts required by the Administrator.

There will probably be at least one test question on any of that information. So, remember, the Administrator can require bonds (liability insurance) to protect investors against sloppy or malicious persons in the industry. The bonding requirement can't exceed what the SEC uses for broker-dealers or investment advisers; a deposit of cash or securities must be accepted by the Administrator (if the securities are on his list as an acceptable deposit); and, if the firm's balance sheet/net capital is already sufficient, no bond is required. Also, the bond is required in case anyone files suit against the person bonded, which means the plaintiff has to file suit within the time constraints we look at elsewhere (two years from discovery, three years, period).

If you get a question about the registration of a successor firm, first of all, your luck is running dangerously low, and, second, remember this passage from the Uniform Securities Act:

> A registered broker-dealer or investment adviser may file an application for registration of a successor, whether or not the successor is then in existence, for the unexpired portion of the year. There shall be no filing fee.

In other words, if Able-Brooks Broker Dealers, LLC, is going to become Able-Brooks, Inc., in early spring, they can go ahead and register the new entity, which can use the rest of the year's registration without paying a fee.

The next snippet points out that while the broker-dealer is responsible for the actions of its principals and agents, there is still a big difference between the firm and any individual who represents it:

> The [Administrator] may not enter an order against a broker-dealer on the basis of the lack of qualification of any person other than (A) the broker-dealer himself if he is an individual or (B) an agent of the broker-dealer.

So, if the owners of the firm are all qualified, the state doesn't get to later come after the firm when it discovers that some of the agents would not be qualified to open their own firms. As long as they're merely acting as agents, what's the problem? None. The Uniform Securities Act makes the same point about the difference between the investment advisory firm and the IARs representing it:

> The [Administrator] may not enter an order against any investment adviser on the basis of the lack of qualification of any person other than (A) the investment adviser himself if he is an individual or (B) any other person who represents the investment adviser in doing any of the acts which make him an investment adviser, an investment adviser representative.

If you pass your license exams and have no regulatory or criminal problems, you get to work as an agent of a broker-dealer or an investment adviser representative of an investment adviser, even if you have zero experience. If not, how would you ever get any experience? As the Uniform Securities Act states:

> The [Administrator] may not enter an order solely on the basis of lack of experience if the applicant or registrant is qualified by training or knowledge or both.

So, that does mean the agent has to prove some knowledge by passing a test and/or going through rigorous training. But, it also means that lack of experience by itself is not a reason to deny an entry level position to an agent or an IAR. There has to be an *entry-level* position, right? Otherwise, there would be no entry. And, as the next snippet says:

> The (Administrator) shall consider that an agent who will work under the supervision of a registered broker-dealer need not have the same qualifications as a broker-dealer and that an investment adviser representative who will work under the supervision of a registered investment adviser need not have the same qualifications as an investment adviser.

You may see a test question about a broker-dealer registering also as an investment adviser. First, know that this is very common. Many firms are both broker-dealers and advisers. The exam requirements are different and the business models/forms of compensation are different, but, still, many firms perform both activities. The exam may point out something from the Uniform Securities Act, which states:

> When the Administrator finds that an applicant for initial or renewal registration as a broker-dealer is not qualified as an investment adviser, he may by order condition the applicant's registration as a broker-dealer upon his not transacting business in this state as an investment adviser.

What the law is trying to say is this: if you're a broker-dealer who also wants to be an investment adviser, the state may say, "No. You can be a broker-dealer as long as you don't try to stretch and hurt yourself acting as an investment adviser, which you, apparently, have no business trying to do." In other words, they don't lose their broker-dealer license just because they also wanted to transact business as an adviser. They simply have to promise not to act as an adviser if they want to keep their broker-dealer license.

Finally, as you probably know, the state securities Administrator can require an exam before granting anyone a license:

> The [Administrator] may by rule provide for an examination, including an examination developed or approved by an organization of securities administrators, which examination may be written or oral or both, to be taken by any class of or all applicants. The [Administrator] may by rule or order waive the examination requirement as to a person or class of persons if the [Administrator] determines that the examination is not necessary for the protection of advisory clients.

As we mention elsewhere Certified Financial Planners (CFPs) and Personal Financial Specialists (PFSs) generally register without having to take an exam, while Certified Public Accountants (CPAs) still have to take the same test everybody else does if they want to be IARs or RIAs in addition to the auditing or tax planning practice. And, the Administrator occasionally waives the exam for a particular individual—maybe she was registered as an IAR for 10 years and was then lied to by the next place, who told her the license was current. Five years later when she tries to get another job, she finds out it's been over two years since her registration/license was active. Many states would waive the exam in that case, and, of course, some would not.

EXEMPTIONS, EXCLUSIONS, THE TRICKY STUFF

Broker-dealers and their agents, as well as investment advisers and their representatives, generally have to be registered with the Administrator so he can keep tabs on them. These professionals can be firms or individuals; either way they are **persons**. A **person** may include an individual, but the definition of "person" is not limited to that. Microsoft is a **legal person**. A Unit Investment Trust is a **legal person**. The estate of a dead person is a person, for crying out loud. Since the definition of "person" includes corporations, partnerships, etc., when the regulators want to refer to an individual, they usually call him a **natural person**. When they simply use the word "person" or "any person," they're referring to any individual, partnership, corporation, etc. These are all "legal persons."

The list of who is a person is too long to complete in just one lifetime, but I can tell you who is *not* a person. A person is *not*:
- Dead
- Declared mentally incompetent
- A minor child

Remember, if they're not dead, declared mentally incompetent, or a child, they're a person who can manage his/her own affairs, sign binding contracts, etc. A broker-dealer or investment adviser could be organized as either a sole proprietorship or a corporation; either way, he/it would be considered a person.

The Uniform Securities Act defines a broker-dealer thusly:

> A broker-dealer is any person engaged in the business of effecting transactions in securities for the account of others or for its own account.

So, of course, the investment in question would have to be a "security" as defined by law, not a fixed annuity, bank deposit, etc. But if any "person" is effecting transactions for the accounts of others in securities, they fit the definition of "broker-dealer." And, if the state finds out they're doing it without a license, they sort of have a real problem with that.

As we have seen, an **investment adviser** is compensated for advising others on securities investments. The Uniform Securities Act defines an investment adviser as:

> ...any person who, for compensation, engages in the business of advising others, either directly or through publications or writings, as to the value of securities or as to the advisability of investing in, purchasing, or selling securities, or who, for compensation and as part of a regular business, issues or promulgates analyses or reports concerning securities. "Investment adviser" also includes financial planners and other persons who, as an integral component of other financially related services, provide the foregoing investment advisory services to others for compensation and as part of a business or who hold themselves out as providing the foregoing investment advisory services to others for compensation.

Do all broker-dealers and investment advisers have to register? Not necessarily, but the main concern of securities law is that investors are not deceived/misled/defrauded. So, whether the firm was registered or required to be registered is one concern. The more important point is this:

> Section 101. [Sales and Purchases.] It is unlawful for any person, in connection with the offer, sale, or purchase of any security, directly or indirectly
>
> to employ any device, scheme, or artifice to defraud,
>
> to make any untrue statement of a material fact or to omit to state a material fact necessary in order to make the statements made, in the light of the circumstances under which they are made, not misleading, or

> to engage in any act, practice, or course of business which operates
> or would operate as a fraud or deceit upon any person

See? Whether somebody fits the definition of broker-dealer, is required to be registered, or is simply hoping the regulators never find out about their activities, the statute above says that if they mislead anybody when offering or selling securities, they can be busted for **fraud**.

Fraud can also take place when somebody is being compensated for providing investment advice. As the Uniform Securities Act says:

> Section 102. [Advisory Activities]
>
> It is unlawful for any person who receives any consideration from another person primarily for advising the other person as to the value of securities or their purchase or sale, whether through the issuance of analyses or reports or otherwise,
>
> to employ any device, scheme, or artifice to defraud the other person, or
>
> to engage in any act, practice, or course of business which operates or would operate as a fraud or deceit upon the other person

And, the Uniform Securities Act states that it is fraudulent to deceive or mislead when soliciting for advisory clients, not just when providing investment advice. So, whether we're talking about offering/selling securities, or advising clients on securities, the person had better not "employ any device, scheme, or artifice to defraud the other person."

Is that really so much to ask? We don't put up with car salesmen misrepresenting the mileage on used cars—why should we put up with similar nonsense in the securities industry?

We shouldn't, and we don't. Later on, when things get more complicated, we'll see that certain firms escape the definition of "broker-dealer" or "investment adviser," or they fit the definition but are excused from registration.

Fine. Nobody is excused from anti-fraud regulations. Doesn't matter if you're in the securities industry or not; if you mislead someone about securities, you will probably end up having to sign for some registered mail with the official seal of the state on it.

If you took your Series 6 or 7, you're in the process of becoming an **agent** of a broker-dealer. The Uniform Securities Act defines an agent as:

> Agent means any individual other than a broker-dealer who represents a broker-dealer or issuer in effecting or attempting to effect transactions in securities.

Investment adviser representatives are the individuals employed by an investment adviser who are involved with selling the services of the firm or managing clients' financial affairs. The Uniform Securities Act defines an investment adviser representative as:

any partner, officer, director or other individual employed by or
associated with an investment adviser that is registered or required
to be registered under this act, or who has a place of business
located in this state and is employed by or associated with a
federal covered adviser; and who does any of the following: (1)
makes any recommendations or otherwise renders advice regarding
securities, (2) manages accounts or portfolios of clients, (3)
determines which recommendation or advice regarding securities
should be given, (4) solicits, offers or negotiates for the sale of
or sells investment advisory services, or (5) supervises employees
who perform any of the foregoing.

So, the broker-dealer is the firm that an agent represents. An investment adviser is the firm that an investment adviser representative represents. Please keep in mind that a broker-dealer is, by definition, not an agent and vice versa. An investment adviser is not an investment adviser representative and vice versa. One is the firm, the other is the individual who represents the firm. So, if the question is saying something like, "Which of the following are securities agents?" you would skip over any choice that started with "a broker-dealer who." Broker-dealers aren't agents, and agents aren't broker-dealers. If the question asks, "Which of the following are investment advisers?" you would skip over any answer choice starting with "an investment adviser representative who." Investment adviser representatives—get this—represent the investment adviser.

Why are all these terms so important? Maybe this will illustrate it. The other day I was visiting several state securities websites and came across an enforcement action taken by a large Midwestern state starting with the letter "M." To save time, I'll summarize the case for us rather than wading through 37 pages of legalese. Seems there was a successful insurance agent with a successful practice writing a whole lot of whole life insurance business and a whole lot of indexed annuity business. He was a guy in his mid-50s who saw no reason to be securities licensed—he was only selling insurance products, after all.

The guy held dozens of free hot lunch seminars primarily for retired investors. He got all his marketing materials from an organization based out of Portland, Oregon, which was lucky since he would not have been willing or able to create even one PowerPoint slide, let alone an entire presentation, himself. The marketing organization also issued a certificate attesting to his ethics and clean background, which looked like a pretty good deal for just $150 plus an annual $50 renewal. So, the guy would pull in 20 or 30 affluent retirees, feed them a nice catered lunch, and then dim the lights for his PowerPoint presentation. As the state securities Administrator pointed out, some of the titles of the slides included:

- Why your $ isn't safe in the bank!
- FDIC's credit rating is D–
- Earn up to 25%, guaranteed!
- Heads you win—tails you win!

Who knows how over-the-top the graphics were, but, clearly the message worked its magic by scaring several dozen investors into liquidating their savings accounts and fixed-income mutual funds in order to buy the indexed annuity product this guy was pitching. All told, he pulled in something like $14 million in annuity investments that year pocketing something like $725,000 in commissions. So far, some readers are probably thinking, good for him! Who *wouldn't* want to earn $725,000 helping retired investors protect their savings with an indexed annuity backed up by a solid insurance company?

Well, not so fast. Here were just some of the problems that the state securities Administrator had with the whole thing:

- The respondent held himself out as an objective, impartial investment adviser when, in fact, he was an annuity salesman.
- The respondent held himself out as an investment adviser without being registered as such or shown to be exempt from registration.
- The respondent failed to disclose the 10-year surrender period on the annuity product that contradicted his many assurances to investors that the product provided "excellent liquidity."
- Several investors have faced financial emergencies leading to losses of up to 10% of their invested principal despite assurances from the respondent that this was a "can't-lose investment opportunity."
- The respondent's sales materials were deceptive and misleading.
- The respondent presented credentials issued by an organization with no objective criteria for certification other than payment of a fee.
- The respondent used high-pressure and misleading sales practices to intimidate and convince senior investors to sell securities in order to purchase his annuity product.

The state securities Administrator was stating all this in the notice of hearing, where they have to explain what the guy did and which sections of state law or securities rules he violated. The hearing would be held at the Administrator's office to determine if the state should issue an order preventing the respondent from ever applying for any type of securities license or offering/selling securities in the state. Also, they were considering filing a petition with the courts to order that restitution be paid to any investor who wanted his/her money back.

So did the guy, like, end up going to jail? Whoa, easy now. This is just a state securities Administrator here. And, the guy did not cash the investors' checks and buy a fleet of Ferraris or anything. He just used some distasteful methods to move their money from perfectly safe bank accounts and fixed-income mutual funds into fixed annuities with steep surrender charges that were never explained.

But, the situation is not cut and dried, either. Securities regulators are lawyers, but the respondent can bring in as much legal talent as he can afford, too…and $725,000 in commission checks should have left this guy with enough cash to cover a legal emergency. The respondent's lawyers are going to attack and twist every definition involved with the case. The Uniform Securities Act's anti-fraud statute says that it's unlawful for any person "connected with the offer, sale, or purchase of any security" to mislead or deceive the investor. But, we contend that our client did not, in fact, make an offer or sale of any security; therefore, no fraud occurred. Maybe the state counters that the respondent in effect was connected to the sale of various bond and money market mutual funds—which are securities—which were required to free up money for investors to purchase his annuity products. But, his attorneys counter that he never advised them on any aspect of the sale, that it's not his problem where investors get the money to buy his insurance product. On another note, the state is contending that the respondent acted as an "investment adviser." They say he was deceptively holding himself out as an objective investment adviser, which is fraudulent, and that he was actually unregistered and not exempt from registration. Then again, the respondent's attorneys argue that since the product he offered and sold is not a security, he cannot be defined as an "investment adviser."

As we're about to see, definitions of terms are extremely important to securities regulations, and to your exam.

Up to now we've been talking about the different "persons" in the securities industry: broker-dealers, agents, investment advisers, and investment adviser representatives. Now we have to drill down much deeper into these definitions, focusing on all the people who either do *not* meet the definition of broker-dealer, agent, investment adviser, or investment adviser representative or are excused from having to register as such.

Nobody wants to register. Registration usually requires somebody to study for at least one difficult exam, fill out a bunch of cumbersome paperwork, pay a bunch of fees, keep a bunch of records, and hope the state regulators never cop an attitude against them. So, let's talk about the folks lucky enough to avoid the hassles of registration. As we've said a few times already, a "broker-dealer" is defined by the Uniform Securities Act as "any person engaged in the business of effecting transactions in securities for the account of others or for his own account."

Not a Broker-Dealer

The Uniform Securities Act then states that:

> **"Broker-dealer" does not include:**
>
> - agent
>
> - issuer
>
> - bank, savings institution, or trust company

That simply means that agents, issuers, banks, savings institutions, and trust companies do not meet the definition of "broker-dealer." They are **excluded** from the definition. And that would be similar to saying that in baseball the shortstop, pitcher, and third baseman are excluded from the definition of "outfielder." When the baseball regulators write rules for outfielders, they aren't talking to shortstops, pitchers, or third basemen. Why not? Because those people are not outfielders.

So, if the question is looking for "broker-dealers," skip over any answer choice that's talking about agents, issuers, banks, savings institutions, or trust companies.

Why?

They're not broker-dealers.

Okay, but why are the regulators pointing this out? I mean, who thought that a bank or savings institution might be a broker-dealer in the first place? Think of it this way: banks, broker-dealers, and investment advisers are all in the financial services industry. Many large firms have divisions that cover all the bases; the securities laws are simply trying to keep all those divisions separate. When your grandmother used to go to the bank as a young woman, she would have never seen any signs about IRAs or mutual fund investing. But these days we all see information on investing in securities while waiting for a teller or an open ATM. That's because the bank and the broker-dealer are related entities. They probably have the same parent company. But the securities regulators are pointing out that if a bank wants to get into the broker-dealer business, they need to establish a separate entity and register it as a broker-dealer. Later we'll see that these full-service financial firms probably also have a registered investment adviser. In that case, there would probably be a public company in which we could own stock and underneath that public company we'd find a bank, a broker-dealer, and an investment adviser. It's like three children of the same parent—they're related but still separate entities. For example, there is a public company that trades under the stock symbol WFC. That's "Wells Fargo" for short. Under that "holding company" we would also find a bank, a broker-dealer, and an investment adviser with similar but slightly different names.

Exemptions

The folks above simply are not broker-dealers. Now let's talk about broker-dealers who are excused from registration requirements in a particular state. A broker-dealer *with no place of business in the state* might not have to register in that state. Please don't forget the italicized phrase there though—no place of business in the state. Why? Because if they DO have a place of business in the state, they'll have to register with the state. We're talking about firms with no place of business in a particular state. See, if I'm the state securities Administrator, I'm registering the broker-dealers who have offices in my state. If I'm the Colorado Administrator, I don't care about the broker-dealers with offices in Nebraska.

Well, not unless and until they start doing securities business with residents of Colorado, that is. I'm out to protect my residents from fraud and other shenanigans, so if you want to do business with my residents, you'll have to register here. However, the out-of-state broker-dealer may only want to do business with my "big kids," known as "institutional investors." If so, I'm not worried about making the firm register. If they try to take advantage of my kids, I'll come after them with everything I've got, but as long as they mind their manners, I'll let them do business exclusively with the following investors in my state without requiring the firm to register:

- issuers of the securities involved in the transactions
- other broker-dealers
- banks, savings institutions, trust companies, insurance companies
- investment companies as defined in the Investment Company Act of 1940
- pension or profit-sharing trusts
- other financial institutions or institutional buyers

So, if the firm has a place of business in my state, they register in my state. If they want to do business with individuals, they'll also have to register, whether they have an office in my state or not. But, if they don't have an office in my state, they will not have to register if their only clients are those in the bulleted list above. Also, a broker-dealer is not required to register in a state if they're dealing with an existing customer who just happens to be visiting the other state temporarily. They can't solicit for new clients in that other state, but the broker-dealer and the agent can definitely do securities business with an existing customer temporarily in another state. That means that if the existing customer stays so long he becomes a resident of that other state, then the broker-dealer and agent would have to register in that state. The flowcharts on broker-dealer and agent registration on pages 63 and 64 should clarify this concept, especially for "visual learners."

Agents

As we saw earlier, the Uniform Securities Act defines an "agent" as "any individual other than a broker-dealer who represents a broker-dealer or issuer in effecting or attempting to effect purchases or sales of securities."

Not Agents

The Uniform Securities Act also points out that if the individual represents the ISSUER of the securities involved, he would not be an agent if:

- The security is exempt
- The transaction is exempt
- And, the individual representing the issuer of the securities is also not being compensated based on successfully selling the security

For example, commercial paper is an exempt security if it meets certain requirements, so if you're the CFO of the company issuing the commercial paper that qualifies for an exemption, you do not have to register as an agent, provided you just receive your CFO salary and no extra compensation based on placing the commercial paper and raising money for the issuing corporation. Or, you could represent the issuer in offering/selling their securities to a bank or other financial institution. Since that's an exempt transaction, and since you represent the issuer, you are not an agent. That assumes that you otherwise don't fit the definition of "agent." You aren't being called in from Morgan Stanley to help the issuer do a private placement in exchange for a commission. You are probably an employee or officer of the issuing company and would otherwise have no connection to securities offerings—this is just a transaction between your firm and a pension fund buying your commercial paper. You don't look and walk like an agent—you're not an agent.

Unfortunately, it's not quite as simple as our little bullet list implies. When we say the individual is not an agent if representing the issuer of an "exempt security," we really only mean an issuer of *these* exempt securities:

- any security (including a revenue obligation) issued or guaranteed by the United States, any state, any political subdivision of a state, or any agency or corporate or other instrumentality of one or more of the foregoing; or any certificate of deposit for any of the foregoing

- any security issued or guaranteed by Canada, any Canadian province, any political subdivision of any such province, any agency or corporate or other instrumentality of one or more of the foregoing, or any other foreign government with which the United States currently maintains diplomatic relations, if the security is recognized as a valid obligation by the issuer or guarantor

- any security issued by and representing an interest in or a debt of, or guaranteed by, any bank organized under the laws of the United States, or any bank, savings institution, or trust company organized and supervised under the laws of any state

- a promissory note, draft, bill of exchange or banker's acceptance that evidences an obligation to pay cash within 9 months after the date of issuance, exclusive of days of grace, is issued in denominations of at least $50,000, and receives a rating in one of the three highest rating categories from a nationally recognized statistical rating organization; or a renewal of such an obligation that is likewise limited, or a guarantee of such an obligation or of a renewal

- any investment contract issued in connection with an employees' stock purchase, savings, pension, profit-sharing, or similar benefit plan

Fortunately, though, when we said "exempt transactions," we meant all of them. But, we also need to add here that an individual who represents an issuer in a transaction with a **qualified purchaser** also is not considered an agent in the state.

The Uniform Securities Act also says that an individual can effect transactions with the issuer's employees, partners, or directors if no commission or other remuneration is paid. Maybe you work in the human resources department and help employees buy their employer's stock for the 401(k) plan. As long as you don't get a commission for the transactions, you're not an agent. But, clearly, if your company offered you, say, $50 for every sale of stock, you might just start pestering and pressuring the employees to buy stock, and that would be a different situation.

But the fact that the individual is representing the issuer of the securities is not the be-all and end-all. If that issuer is not exempt, or if the transaction does not qualify for an exemption, that individual is an agent of the issuer and must register. One usually thinks of an agent as representing a broker-dealer, because that is definitely the usual case. But, there are also "issuer agents" for whom the issuer files a U4 with the Administrator. I've seen many enforcement actions recently involving unregistered agents selling securities issued by fly-by-night companies that qualify for no exemption imaginable. Of course, the unregistered agent selling the unregistered, non-exempt securities always manages to mislead investors, who then inform the state securities regulators. This potential for abuse is why registration of an agent is always required, except in the many cases when it isn't.

Some of you readers own your own firms. If that describes you, you almost certainly cannot hire somebody to go around rounding up investors in exchange for 10% of the money raised selling your firm's securities, unless the individual is registered as an agent of the issuer—your firm. That lets the state look into the individual's past, and when you register the securities the state will get to see all of your advertising materials, a specimen of the security, the amount of proceeds to be raised, the amount of compensation to the agent, et cetera, et cetera.

Okay, for simplicity's sake I indicated that the individual is not an "agent" if he represents the issuer of an exempt security or represents the issuer in an exempt transaction. Turns out, it's not quite that simple. Here's the full story—if the individual represents the issuer in an exempt transaction, he is not an agent. If the individual represents the issuer of an exempt security, there are actually only five exempt securities that qualify for an exemption for the individual selling them. Those are the securities "exempted by clause 1, 2, 3, 10, or 11 of Section 402(a)," which include:

- US Treasury and municipal securities
- Foreign government with diplomatic relations (national level only), or any Canadian government, securities
- Securities issued by a bank, savings institution, or trust company
- Short-term debt if $50,000+ denomination, rated in top 3 credit tiers, 9 months maximum maturity
- Investment contract issued in connection with an employees' stock purchase, savings, pension, profit-sharing, or similar benefit plan

Finally, the Uniform Securities Act says:

> A partner, officer, or director of a broker-dealer or issuer, or a person occupying a similar status or performing similar functions, is an agent only if he otherwise comes within this definition.

Wow, so if he's not an agent, he's not an agent?

That's pretty much what they're saying. If the individual is on the board of directors for a broker-dealer, is he automatically an agent? No. Not unless he wants to start offering/selling securities. If he just wants to sit on the board, he's a board member. If he wants to act like an agent, he's an agent. And, if this person *will* act as an agent, his registration is effective when the firm's registration is effective; there is no need to register him or her as an agent separately.

Notice how the whole idea of squirming out of the requirement to register as an agent is predicated on the fact that the individual represents a particular ISSUER. What if the individual represents a broker-dealer? Then, he will have to register if:

- he and/or the broker-dealer have a place of business in the state
- the investors are individuals (not institutions)

Remember that an agent who sells municipal securities on behalf of a broker-dealer still has to get licensed, even though he, by definition, is offering and selling exempt securities. The municipal bonds don't have to be registered; the agent offering and selling them does.

Exemptions

Just like for the broker-dealer he represents, if the agent has no place of business in the state, and the customers are all institutional investors, he does not have to register in that state. He is exempt from registration, we could say. Also, the agent can do business with an existing customer who is not a resident of the state without having to register. If you're an agent in Nebraska, one of your existing customers might go on vacation in Florida. If so, you can contact your customer without having to register in Florida. Same way you could drive your rental car in Florida without having to get licensed. Of course, if your customer becomes a Florida resident, that's completely different. And, just like with the rental car, even though you don't have to be licensed, if you break the law, Florida can bust you. Florida has authority over any offer or sale of a security that is directed into or accepted in their state. So, while you don't have to register when talking to your existing customer who's just visiting the Sunshine State, watch what you do and say, okay?

Investment Adviser Exclusions

Here is the verbatim, legalistic definition of "Investment Adviser" under the Uniform Securities Act:

> "Investment adviser" means any person who, for compensation, engages in the business of advising others, either directly or through publications or writings, as to the value of securities or as to the advisability of investing in, purchasing, or selling securities, or who, for compensation and as a part of a regular business, issues or promulgates analyses or reports concerning securities. "Investment adviser" also includes financial planners and other persons who, as an integral component of other financially related services, provide the foregoing investment advisory services to others for compensation and as part of a business or who hold themselves out as providing the foregoing investment advisory services to others for compensation.

In a second we'll see who does and does not fit within that rather complicated definition above by applying the so-called "three-pronged test." But first let's see who is excluded outright from the definition of "investment adviser" by the Uniform Securities Act:

> "Investment adviser" does not include (1) an investment adviser representative; (2) a bank, savings institution, or trust company; (3) a lawyer, accountant, engineer, or teacher whose performance of these services is solely incidental to the practice of his profession; (4) a broker-dealer or its agent whose performance of these services is solely incidental to the conduct of its business as a broker-dealer and who receives no special compensation for them; (5) a publisher of any bona fide newspaper, news column, newsletter, news magazine, or business or financial publication or service, whether communicated in hard copy form, or by electronic means, or otherwise, that does not consist of the rendering of advice on the basis of the specific investment situation of each client; (6) any person that is a federal covered adviser; or (7) such other persons not within the intent of this subsection as the [Administrator] may by rule or order designate.

First, an investment adviser is not an investment adviser representative and vice versa. One is the firm, the other represents the firm. We saw the same relationship between the broker-dealer firm and the agent who represents it. Some states go so far with this separation that they require an investment adviser set up as a sole proprietor or single-member LLC to register as *both* the investment adviser *and* the investment adviser representative. And then that leads to rather bizarre and comical statements from the regulators such as, "If you are both the adviser and the adviser representative, you are not required to file a report of securities holdings with yourself or receive authorization from yourself."

Anyway, the RIA and the IAR are two different entities.

As with the definition of broker-dealer, the following entities are also excluded from the definition of investment adviser: banks, savings institutions, and trust companies. They may be related to the investment adviser, with the same parent company and everything, but the investment adviser is not the bank or the savings & loan and vice versa. If a bank or other savings institution wants to get into the managed funds business, they set up a separate entity and register that entity as an investment adviser, just as they have to do if they want to set up a broker-dealership. Since I own a few shares of Wells Fargo common stock, I decided to look up the Form ADV information on their investment adviser. As their registration information indicates, Wells Capital Management is the investment advisory subsidiary of Wells Fargo Bank. The bank is not an adviser. The adviser is not a bank. Related, sure. But separate entities.

Lawyers, accountants, teachers, and engineers could all end up talking about securities or the value of securities, or having conversations with investment implications. Lawyers could be doing estate planning and trying to determine the value of some oil & gas partnership that nobody knew anything about. An accountant could be "advising" somebody to make a maximum 401(k) contribution. A teacher could be teaching about the value of IBM stock. And an engineer or geologist could be rendering his opinion that there is, in fact, oil or natural gas worth drilling for on a particular patch of ground, but in none of those cases is the professional acting as an investment adviser. For example, making your maximum 401(k) contribution could help your tax situation; as long as the accountant isn't charging you to help you select the investments for that contribution into your 401(k), she's just acting as an accountant. So, if their advice is "solely incidental" to their profession, they escape the definition of "investment adviser." Be careful how you read the test question, though—if the lawyer or accountant (teacher or engineer) is clearly providing investment advice for compensation, then they are acting as investment advisers. It's just that their professions might require them to deal with securities' values to some extent. But as long as it's within the scope of their profession, they're not acting as investment advisers.

Broker-dealers and their agents definitely do advise clients on how to invest. But, as the above language states, as long as they don't get compensated for the advice itself, and only get paid by commissions or markups/markdowns on the sale of securities, then they are still just acting as broker-dealers and/or agents. Now, that doesn't mean that because somebody is an agent he is automatically not an investment adviser. If a securities agent starts providing financial planning services on the side, he would be an investment adviser who needs to register and let the broker-dealer know what the heck he's up to. So, basically, just ask yourself if the agent is trying to get compensated for selling securities or for providing investment advice. He's only registered to do the former; to do the latter, he'd need a separate registration.

The Wall Street Journal and *Forbes* pass out all kinds of general investment advice in exchange for the subscription or newsstand price. That doesn't make them an investment adviser. You'd have to be rendering specific advice based on a specific situation and getting compensation for it before anyone would accuse you of being an investment adviser. This point of distinction could lead to confusion, unfortunately. A publication of general and regular circulation does not meet the definition, but what if the circulation is irregular, based on market movements or market signals? In that case, the regulators usually consider the newsletter writer to fit the definition of "investment adviser." There is a big difference between, on the one hand, writing general articles on investing and, on the other, charging people money to tell them when to buy and sell stock through email or text messaging, or even targeted mailings based on market conditions. The definition of investment adviser includes this phrase "any person who, for compensation, engages in the business of advising others, either directly or through publications or writings, as to the value of securities or as to the advisability of investing in, purchasing, or selling securities." That means that if you have, say, 30 clients and rather than meet with them face-to-face you, instead, send them written recommendations, you are definitely acting as their investment adviser. When the advice is specific to the client's needs, you're an adviser. If you're writing a newsletter, newspaper, magazine, etc., that goes to a general audience on a regular publication schedule, you're not an adviser. Notice it's not the terminology we use that makes us an adviser or not. It's not whether or not you call the publication a "newsletter" that determines if you're an investment adviser. It's the *function* of that "newsletter" or "financial publication" or of your written recommendations that determines things. Are you publishing information on small-cap stocks in general to a general audience who receives the publication regularly? Or, are you dressing something up as a "newsletter" when, in fact, you're just charging people to tell them which securities to buy and sell and when to buy and sell them? You don't have to meet with someone to "advise" them, remember. If your sophisticated website takes the financial data that visitors enter and delivers a tailor-made investment recommendation, you are an investment adviser if you get any sort of compensation as a result of this "self-serve" website. But, again, if you're just writing articles about investing, chances are you do not meet the definition of an investment adviser.

A federal covered adviser is defined as an adviser under the federal Investment Advisers Act of 1940 and, therefore, not defined under the state securities law as an investment adviser. Finally, the Administrator also has the authority to name other individuals and entities that he considers outside the scope of regulation as an "investment adviser."

Investment Adviser Exemptions

So those folks are excluded from the definition of "investment adviser." Whatever an investment adviser may—or may not—be able to do doesn't apply to them. They are NOT investment advisers.

If you are granted an "exemption," on the other hand, that basically means that you are an adviser, but you get an exemption (you're excused) from having to go through the process of registration. Bottom line is, whether you're excluded or exempted, it means you don't have to register. But, you might have to tell the exam that an adviser who is *excluded* from the definition of "investment adviser" under the Investment Advisers Act of 1940 is also *excluded* at the state level. However, the fact that someone gets an SEC *exemption* does not mean that the person necessarily gets a free hall pass at the state level.

I'm not convinced that the exam is all that concerned about SEC exemptions, but since there would be no way for you to, like, guess at the testing center if I'm wrong, I sort of have to include them. Sorry about that. I've decided in this version of the book to only mention the new exemptions that the SEC has come up with. Here we go:

- Advisers to private funds (private equity, hedge funds) with less than $150 million of assets under management are now exempt from registration, but are considered to be "exempt reporting advisers," meaning they must submit reports to the SEC and maintain certain scaled-down books and records, even though they don't have to register.

- Advisers to private funds (private equity, hedge funds) with $150 million of assets under management or more will be required to <u>register</u> with the SEC and will notice file with the states in which they have a place of business.
- Finally, advisers to VC (venture capital) funds are exempt, and here is how the SEC defines a "venture capital fund."

> a private fund that: (i) Holds no more than 20 percent of the fund's capital commitments in non-qualifying investments (other than short-term holdings) ("qualifying investments" generally consist of equity securities of "qualifying portfolio companies" that are directly acquired by the fund; (ii) <u>does not borrow or otherwise incur leverage, other than limited short-term borrowing;</u> (iii) <u>does not offer its investors redemption or other similar liquidity rights except in extraordinary circumstances;</u> (iv) represents itself as pursuing a venture capital strategy to its investors and prospective investors; and (v) is not registered under the Investment Company Act and has not elected to be treated as a business development company ("BDC").

So, if the investment adviser advises *only* venture capital funds—funds that meet the definition above—the adviser qualifies for an SEC exemption. The state regulators will likely also play along, not that they have to.

More important, let's focus on the exemptions under the Uniform Securities Act. The following persons might be investment advisers, but they don't have to register in the state:

- person who has *no place of business in this state* if his only clients in this state are other investment advisers, broker-dealers, banks, savings institutions, trust companies, insurance companies, investment companies as defined in the Investment Company Act of 1940, pension or profit-sharing trusts, or other financial institutions or institutional buyers
- person who has *no place of business in this state* if during any period of twelve consecutive months he does not direct business communications into this state to more than 5 clients other than those specified above

Again, notice how I put the phrase "no place of business in this state" in italics. If the firm has a place of business in the state, the firm will always have to register in the state.

Except when it doesn't.

Before we move on, remember that receiving an exemption or registering under the Act is just peachy, but neither one implies that the Administrator has determined you to be a good professional or the security offered to be a good investment. In fact, the Administrator does not even determine that a registration statement is true, complete, and accurate. As the Uniform Securities Act makes clear:

> (a) Neither (1) the fact that an application for registration or notice filing under Part II or a registration statement or notice

> filing under Part III has been filed nor (2) the fact that a person or security is effectively registered constitutes a finding by the [Administrator] that any document filed under this act is true, complete, and not misleading. Neither any such fact nor the fact that an exemption or exception is available for a security or a transaction means that the [Administrator] has passed in any way upon the merits or qualifications of, or recommended or given approval to, any person, security, or transaction. (b) It is unlawful to make, or cause to be made, to any prospective purchaser, customer, or client any representation inconsistent with subsection (a).

So, if you get a question about somebody telling a prospective investor something like, "Well, of course this stock is safe—it's federal covered," understand that this would be a misleading/deceptive/fraudulent statement. Plenty of stocks on NASDAQ, NYSE, or AMEX could easily cause a sudden and traumatic loss of value, making the statement totally misleading. A US Treasury Bond is exempt from registration, but you can't tell the investor, "Well, it's exempt from registration, so you know there's no risk there." Careful now—what about interest rate risk? Purchasing power/inflation risk? Reinvestment risk? A US Treasury Bond does not have default risk, but it retains every other risk known to debt securities. To focus solely on the rather unimportant fact that it escapes registration would be a really bad idea.

NSMIA

The National Securities Markets Improvement Act of 1996 decided that certain advisers should be "federal covered." That means that these folks register with the SEC. So, if you had an office in Albany, New York, you would not register with the State of New York if you were a federal covered adviser. You would, instead, register with the SEC. Either way, you'd fill out Form ADV, but you would indicate on it that you were registering with the SEC, who will provide a notice filing to the State of New York. But a notice filing is simply a filing of notice that sounds much more official when we say it backwards.

Remember that federal covered advisers are still subject to the state's power to enforce anti-fraud regulations. But as long as they don't plan on defrauding investors, they can have an office in the state without registering with the state. The firm just needs to have the SEC send the state regulators a copy of Form ADV and all required schedules and pay a notice filing fee. This is done, by the way, through the convenient IARD system. The state can also demand a "consent to service of process."

What about the investment adviser representatives working for a federal covered adviser? Those individuals still register with the states. The investment advisory firm registers with the SEC if they're federal covered, but the individuals register with the states where they maintain a place of business. Just to keep everything nice and simple. Again, I suggest you take a look at the flowcharts for investment adviser and investment adviser representative registration on pages 64 and 65.

Also remember that the officers, partners, and directors of the adviser are automatically registered as investment adviser representatives when the firm registers with Form ADV. This is similar to the fact that partners, officers, and directors of a broker-dealer who will act as agents are automatically registered as agents when the broker-dealer registers.

SEC RELEASE IA-1092

Some readers would probably think that after the regulators went to the trouble of spelling out all those details, it's now crystal clear who is and is not an investment adviser and who does and does not have to register. However, that is not the case. In fact, it is so unclear that the SEC is frequently responding to letters from attorneys of various clients trying to figure out if it's okay to do what they're proposing to do without actually registering as an investment adviser. In case the exam goes crazy and asks about it, those requests are called "requests for no-action relief." That means that the attorney for the client is seeking verification from the SEC or the securities Administrator that his client is okay to do what he proposes to do without registration and the regulators will take no action. Sometimes the regulator can grant "no-action relief," sometimes they can't.

What kind of facts would the regulators use to determine if somebody is acting as an investment adviser? All relevant facts, actually, but there are three "prongs" that we need to look at, which help the regulators determine if somebody meets the definition of "investment adviser" or not.

Why is it so hard to make such a determination? Well, some professionals provide investment advice in connection with other financial services, and maybe they don't think of the advice as being an important part of the business. For example, a financial planner who focuses almost exclusively on insurance products could still be considered to provide investment advice if he told clients to sell their mutual funds in order to buy his fixed annuity. Hey—that relates to the guy who got in hot water with the retirees, right? Bingo. Many sports and entertainments agents are attorneys who negotiate contracts for star athletes and performers; they also end up telling clients how to invest their money. Many pension fund consultants are hired by pension funds to help select all the investment advisers for the fund; are those people investment advisers or not?

Since it's not always clear if a professional meets the definition of "investment adviser," the SEC put out a release back in 1987 that attempts to help explain their thought process when determining if somebody is or is not an investment adviser. This release made clear that the "three-pronged" test to determine if someone is an investment adviser involves the following:

- Does the professional provide investment advice?
- Is he/she in the business of providing advice?
- Do they receive compensation for this advice?

If the answer to all three questions is "yes," then the person is an adviser and must register unless he/they can claim a specific excuse known as an **exemption**. So, first, does the professional provide investment advice? Generally, if someone is helping someone decide on whether to invest in securities or how to allocate a portfolio based on the client's particular needs, that person is providing investment advice. The advice in this case doesn't have to be on a specific security. If a financial planner or sports agent is helping clients pick investments in securities *in general* as an alternative to an investment in real estate or insurance-based products, then he/she

IS an investment adviser. In fact, if we rewrote that sentence in the other direction—the professional is helping clients pick insurance-based products or real estate as an alternative to investing in securities—same deal.

Pension consultants who help pension plans decide on either *which* securities to invest in or *whether* to invest in securities over some other asset are advisers. The consultants who help the funds determine which investment advisers to hire or retain are as well.

What does it mean to "be in the business of providing advice"? The SEC and NASAA determined that a person is in the business of providing advice if he or she gives advice on a regular basis and that advice "constitutes a business activity conducted with some regularity." The frequency is a factor, but it's not the only factor in determining if the person is "in the business" or not. In other words, the regulators can take it all on a case-by-case basis. What are the relevant factors in the case of this particular adviser who claims they don't have to register? Does it look like something that's part of a regular business or not? Providing advice doesn't have to be the main activity of the person, either. You could be a CPA doing tax work and only provide investment advice if a client asks for it—that's close enough for the regulators; you're an adviser. If the person "holds himself out to the public" as one who provides investment advice—via business cards, Yellow Page® ads, billboards, letterhead, office signage, etc.—then he/she is in the business and is an adviser.

What about the compensation question, the third prong? Some folks would like to think they're not advisers because they don't receive money for their advice. But regulators wouldn't leave a loophole that big—they use the broader term "compensation" to determine who is and isn't an investment adviser. Compensation is any economic benefit, not necessarily just money. Compensation can come in the form of "soft dollars," such as receiving goodies from broker-dealers when you direct clients to put trades through the firm. Goodies such as research reports, custodial and clearing (trade processing) services, and special software aiding in research represent compensation are considered soft-dollar compensation, so if you receive anything like that in exchange for providing investment advice of any kind, you're probably an adviser. These soft-dollar compensations are allowable, though they must be disclosed to clients. But the regulators won't let anybody receive the following soft-dollar compensation arrangements: furniture and office equipment, salaries or overhead, vacations, cell phones…you know, the stuff you might actually want.

Allowable:
- Research reports
- Custodial and clearing (trade processing) services
- Special software aiding in research

Non-allowable:
- Furniture and office equipment
- Salaries or overhead
- Vacations
- Cell phones

Surprisingly, even if the compensation is paid by someone other than the client, you're still an investment adviser. For example, if you advise Coca-Cola's employees on how to allocate their 401(k) investment dollars, and you bill the company, you're an adviser.

Some securities agents with a Series 6 or 7 actually function as financial planners, even if they don't call themselves that. Many of these planners figure that they can just put together a financial plan for free and only get paid off any resulting commissions to avoid being defined as investment advisers. Unfortunately, Release IA-1092 says they would likely be considered "investment advisers" because they receive an economic benefit as a result of their advice. The compensation might come directly or indirectly as the result of providing specific investment advice to clients. However it comes, the regulators will probably require such people to get registered. I mean, the business standard is pretty easy to establish. If it is actually investment advice or not is probably the toughest of the three prongs to nail down, but once that's established, the compensation issue is darned easy to determine. Any economic benefit that you receive as a direct or indirect result of giving investment advice equals "compensation." Notice how it's not about the language one uses; it doesn't matter whether the compensation is called a "commission" or a "fee." The compensation doesn't have to be listed as a separate item. The regulators, as always, look at how things function to determine if the activity meets a particular definition. If it were based on terminology, the folks who wanted to escape registration could just use different terms.

Anyway, because of Release IA-1092, even people who might not have thought in the past that they were advisers must now take great care to disclose conflicts of interest.

If the investment adviser advises, say, that someone purchase technology stocks, he/she/they will have to disclose the fact that his/her spouse just happens to be on the boards of several technology companies that might be recommended for purchase.

If the professional is receiving soft-dollar compensation from a broker-dealer in exchange for placing trades and/or clearing through a particular broker-dealer, that needs to be disclosed.

And, if an agent of a broker-dealer also does some financial planning/advising business on the side, she must inform clients that these services are performed outside the scope of her employment at the broker-dealer. Wouldn't be exactly fair for a brand-new rep of some major Wall Street firm to set up shop as an adviser on the side and imply that the advice is being given under the umbrella of the broker-dealer.

Many advisers and planners make commissions from broker-dealers when they place or tell customers to place trades through them. That needs to be disclosed to clients. And the adviser needs to tell clients they don't have to use the particular broker-dealer in cahoots with the adviser—they might be able to get lower commissions using somebody else.

If the planner only recommends products offered by his/her employer, that needs to be disclosed. Wouldn't you feel better getting a recommendation for a mutual fund based on its performance rather than on the fact it's the only one the planner can recommend or the one that pays the best commission?

FLOWCHARTS

Some people learn best by reading; many people prefer pictures, and still others prefer both. Whatever the case, it might help to look at some flowcharts that summarize what we just discussed in terms of exemptions/exclusions for agents and broker-dealers, and for the investment advisory business.

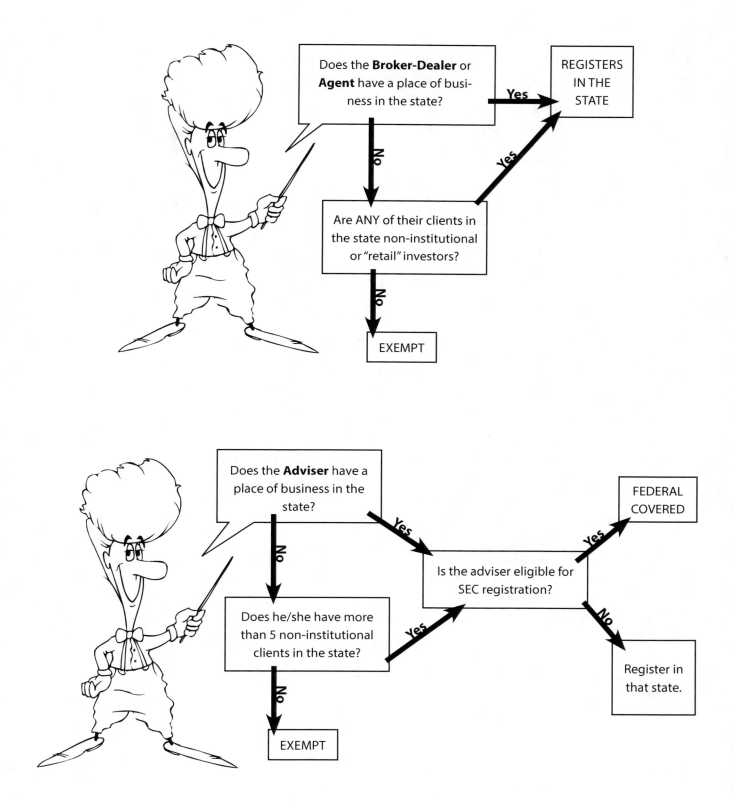

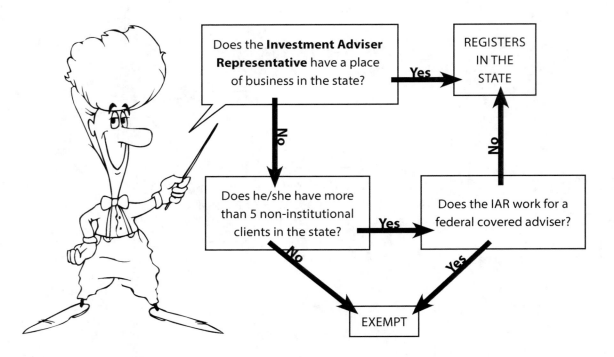

COMMENT: So, if the test question says that the IAR working for a federal covered adviser meets with clients "only once a month" in State B, make sure the IAR gets registered in State B because he/she has a "place of business" in State B. Also notice how meticulously the regulations are worded—because the above passage is so carefully crafted, whether the IAR actually meets with clients regularly at that office or merely makes it known that the office is a location where advisory services are provided or solicited, he has a "place of business" in that state and needs to be registered. Remember that there is a big difference between having an office in State A, with 5 or fewer clients who reside in State B, and actually having a "place of business" in State B. In the first case, no registration is required in State B; in the second case, registration is required. As always, read the exam questions very carefully..

CHAPTER 2 REVIEW QUIZ

1. When a securities agent registers initially with the Administrator, she authorizes the Administrator to receive court documents in connection with any non-criminal suit by filing a
    A. W-9
    B. Affidavit of loss
    C. U4
    D. Consent to service of process

2. If a broker-dealer has its licensed revoked, what is true of the agents' licenses?
    A. They are summarily suspended
    B. They are revoked
    C. They are not currently in effect
    D. They are transferred to another FINRA-member firm's OSJ

3. Which of the following is an accurate statement of financial planners?
    A. They are defined as federal covered investment advisers
    B. All professionals who call themselves "financial planners" must register as investment advisers
    C. All professionals who call themselves "financial planners" must register as securities agents
    D. If any part of their financial plans involves securities, they must register as investment advisers

4. An Investment Adviser Representative registers via which form?
    A. Form ADV
    B. Form U4
    C. Form U5
    D. Form ADV-IAR

5. All of the following are registered in the state where they maintain a place of business except
    A. Investment adviser representatives
    B. Federal covered investment advisers
    C. Securities agents
    D. Financial planners

6. **If a broker-dealer registers on the first business day following Halloween, which of the following is an accurate statement?**
   A. The firm must remit all of the current year's fee
   B. The firm must remit all of next year's fee only
   C. The firm must remit all of this year's and next year's fee
   D. No registration fee is due until December 31st

7. **Form U4 requires an applicant to list all of the following but not:**
   A. Convictions for shoplifting 15 years earlier
   B. 5-year residential history
   C. 10-year educational history
   D. 10-year employment history

8. **You and two friends form a broker-dealer organized as an LLC. You are all managing members of the LLC and intend to sell securities for compensation. Therefore,**
   A. When the firm's registration is accepted, you and the other managing members are automatically registered as agents of the firm
   B. The three managing members must also submit U4 applications with the firm's Form BD
   C. A managing member cannot also be an agent but only a principal/supervisor of the firm
   D. Only one of the managing members may also perform work as a registered agent of the firm

9. **Which of the following is true of net capital requirements?**
   A. Only investment advisers with custody have minimum net capital requirements
   B. Net capital requirements are for the brokerage but not the advisory industry
   C. The Administrator must set net capital requirements lower than those imposed by the SEC
   D. Deficiencies in minimum net capital must be reported by close of business the following day

10. **Which of the following must register as a broker-dealer in State B?**
    A. A securities agent offering non-exempt securities to residents of State B
    B. An individual selling the services of a federal covered adviser from an office in State B
    C. A firm with an office in State B that raises capital for corporate clients by underwriting equity offerings
    D. A firm with an office in State A executing transactions for large pension funds in State B

11. **Jo Ellen would register with the Administrator of State B if**
    A. She had no place of business in State B and only 7 advisory clients living there
    B. She was a broker-dealer organized as a sole proprietor
    C. She was a financial planner with two or more clients residing in State B
    D. She had a place of business in State B and managed assets of $124 million

12. Records required to be retained by investment advisers include
A. Originals of all written communications received by the investment adviser relating to recommendations/advice
B. Copies of all written communications sent by the investment adviser relating to recommendations/advice
C. Bank statements for the firm
D. All choices listed

13. A client sends a letter to you, the IAR overseeing her account, complaining about the performance of the account. After opening the letter, you receive a phone call from the client requesting that you send the letter back to her. Therefore, you should
A. Keep the original letter and send the client a copy
B. Make and keep a copy of the letter and then return the original to the client
C. Ask the client for an affidavit and once received discard the letter
D. Return the letter to the client within 48 hours

14. All of the following information would be updated with an investment adviser's annual updating amendment except one of these, which must be updated promptly whenever the change occurs. That change would be that
A. The firm has hired three IARs since its last annual updating amendment
B. The firm's assets under management have dropped
C. The firm's assets under management have increased
D. The firm inadvertently received client securities in the mail and returned them via registered mail within 5 business days

15. Under the Uniform Securities Act registrations of persons expire
A. 12 months from the issue date
B. On December 31st unless properly renewed
C. On the third anniversary of initial registration and on the second anniversary thereafter
D. Only if the registrant is the subject of an Administrative order

16. Under the Uniform Securities Act registrations of persons are granted
A. By noon of the 30th day following application unless a proceeding is pending
B. On December 31st
C. Immediately upon passage of the appropriate pre-licensing exam
D. Only upon review by a competent court of law

17. **An investment adviser in State A manages part of a mutual fund portfolio for a registered investment company in State B. Therefore, the investment adviser**
   A. Is not eligible for SEC registration
   B. Is not subject to registration in State A or State B
   C. Need not register as an investment adviser
   D. Must provide the client with a disclosure brochure prior to signing the advisory contract

18. **A broker-dealer in State A has only 3 retail customers in State B. Therefore**
   A. The broker-dealer must register in both states
   B. The broker-dealer is exempt from registration requirements in State B
   C. The broker-dealer is exempt from registration requirements in State A
   D. The broker-dealer is exempt from registration requirements in State B unless and until their sixth customer is acquired

19. **Which of the following statements best addresses the terms "licensed" and "registered"?**
   A. A new securities agent is registered as soon as she passes the exam and licensed when the registration is accepted by the state securities Administrator
   B. A new securities agent is licensed as soon as she passes the exam and registered when the registration is accepted by the state securities Administrator
   C. The terms are synonymous
   D. States use the term "licensed," while the SEC uses the term "registered"

20. **Which of the following is an inaccurate statement concerning an investment adviser's Form ADV Part 2?**
   A. It must be delivered to all clients of an investment adviser
   B. It is now completed in narrative (vs. checkbox) form
   C. A supplement on IARs managing affairs for clients is required
   D. Plain English is now the standard required

21. **A broker-dealer is required to keep all of the following records except**
   A. A list of securities held for client accounts cross-referenced with a list of positions by customer
   B. Copies of sales literature
   C. Copies of advertising materials
   D. List of all other accounts held by each customer of the firm

22. **Janice leaves Broker-Dealer A in order to work closer to home, for Broker-Dealer B. Therefore, who must notify the state securities Administrator?**
    A.   Only Janice
    B.   Only Broker-Dealer B
    C.   Only Broker-Dealer A
    D.   Janice, Broker-Dealer A, and Broker-Dealer B

23. **Peter is a Canadian citizen working in Seattle, Washington, this year. If he wants to keep his current Canadian broker-dealer, which of the following best addresses this situation?**
    A.   The Canadian broker-dealer must already be registered in the State of Washington
    B.   The Canadian broker-dealer must register in the State of Washington promptly
    C.   The Canadian broker-dealer is exempt from registration in the State of Washington based on these facts
    D.   Peter must also select an American broker-dealer to serve as co-counsel on the account

24. **Which of the following is an accurate statement concerning the registration of securities professionals?**
    A.   All investment adviser representatives must pass either the Series 65 or Series 7/66 combination
    B.   Certified Public Accountants are not subject to registration as investment advisers
    C.   Certified Financial Planners typically do not have to take the Series 65 or 66 in order to register as IARs or RIAs
    D.   Certified Public Accountants are not subject to the license exam requirements for the Series 65/66

CHAPTER 2 REVIEW
QUIZ ANSWERS

1. **ANSWER:** D

    WHY: this is a brief form filed with an initial application doing just what the question says.

2. **ANSWER:** C

    WHY: an agent is only agent if/when he's associated with a properly registered broker-dealer (or issuer).

3. **ANSWER:** D

WHY: a financial planner could possibly steer clear of securities and not be considered an investment adviser. They register with state regulators usually, as they don't really have assets under management for purposes of reaching SEC eligibility.

4. **ANSWER:** B

   WHY: both securities agents and IARs associate with their employers through a U4 and terminate through a U5.

5. **ANSWER:** B

   WHY: by definition, a federal covered investment adviser does not register with any state. In fact, they are excluded from the definition of "investment adviser" under the Uniform Securities Act. They merely file copies of their SEC registration information through a "notice filing."

6. **ANSWER:** A

   WHY: it's really simple—if you want to register for 2013, you pay the whole year's fee, whenever you get around to getting registered. Could be January, March, or November; the same fee applies.

7. **ANSWER:** C

   WHY: Form U4 asks if you have *ever* been convicted of any felony or any misdemeanor such as shoplifting/theft/wrongful taking of property. It also asks about the employment and residential history as indicated in the question.

8. **ANSWER:** A

   WHY: to get the broker-dealer registered, the three managing members will have to provide information on themselves on Form BD, so the U4 would be redundant.

9. **ANSWER:** D

   WHY: both broker-dealers and advisers have net capital requirements determined by the Administrator depending on their activities. The Administrator cannot make his requirements higher than what the SEC requires of broker-dealers and advisers, which is not the same thing as saying the requirements "must be lower."

10. **ANSWER:** C

    WHY: investment bankers are broker-dealers, period. Also, an agent is not a broker-dealer, period. The firm in State A is exempt since they have no physical presence in State B and only deal with institutional investors.

11. **ANSWER:** A

    WHY: an out-of-state adviser or IAR can have only 5 clients without registration.

12. **ANSWER:** D

    WHY: some things do involve memorization, and the test has been known to sweat people about whether the adviser keeps the original letter from the client or a copy.

13. **ANSWER:** A

   WHY: advisers keep originals of correspondence received from others and keep copies of the correspondence they send.

14. **ANSWER:** D

   WHY: if the firm suddenly has custody, that's a really big deal that has to be disclosed to the Administrator promptly. The other items are routinely altered each year when the adviser updates all answers to Form ADV Part 1.

15. **ANSWER:** B

   WHY: persons are licensed on a calendar-year basis. Securities, on the other hand, are granted 1-year registrations going forward for one year, regardless of when they're granted.

16. **ANSWER:** A

   WHY: the Administrator can't keep the applicant guessing forever. If there's no proceeding against him to deny the license, grant him the license in a reasonable time frame.

17. **ANSWER:** B

   WHY: if the adviser manages mutual fund portfolios, it/they are federal covered. They also don't have to provide a brochure to a registered investment company client, as the mutual fund company will do due diligence all by itself on the pros and cons of using this adviser.

18. **ANSWER:** A

   WHY: the broker-dealer registers in State A because it has a place of business there. If the broker-dealer has any non-institutional clients in State B, the firm must register there, whether it has a physical presence there or not. There is no "under 6 de minimis rule" for broker-dealers, and this question is trying to confuse you over that.

19. **ANSWER:** C

   WHY: some states refer to you as being "licensed," some as being "registered."

20. **ANSWER:** A

   WHY: two types of clients who don't require the adviser's brochure: registered investment companies, impersonal advisory clients.

21. **ANSWER:** D

   WHY: while the broker-dealer will inquire about assets held at other firms, there is no requirement to keep a list.

22. **ANSWER:** D

   WHY: broker-dealer A and Janice will submit a U5; broker-dealer B and Janice will submit a U4.

23. **ANSWER:** C

WHY: think of a Canadian broker-dealer as a firm in a state even farther north than Minnesota or Montana. They're not in the state, but a Canadian citizen needs them to carry his account. No problem—exemption. If the client was an existing client, or if he's in a self-directed IRA... and the firm has no office in the state...exempt. The exam might say the Canadian BD or agent is "subject to limited registration," which is more accurate than calling them "exempt." Because they are subject to limited registration, they must provide clients with a statement to that effect.

24. **ANSWER:** C

WHY: the Administrator can waive the exam for any class of applicants as he sees fit. Most states realize that the CFP process is far beyond the Series 65/66 and so those folks must only register— not pass a qualifying exam. The CPAs don't get the exam waived as a general rule. Why wasn't Choice A true? Because Choice C is true...look for the "internal logic" of the question.

CHAPTER 3

Securities

(6 Questions)

You probably noticed that the definitions of investment adviser, broker-dealer, and agent all included the word "securities." That means if the investment does not meet the definition of a "security," the Uniform Securities Act has nothing to say about it. I mean, even the anti-fraud statute does not apply in that case. A **security** involves an investment of money, but not every investment of money is a security. A security is not an insurance product, a bank account, or a commodity. You can "invest" in a condominium or townhouse, but so far that does not meet the definition of a security. The following are not securities and are not being regulated by the Uniform Securities Act:

- Fixed annuity
- Whole life insurance, term life insurance, universal life insurance, endowment policy
- Commodity futures contract

That means that you could not possibly commit *securities* fraud selling those things deceptively. Why not? Because they are not **securities**. That lays the groundwork for one of the few easy questions on the exam. If the test asks, "Which of the following is not a security?" look for one of the bulleted items above. Or maybe they'll make you stretch a bit further and ask you, "Which of the following is least likely to be an investment adviser?" If so, remember that if the advice is on one of the bulleted items, we're not talking about an investment adviser. Why? Investment advisers give advice on securities.

Like the federal Securities Act of 1933 and the Securities Exchange Act of 1934, the Uniform Securities Act is kind enough to list examples of securities:

- note
- stock
- treasury stock
- bond
- debenture
- evidence of indebtedness
- certificate of interest or participation in any profit-sharing agreement
- collateral-trust certificate
- pre-organization certificate or subscription
- transferable share
- option on commodity/futures contract

- investment contract
- voting-trust certificate
- certificate of deposit for a security
- certificate of interest or participation in an oil, gas, or mining title or lease or in payments out of production under such a title or lease
- in general, any interest or instrument commonly known as a "security"
- warrant, right, or option for a security
- variable annuity or variable life insurance policy

So, of course, the exam may try to mess with you about commodity futures contracts. While the commodity futures contract is not a security, the *option* to buy or sell that contract is a security. So the "December wheat" or "November corn" futures contract is not a security, but the puts and calls traded *on* those commodities futures contracts *are* securities. Also, watch out for this: a "single <u>stock</u> futures contract" is considered a security. Oy!

If you've been reading through any enforcement actions through "contact your regulator" at <u>www.nasaa.org</u>, you have surely seen phrases such as, "The stock referenced in paragraph 6 is a 'security' as that term is defined" in some specific section of the state securities law. The regulators first explain that the investment fits the definition of "security" so that they can at least enforce the anti-fraud statute. Then, since it is a security, it therefore needs to be registered unless shown to be exempt, as do the people offering and selling it.

Did you happen to notice the bulleted item identified as "in general, any interest or instrument commonly known as a 'security'"? That casts a wide net, doesn't it? Just means that if court cases and/or securities regulators have already deemed something to be a security, guess what—it's a security. You may also have noticed **investment contract** above. That was what the **Howey Decision** defined for us. The Howey Decision says that an "investment contract" is:

- `investment of money due to`

- `an expectation of profits arising from`

- `a common enterprise`

- `which depends solely on the efforts of a promoter or third party`

So, the SEC uses a three-pronged approach to determine if somebody is an investment adviser. The SEC and other state securities regulators use the Supreme Court's four-pronged approach to determine if something is a security. The "depends solely on the efforts of a promoter or third party" above means that this person is providing money, not labor, to the enterprise. The fact that the seller had no pre-existing relationship with the buyer would factor in, as well. For example, if you have been a trusted farm hand for many years and the farmer then sells you a part-ownership of his dairy farming operation, you could just be a managing member of the LLC. But, if a farmer is rounding up investors and offering them 10% ownership certificates in which they provide money (but no labor or managerial work) in exchange for a share of the farm's profits, now that is a security and the individuals are simply investors, not farm hands. It fits all four prongs above, right? It's an investment of money in a common enterprise in which the investor would expect to profit solely through the efforts of others. Since the thing being offered is a "security," the farmer could end up committing securities fraud, whether he's in the securities industry or not. If he, for example, gave investors an offering document representing that he owns 300 head of cattle, when it's really only 100 that he keeps shuffling around when their backs are turned, that would be misleading. Same thing if he gives investors an income statement or balance sheet full of bogus numbers. Or fails to disclose a large bill for fuel and fertilizer he can't possibly pay, etc.

And, since this thing fits the definition of a "security," it probably needs to be registered. Remember the very first phrase in the Uniform Securities Act, which explains that the whole thing is designed to prevent fraud and to make securities get registered before they're offered and sold to investors.

REGISTERING SECURITIES

Not all securities have to be registered at the state level, but we haven't messed with that yet. Don't worry, it's coming up. We're still talking about the securities that do have to be registered. If the security has to be registered with the state, this is what the state wants from the person filing the registration statement:
- Filing fee (big surprise)
- Total amount of the offering
- Amount of securities offered in their state
- Names of other states where securities will be offered (not the amount offered in each state)
- Any adverse order, judgment, or decree entered by a court, the securities agency or Administrator in any state, or the Securities and Exchange Commission in connection with the offering

Also, know that:
- Registrations are effective for one year
- Securities offered by coordination or qualification may require an escrow account whose proceeds are impounded by the Administrator and not released to the issuer/underwriters until they have raised the specified amount
- Securities offered by coordination or qualification may need to be sold through a specified form as stipulated by the Administrator
- The securities registration statement must include consent to service of process
- Underwriters can file the registration on behalf of the issuer

At www.nasaa.org, you can take a look at a uniform securities registration form, which will show you pretty much what I just listed above. Do note that securities registrations are effective for one year going forward from the effective date. See, if an agent gets registered on August 15th, her license is still going to expire on December 31st unless properly renewed. But if a security's registration is declared effective on August 15th, it will be effective for one full year going forward. Also, issuers often apply for a "shelf offering," in which they register the securities now and then sell them gradually over two years, or maybe longer. If the offering drags on and on, the Administrator may require progress reports from the issuer, but no more often than quarterly.

As you may have noticed, this exam covers a lot of details. It can't cover all of them on your particular 60-question exam, but it will pull from an amazing variety of topics mentioned on the NASAA exam outline and, therefore, this book. But I'm not sure the exam wants or expects you to know everything ahead of time—this exam actually wants to see if you can *think* on the spot, with the camera and audio recording devices bearing down on you.

When we say that a security or offering of securities must be registered/filed with the Administrator, know that the state securities Administrator can also require a copy of any of the following documents connected to the offer: any prospectus, pamphlet, circular, form letter, advertisement, or other sales literature or advertising communication addressed or intended for distribution to prospective investors. So, if a question is talking about the requirement to "file sales literature or advertising," that is just part of the requirement to register securities with the state securities Administrator.

ADMINISTRATIVE STOP ORDERS

Anyway, as long as you fill out your little securities registration statement and pay your little filing fee, you'll get to issue your little securities, right?

Maybe, maybe not. The Administrator gets really nervous when some little company decides it would be really cool to raise a bunch of money by selling securities to people who don't know any better. Most of those enforcement actions you've read by now have involved people selling promissory notes or preferred stock in some company that has no ability to pay interest or dividends and no intention of bothering to register the securities.

Which is pretty rude, since the Uniform Securities Act goes so far out of its way to point out how important it is to register a security in the state before even trying to sell it. When you register a security, the state is going to want to see all the sales literature and advertising to be used in connection with the offering. They'll probably want to see a specimen of the security and, of course, all the offering documents. They'll want to know if the security has been registered with the SEC and if any other regulator—including the courts—might have a problem with it. They'll want to see a copy of the agreement between the issuer and the underwriters, as well as the agreement among the underwriters. That point seems to shock many students, but, trust me, the regulators want to know if the underwriters and/or promoters of the whole scheme are simply planning to get rich taking money for nothing while everybody else is left holding some high-risk security not worth the paper it's printed on.

If so, no dice.

Yes, that's right. Just as he can do with the registration/application of an agent, broker-dealer, or investment adviser, the Administrator can prevent a security from getting registered. Why would he do a thing like that?

Because it's in the public interest and:
- The registration statement contains any statement that is incomplete, misleading, or false
- Any provision of the Uniform Securities Act, or any rule or order by the Administrator, has been willfully violated in connection with the offering
- The security registered or sought to be registered is the subject of an administrative stop order or a court injunction entered under any other federal or state act applicable to the offering
- The issuer's enterprise includes or would include activities which are illegal where performed

- The offering has worked or tended to work a fraud upon purchasers (or would so operate)
- The offering has been or would be made with unreasonable underwriter compensation or excessive promoters' profits, or unreasonable amounts or kinds of options
- A security seeking to be registered by filing is not eligible for such registration
- A security seeking to be registered by coordination has failed to comply with the requirements of that process
- The proper filing fee has not been paid (but only a denial order can be entered and shall be vacated once the fee is paid)

As with registrations of persons, before a deny, suspend, or revoke order is entered, the issuer would get a prior notice of an opportunity for a hearing and all the written findings of fact and conclusions of law. Of course, as before, there are emergency cease & desist orders and there are also "summary suspensions pending final determination of a proceeding." It'd be interesting to see what kind of nonsense a would-be issuer would be up to that would make the Administrator go and do a thing like that.

Also, did you notice the thing about illegal operations? That means that if Crystal MethCorp decides to do an IPO, they'll probably run into some serious snags with the Administrator.

METHODS OF REGISTRATION

There are three different ways to register securities with the state securities Administrator. Let's start with **Registration by Coordination**.

Coordination

Why would they call this method "registration by coordination"? Because the issuer has to first register the securities with the SEC under the Securities Act of 1933, and then they can coordinate the process with the states where the securities will be offered for sale. What if the issuer is not going to register with the SEC? Then they can't use this method. Also, the securities can generally not already be declared effective by the SEC. Actually, the Administrator could allow that to happen, but the greater the interval between the SEC declaration of effectiveness and the filing with the state, the more likely the Administrator will deny the registration.

Typically, the test question would indicate that the company is doing an interstate IPO. The prefix "inter" means "between" or "among." Since these securities are being sold among many states, this is interstate commerce, which the federal government typically feels is their business. You have probably noticed that some of the road signs in your state indicate the name of your state, but if you're driving on I-80, I-57, I-10, I-95, etc., the signs are suddenly red, white, and blue. Why? Those are interstate highways, the domain of Uncle Sam.

So, the issuer of an interstate offering is subject to registration with the SEC under the Securities Act of 1933, and, since the issuer is not big enough to be granted a break at the state level, they also have to register with the states.

As the Uniform Securities Act indicates, "A registration statement under this section shall contain the following information and be accompanied by the following documents in addition to the [requirements of all registrations] and a consent to service of process."

And those documents are:

- Three copies of the prospectus and all amendments filed with the SEC under the Securities Act of 1933
- If the Administrator requires it, a copy of the articles of incorporation and bylaws currently in effect, a copy of any agreements with or among underwriters, a copy of any indenture, and a specimen/copy of the security

So, as you can see, the issuer and its underwriters are really sweating it out with the SEC and also showing the state regulators what they've shown the federal regulators. The state wants to see what the stock or bond actually looks like, and they'd like to see how much the underwriters are going to make by selling securities in their state. The effective or release date, which is the day that the underwriters can sell to investors, will be declared by the SEC. Just means that as long as you meet the following conditions, your effective/release date at the state level will be whatever day the federal regulators (SEC) declare:

- No stop order is in effect and no proceeding is pending (deny, suspend, revoke)
- The registration statement has been on file with the Administrator for at least 10 days
- A statement of the maximum and minimum proposed offering prices and the maximum underwriting discounts/commissions has been on file for two full business days

Filing/Notification

Just to add to the confusion, we can call this next method either **registration by filing** or the more archaic "registration by notification." Securities registered under this method also must be registered with the SEC, as with registration by coordination. As long as the issuer and any predecessors have been in continuous operation for at least five years, registration by notification/filing for their additional offering is available if:
- There has been no default during the current fiscal year or within the three preceding fiscal years in the payment of principal, interest, or preferred dividend
- The issuer and any predecessors during the past three fiscal years have had average net earnings, in accordance with generally accepted accounting practices (GAAP), of 5% of either the maximum offering price or the market price within 30 days of filing, whichever is higher

By the way, what if the issuer's securities meet the requirements for both coordination and filing/notification? The issuer uses its discretion, meaning they can choose the method to use.

As the Uniform Securities Act says, "a registration statement under this section shall contain the following information and be accompanied by the following documents in addition to the [general requirements for all securities] and the consent to service of process":
- A statement demonstrating eligibility to use this method
- Name, address, form of organization, the state or foreign jurisdiction where the issuer is organized and the date of organization, and the general character and location of its business
- If some/all of the securities are being sold by someone other than the issuer (non-issuer distribution), the name and address of the person, the amount of securities held by him as of the date of filing, and a statement of his reasons for making the offering
- A description of the security being registered
- If the issuer has not been in business continuously for five years—a balance sheet as of a date within four months prior to filing and a summary of earnings for each of the two fiscal years preceding the date of the balance sheet

If no stop order is in effect and no proceeding is pending, a registration statement under this section automatically becomes effective at 3 o'clock Eastern Time in the afternoon of the second full business day after filing the registration statement or the last amendment, or at such earlier time as the Administrator determines.

And now, in order to end the suffocating suspense, we will move on to the third and final method of registering securities at the state level.

Qualification

As the Uniform Securities Act declares, any security may be registered by **qualification**, but, as we'll see, this is the most arduous method of registering securities at the state level. In addition to the requirements for securities registration in general, a registration statement under qualification must contain the following amazingly dense bulleted list:

- The following information on the issuer: name, address, form of organization, state/foreign jurisdiction where organized and date of organization, description of physical properties and equipment, and a statement of the general competitive conditions in the industry in which it is or will be engaged

- With respect to every director and officer of the issuer: name, address, principal occupation for the past five years, amount of securities of the issuer held by him as of a specified date within 30 days of filing, the amount of the securities covered by the registration statement to which he has indicated his intention to subscribe

- Remuneration paid during the past 12 months and estimated to be paid during the next 12 months by the issuer to the directors and officers mentioned above

- For the folks who own 10%+ of the issuer's securities, indicate the amount of securities of the issuer held by them as of a specified date within 30 days of filing and the amount of the securities covered by the registration statement to which they have indicated their intention to subscribe

- If anyone is doing a non-issuer distribution connected to this offering, give the same information asked for under registration by filing/notification

- Capitalization and long-term debt of the issuer

- Kind and amount of securities to be offered, proposed offering price, estimated underwriter compensation and finders' fees to be paid

- Estimated cash proceeds to be received by the issuer, purposes for which the proceeds will be used and the amounts to be used for each purpose, source of any proceeds to also be used to achieve the purposes listed

- Description of any stock options outstanding or to be created in connection with the offering together with the amount held or to be held by every person required to be listed above (officer, director, 10%+ owners)

- Copy of any prospectus, pamphlet, circular, form letter, advertisement, or other sales literature to be used

- Specimen/copy of the security being registered, copy of articles of incorporation and bylaws, and copy of the indenture if applicable

- Signed statement of a legal opinion

- Balance sheet as of a date within four months prior to filing, income statement for each of the three fiscal years preceding the date of the balance sheet, and if any part of the proceeds of the offering will be used to purchase another business, the same financial statements on that business

- Small, brown bag of cash left surreptitiously near a locked emergency exit of the offices of the Administrator

As the Uniform Securities Act then indicates, the securities registered under this method are effective when the Administrator so orders. Therefore, a test question might ask, "Which of the following methods requires a specific response from the Administrator?" The answer would be "registration by qualification." The other two methods—coordination and filing—lead to a release/effective date determined by the SEC.

REGISTRATION OF SECURITIES, GENERAL PROVISIONS

Coordination, filing, and qualification all have several provisions in common:

- First, there is no big surprise that the Administrator requires a filing fee when registering securities. The fee is usually a minimum dollar amount or a percentage of the offering, whichever is greater.

- What is contained in the registration statement in general, whether using coordination, filing, or qualification? As the Uniform Securities Act states: Every registration statement shall specify (1) the amount of securities to be offered in this state; (2) the states in which a registration statement or similar document in connection with the offering has been or is to be filed; and (3) any adverse order, judgment, or decree entered in connection with the offering by the regulatory authorities in each state or by any court or the Securities and Exchange Commission. So, the State of Kansas needs to know how much of the total offer will be offered in Kansas and needs to know that the securities will be offered also in Missouri. The Kansas Administrator does not, however, need a state-by-state total of how many securities or what dollar amount is to be raised in each state.

- The Administrator can permit an applicant to omit any document that is ruled to be unnecessary, and any document filed with the Administrator within the previous 5 years that is still accurate can be incorporated by a reference to it as opposed to reproducing the document. So, if the issuer already filed a balance sheet for the previous fiscal year in an earlier filing, for example, they can just refer to it by name in the next filing—incorporated by reference.

- The Administrator has the authority to require standardized forms and documents in connection to an offer of securities. As the Uniform Securities Act states:

  The [Administrator] may by rule or order require as a condition of registration that any security registered by qualification or coordination be sold only on a specified form of subscription or sale contract, and that a signed or conformed copy of each contract be filed with the [Administrator] or preserved for any period up to three years specified in the rule or order.

Again, no big surprise that the state may require specific forms to be used.

- This next one, though, can be a little confusing at first glance:

  The [Administrator] may by rule or order require as a condition of registration by qualification or coordination (1) that any security issued within the past three years or to be issued to a promoter for a consideration substantially different from the public offering price, or to any person for a consideration other than cash, be deposited in escrow; and (2) that the proceeds from the sale of the registered security in this state be impounded until the issuer receives a specified amount from the sale of the security either in this state or elsewhere.

Okay, just in case the exam goes anywhere near that, understand that some of the fraud taking place involves an issuer seeming to issue stock to public investors but, in fact, really just trying to make a few key players wealthy. So, as the Act states, if a security has been or will be issued to a promoter for some amazingly sweet price (either stock price or via opaque little options/warrants), the Administrator may want to make sure the thing goes into an escrow account. That way, if the whole thing turns out to be a fraud, the promoter won't be getting that economic benefit out of escrow after all.

- After the registration statement has been filed, can any part of it be altered? As the Uniform Securities Act states:

  a registration statement may be amended after its effective date so as to increase the securities specified to be offered and sold, if the public offering price and underwriters' discounts and commissions are not changed from the respective amounts of which the [Administrator] was informed. The amendment becomes effective when the [Administrator] so orders. Every person filing such an amendment shall pay a late registration fee of [$25] and a filing fee, calculated in the manner specified in subsection (b), with respect to the additional securities proposed to be offered.

So, similar to the previous point, the state securities Administrator is making sure that some special securities are not suddenly being "added on" that sell for, like, 1/100ᵗʰ of what ordinary investors will actually pay. But, other than that, to increase the number of securities being offered—as long as they're being offered on the same terms the Administrator was informed of—is not considered a big deal.

EXEMPT SECURITIES

So, if the issuer has to register the securities being offered and sold, the methods available are coordination, filing, and qualification. And, turns out it's a big "if." Many securities are excused from being registered, and the fancy word we use for "excused" is "exempt." Remember, the word "exempt" means "excused." Now, what would the word "non-exempt" mean, then? Exactly right—*not excused*. So, if a security is an **exempt security**, then it is excused from the filing/registration requirements we just had a lot of fun discussing. If the security is "non-exempt," it is not excused from the filing/registration requirements.

Okay, so which securities have to be registered with the state? Well, certainly not the exempt ones. The only securities that have to be registered are the non-exempt ones. Why do non-exempt securities have to be registered? Because they are not excused—non-exempt.

The following exempt securities are still securities (subject to anti-fraud), but they are excused from <u>registering</u> under the Uniform Securities Act:
- any security issued/guaranteed by US Treasury/US Government
- municipal securities
- any security issued by ANY Canadian government
- any security issued by a foreign government with diplomatic relations (national/federal only…except Canada, eh?)
- bank, savings institution, trust company security (not bank holding company)
- savings & loan, building & loan securities, credit union securities
- debt securities issued by an insurance company
- securities issued by railroad or other common carrier, public utility, or holding company subject to Interstate Commerce Commission, or the Public Utility Holding Co. Act of 1935
- a federal covered security
- non-profit securities (e.g., religious, educational, fraternal, charitable, social, or trade/professional associations)
- promissory note maturing in 9 months/270 days or less, issued with denominations of $50,000+, and rated in top 3 credit tiers by a nationally recognized statistical rating agency
- investment contract issued in connection with pension/employee benefit program

Two of those securities could actually lose their exemption if they aren't careful. Those two would be:
- investment contract issued in connection with pension/employee benefit program
- non-profit securities (e.g., religious, educational, fraternal, charitable, social, or trade/professional associations)

Why are the securities above exempt in the first place? Because the Uniform Securities Act says so. And, if you look at the list, you find a lot of government securities, right? They're either the direct obligation of a federal government, or covered by some federal act like the Public Utility Holding Company Act of 1935, or covered by some federal agency such as the now-defunct Interstate Commerce Commission, which had jurisdiction to set rates for services provided by railroads, trucking companies, bus lines, freight forwarders, water carriers, oil pipelines, transportation brokers, and express agencies. Fine, the state regulators have enough trouble trying to stop all the shady characters trying to sell shares of 17% preferred stock that trades on exactly zero secondary markets and has as much likelihood of paying out as a lottery ticket. Let the federal regulators deal with federal government securities and securities covered by various federal laws. We'll deal with the little companies nobody's ever heard of. See, those "federal covered securities" are more easily regulated by the SEC, but the weird little promissory notes that pop up in Opp, Alabama, are better spotted and regulated by the state regulators in Alabama. Those are really the securities that have to be registered with the states—the ones that are not trading on a national exchange or issued by a government, a bank, savings & loan, credit union, or insurance company.

FEDERAL COVERED SECURITIES

So, all securities will have to be registered at the state level, except for all the securities that don't have to be registered at the state level. If the Uniform Securities Act declares a security to be exempt, that means it does not have to be registered and is not subject to the filing of advertising materials, sales literature, the prospectus, etc. The security and the offer and sale of it are still subject to anti-fraud rules, of course, but not subject to registration requirements. We saw above that one type of exempt security is a "federal covered security." Like a federal covered investment adviser, **federal covered securities** don't have to be registered with the states. As their name suggests, these securities are <u>covered</u> at the <u>federal</u> level. The **National Securities Markets Improvement Act** of 1996 (**NSMIA**) created this special class of security. This Act also reminds us that while the SEC plays the very important role of providing necessary protection to investors, they also play the important roles of promoting capital formation and encouraging efficiency and competition in the securities markets. See, the SEC exists because of the "commerce clause" of the US Constitution. They have the power to oversee interstate commerce, and since the securities markets function through interstate commerce and affect the banking system, the economic health of the nation, and even the amount of tax receipts the federal government takes in, the federal government saw a need to regulate the securities markets. Are they out to protect the investor per se? Probably not. They're out to protect the securities markets from getting so corrupt that nobody wants to play anymore. They want investors to feel confident enough in the integrity of the markets that they will keep putting up money for stocks and bonds that allow companies to expand, which keeps the economy, banking system, and federal tax rolls healthy as well. So, whenever they make rules, they try to balance the need to provide investor protection with the need to help issuers raise capital and the need to make the markets as efficient and competitive as possible. With this in mind, the federal regulators decided that investors would be plenty protected and the markets would become more efficient if certain securities registered only with the SEC. So, registration of the following federal covered securities is covered at the federal level only:

> Securities listed, or authorized for listing, on the New York Stock Exchange or the American Stock Exchange, or listed on the Nasdaq Stock Market (or any successor to such entities)
>
> Securities listed, or authorized for listing, on a national securities exchange that has listing standards that the Commission determines are substantially similar to the listing standards applicable to securities described in subparagraph (A); or
>
> Securities of the same issuer that are equal in seniority or that are a senior security to a security described in subparagraph (A) or (B)
>
> Securities issued by an investment company that is registered, or that has filed a registration statement, under the Investment Company Act of 1940
>
> SALES TO QUALIFIED PURCHASERS—A security is a covered security with respect to the offer or sale of the security to qualified purchasers, as defined by the Commission by rule. In prescribing such rule, the Commission may define the term 'qualified purchaser' differently with respect to different categories of securities, consistent with the public interest and the protection of investors.

Why should these securities automatically be on the federal government's turf? Well, if the security is trading on a national exchange, first, we're talking about interstate commerce, which is the federal government's domain. Just as there are state highways and also federal highways, some securities are on the state's turf and some are on the federal government's turf. Second, the security has to provide lots of disclosure and meet all kinds of rigid criteria just to be trading on this national exchange—notice the phrase "has listing standards that the Commission determines are substantially similar to the listing standards applicable to securities described in subparagraph (A)." The "Commission" (SEC) also reserves the right to determine that exchanges created in the future have similar criteria. If so, those securities are federal covered, too. And, if your common stock is federal covered, so is your preferred stock and so are your bonds (senior securities). Investment company securities include open- and closed-end funds, UITs, ETFs, and variable contracts. Those are federal covered. They might do a notice filing, but that's just a filing of notice with the states. Note that there is a uniform notice filing for investment company shares at www.nasaa.org.

So, nobody said that a federal covered security doesn't have to be registered. What we're saying is that a federal covered security doesn't have to be registered with the states. All these issuers have to worry about is the Securities and Exchange Commission (SEC), which is plenty to worry about, as it turns out.

Now, let's apply the concept. Since these securities such as IBM, Microsoft, or variable annuities are federal covered, the states, therefore, have no power to enforce anti-fraud regulations on any offer or sale, right?

Right? Well, how does the fraud definition go again? Does it say that it's unlawful to employ any device, scheme, or artifice to defraud in connection with any security that has to be registered with the state?

No, remember that it says "any security." IBM doesn't have to register with the states—so what? If anybody makes a fraudulent offer or sale of IBM, the states can still enforce anti-fraud regulations. IBM is still a "security."

Just like a fixed annuity, right? Right? Good call—a fixed annuity is not a security. The exam might even point out that if the thing is not a "security," it's not subject to anything under the Uniform Securities Act. That answer drives most test takers crazy, which is why NASAA loves to throw it into the mix. But, if the thing is a security, it is always subject to at least the anti-fraud statutes. So, whether the security has to be registered or not is one concern. If the issuers can claim an exemption, the issuers are happy about not having to fill out as much paperwork and pay a bunch of unnecessary fees. But registration has nothing to do with the f-word, fraud. If the thing fits the definition of a "security," the anti-fraud statutes apply. And, if the thing isn't even a security, then what the heck are we even talking about it for?

EXEMPT TRANSACTIONS

Okay, so we can now draw a few very clear conclusions:
- If it is a security, it is subject to the Uniform Securities Act's anti-fraud regulations
- If it is a security, it has to be registered
  - Unless the security or the transaction is exempt

Federal covered securities are exempt from state-level registration. Other exempt securities such as bank securities and religious organization securities are excused from the requirements to register and file sales and advertising materials with the regulators. So, if it is an exempt security, it is a security that does not have to be registered. If anybody sells it fraudulently at any time, that's a whole different issue. It would be securities fraud because the thing in question would be a security, whether it's exempt or not.

But exempt securities do not have to be registered. That's all that the term "exempt security" means. Non-exempt securities, of course, would always have to be registered.

Except when they wouldn't.

Just like federal law, the Uniform Securities Act lists securities that are exempt from registration requirements and calls them "exempt securities." Then, the Uniform Securities Act lists transactions that make the security exempt from registration and calls them **exempt transactions**. Why don't these non-exempt securities have to be registered? Because they're being sold in an exempt transaction, such as:
- any sale or offer to a bank, savings institution, trust company, insurance company, investment company, pension or profit-sharing trust, or other financial or institutional buyer, or to a broker-dealer
- private placements
  - No > 10 non-institutional buyers in the state per 12-month period
  - Seller believes that all non-institutional buyers hold for "investment purposes"
  - No commissions paid for soliciting any non-institutional buyer

- transactions between issuers and their underwriters
- transactions by fiduciaries: executors, administrators, sheriffs, marshals, receivers/trustees
- pledges
- unsolicited non-issuer transactions effected through a broker-dealer
- isolated non-issuer transactions
- any transaction to existing security holders of the issuer, if no commission is paid for soliciting buyers
- offerings of pre-organization certificates
  - No more than 10 buyers, period
  - No commissions paid for soliciting any buyer
  - No payment made by any subscriber
- any offer (but not a sale) of a security for which a registration statement has been filed under the Uniform Securities Act and the Securities Act of 1933 if no stop order is in effect. Sales may only take place after registration is effective
- any transaction in a bond secured by a real mortgage or deed of trust provided that the entire mortgage or deed of trust, together with the bonds, are offered and sold as a unit
- non-issuer transactions in securities subject to reporting requirements of the Exchange Act of 1934, or in securities registered under the Investment Company Act of 1940, or in securities where the issuer has filed with the Administrator information substantially the same as that required for registered issuers by the Securities Exchange Act of 1934 for a period of at least 180 days prior to the transaction

So, if you can't find an exemption to registering your securities, chances are you aren't trying hard enough. It goes like this: your company wants to raise a mere $3 million to expand. You do not want to register the securities, so you call in your attorneys. What do we pay attorneys for? Getting us out of stuff. We want to get out of the huge hassle of registering securities with the Administrator and paying registration fees—can't you guys find a way to get us out of it?

They can try. Looking at the list of exempt securities, they don't see anything there for us. We're not federal covered—not even close. We not only don't trade on a national exchange, but the securities won't trade on any exchange after the offering.

Hmm, so I guess we're stuck registering the stock?

Not so fast. At $300 an hour, our attorneys see no reason to rush. They point out that we could offer the securities to a bank or other financial institution. Since those guys are big boys and girls, this describes an exempt transaction. Cool—can we get a bank to cut a check for $3 million for "stock" in our unprofitable company?

Next idea? Our attorneys know a broker-dealer who has a few high-rollin'-type investors. If we could get 10 of them to pony up $300,000 each, we could raise us the $3 million and call it a private placement. What if the 10 investors only want to put in $50,000 each? Then, we'll need to line up some institutional buyers, which puts us pretty much back where we started.

What if we put out the word that if anyone would like to call up and request the opportunity to make a $300,000 investment, we might fill their unsolicited order for them? No—that would be an issuer transaction. The exempt transaction is a "non-issuer" transaction, meaning "not for the benefit of the issuer," but a transaction between two investors.

So, there are ways around having to register our common stock, but it's not necessarily going to be easy qualifying for an exempt transaction. If we dig below the surface, we can see the logic to most of these exemptions, too. For example, we can easily see why the transactions by fiduciaries—executors, administrators, sheriffs, marshals of the court, receivers/trustees in a bankruptcy liquidation of assets—qualify for a more relaxed treatment by the Administrator. They're all being supervised by the courts, whether it's an executor disposing of the estate assets or an accounting firm "marshaling the assets" of a deadbeat company. A receiver placed in charge of a bankrupt entity's assets might liquidate those assets, some of which could be unregistered, non-exempt securities. Oh, well, it's not like this receiver/trustee/marshal in a bankruptcy is a securities dealer trying to skirt the registration requirements.

Recently, I actually heard of an investment advisory firm getting a call from a Texas broker-dealer, who said, "By the way, one of your managers bought a stock that was never blue-skied in Texas." What this rather cryptic remark meant was that a portfolio manager with discretion over an account bought stock in a really small company for a "microcap" portfolio. But, since nobody called up and solicited the client, it was an "unsolicited, non-issuer transaction effected through a broker-dealer." The word "non-issuer" means it was not part of an IPO or other offering where the issuer is raising money.

So, the broker-dealer had the customer sign the unsolicited order acknowledgment, and they had themselves an exempt transaction. And I had myself an amusing story that, so far, has been extremely difficult to work into polite conversation.

But, there you have it. By the way, tell the test that "non-issuer" and "secondary" both mean that the transaction is "not for the benefit of the issuer."

Another item mentioned that an offer for a security that is in the process of registration is okay. Here we're talking about those "indications of interest" you might have learned about for the Series 6 or 7. As long as the issuer has filed the registration statement, they can take the indications of interest, providing investors with a preliminary prospectus. They just can't make a sale until the effective date.

OFFERS AND SALES

As the Uniform Securities Act states:

> "Offer" or "offer to sell" includes every attempt or offer to dispose of, or solicitation of an offer to buy, a security or interest in a security for value.

An **offer** is an attempt to sell somebody a security, or an attempt to get them to, like, beg you to please, please let them buy a security from you (solicitation of an offer to buy).

A **sale** is defined this way:

> "Sale" or "sell" includes every contract of sale of, contract to sell, or disposition of, a security or interest in a security for value.

Why are these definitions important? Because the most important part of the Uniform Securities Act is the very beginning. In the beginning, the Uniform Securities Act said:

> It is unlawful for any person, in connection with the offer, sale, or purchase of any security…to employ any device, scheme, or artifice to defraud.

So, the guy who is the subject of an Administrative action might hire an attorney to argue that the conduct in question did not fit the definition of "offer" or "sale." Because, if the conduct in question does fit the definition of an offer and/or a sale of securities, it is subject to the anti-fraud statutes and might require some people to get registered.

NOT OFFERS

Now we get to look at some examples of things that are *not offers* of securities, which means they would not be subject to registration requirements. As the Uniform Securities Act states, the following are not considered to be *offers* of securities:

- any bona fide pledge or loan of a security

- any stock dividend if nothing of value is given by stockholders for the dividend

- any act incident to a class vote by stockholders…on a merger, consolidation, reclassification of securities, or sale of corporate assets in consideration of the issuance of securities of another corporation

- any act incident to a judicially approved reorganization in which a security is issued in exchange for one or more outstanding securities, claims, or property interests

First, if you're pledging securities as collateral, you are not making an offer to sell securities. So, you can pledge a security as collateral even if the security isn't registered. A stock dividend, as you saw on the Series 6 or 7, is really a non-event. The issuer used to cut the big earnings pie into 10 million slices; now they're going to give everybody more slices by cutting the pie into 15 million smaller slices and having everybody pretend they've gained something. That is not an offer—just a way of pushing down the market price for the stock to entice investors to buy more of it. When a corporation merges with another corporation, the acquiring company is not really offering their securities to the other shareholders—the two companies are simply going to become one. And the last bullet point has to do with a bankruptcy proceeding. The bankruptcy judge will approve the plan to wipe out the current shareholders and give the stiffed bondholders shares in the newly organized entity. So, that's a way of dealing with some mighty ticked-off creditors, not an offer of securities.

D-O-A

So, the next question is, "When has an offer been made in a particular state?" Luckily the Uniform Securities Act tells us that:

> …an offer to sell is made in this state when the offer originates from this state, or is directed by the offeror to this state.

If you get a test question stating that an agent in State A calls an investor in State B trying to interest the investor in some securities, tell the exam that an offer to sell a security has been made in both states. The Uniform Securities Act also gives the Administrator authority when an offer has been accepted in the state. An offer to sell "is accepted in this state when acceptance is communicated to the offeror in this state and has not previously been communicated to the offeror outside this state." That communication could be by phone, text message, email, fax, etc., by the way.

As usual, this is much simpler than it first appears. If an agent in North Dakota calls a customer vacationing in South Dakota and asks if she'd like to buy a variable annuity, an offer to sell a security has been made in both states. If the buyer isn't sure, maybe she calls back a few days later while visiting her Aunt Lorraine in Lincoln, Nebraska. "Sure," she says, "I'd like to communicate my acceptance of said variable annuity to you, the offeror." Now the offer has been accepted in Nebraska. Using our nifty little "D-O-A" mnemonic device thing, you can get the test question right. The offer was D-directed into South Dakota, O-originated in North Dakota, and A-accepted in Nebraska. Who's got jurisdiction if the agent is scamming the customer? Could be any or all of the three states involved.

What if the investor cuts a check while kickin' it up in Branson, Missouri? Nobody cares where the check is cut. It's all about where the offeror and offeree were when they were communicating. Also, if the agent had been offering shares of General Electric, headquartered in New York, that would not imply that the New York Administrator is somehow involved. GE almost certainly has nothing to do with this North Dakota agent.

Please remember that in another section we'll be saying that the North Dakota agent can call an existing customer who's just visiting the state of South Dakota without having to register as an agent in South Dakota. Fine. The agent could also get into his pickup truck and drive to the other state without getting a South Dakota driver's license. But, in either case, if the dude starts violating the law, the State of South Dakota can nail him. What if the agent doesn't like that fact?

Tell him to stay the heck out of South Dakota.

No idea why the test would even think of asking this, but you might need to know the following trivia from the Uniform Securities Act:

> An offer to sell or to buy is not made in this state when (1) the publisher circulates or there is circulated on his behalf in this state any bona fide newspaper or other publication of general, regular, and paid circulation which is not published in this state, or which is published in this state but has had more than two-thirds of its circulation outside this state during the past twelve months, or (2) a radio or television program originating outside this state is received in this state.

So...if a copy of the *New York Times* ends up in Sedona, Arizona, an offer to sell securities published in that newspaper is not being made in Arizona. Or, if there is a newspaper which simply has a printing plant in the State of Iowa, but more than 2/3 of the circulation is outside the state of Iowa, no offer to sell securities has taken place in Iowa. And, any offer to sell securities coming in from a radio or TV program originating outside the state was not made in the state but was, rather, made in the state from where the broadcast was transmitted.

CHAPTER 3 REVIEW QUIZ

1. **Which of the following investments is not subject to the anti-fraud statutes of the Uniform Securities Act?**
   A. Variable Annuity
   B. Equity Indexed Annuity
   C. Variable Life Insurance
   D. None of these choices

2. **An investment contract is**
   A. A security
   B. Defined by the Supreme Court's Howey Decision
   C. Subject to anti-fraud statutes of the Uniform Securities Act
   D. All of these choices

3. **Registration by coordination is made possible under which federal securities act?**
   A. Securities Exchange Act of 1934
   B. National Securities Markets Improvement Act
   C. Investment Company Act of 1940
   D. Securities Act of 1933

4. **A Non-NASDAQ company doing an interstate initial public offering would most likely use which registration method for their issue of common stock?**
   A. Notification
   B. Qualification
   C. Coordination
   D. Notice Filing

5. **An exempt security is**

    A. A security that escapes registration due to the manner in which it is offered and sold

    B. A security deemed to be of investment quality by the securities Administrator

    C. Not subject to the Administrator's requirement to file advertising and sales literature

    D. A security that relieves the broker-dealer from all registration and suitability requirements

6. **An unregistered, non-exempt security may be offered legally in the state if**

    A. It is offered and sold through an exempt transaction

    B. The agent is properly registered in the state

    C. The broker-dealer is properly registered in the state

    D. The investor signs a valid waiver of compliance

CHAPTER 3 REVIEW
QUIZ ANSWERS

1. **ANSWER:** B

    WHY: all securities are subject to the Uniform Securities Act, but an equity indexed or fixed annuity is not a "security." Yes, the test can be exactly this tricky—for a few questions.

2. **ANSWER:** D

    WHY: the "investment contract" was considered to be a security even before the Howey Decision defined what the heck it was. Seriously. Any security is subject to anti-fraud statutes. Period. See the important difference between this and the previous question? One was not a security, one was. Look at these questions from more than one angle.

3. **ANSWER:** D

    WHY: the issuer must register with the SEC under the Securities Act of 1933 and then coordinate the process with the states where the offering is to be made.

4. **ANSWER:** C

    WHY: this company will register with the SEC since the offer is interstate commerce. They will also register by coordination with the states since they are not federal covered.

5. **ANSWER:** C

    WHY: exempt securities escape registration; they do not need a transactional exemption. The Administrator does not make judgments about the investment merit of any security.

6. **ANSWER:** A

WHY: if the security is exempt, the issuer doesn't need to claim a transactional exemption. If the security is non-exempt, it must either be registered or offered/sold through an exempt transaction.

CHAPTER 4

Ethical Practices and Fiduciary Obligations

(24 Questions)

BUSINESS PRACTICES FOR INVESTMENT ADVISERS AND IARs

FRAUD

The main concern of all state securities regulators is protecting their residents from getting ripped off. The folks who pose a potential threat to the residents of any state include agents, broker-dealers, investment advisers, investment adviser representatives, plus all the entrepreneurs out there trying to raise money for shaky little enterprises that put residents at extreme financial risk. Whether registered in the industry or not, any person who is connected with the offer, sale, or purchase of any security is prohibited from making any misleading statements or leaving out important information in a way that is misleading. We're talking about the f-word here, people. **Fraud**. Fraud is a financial crime in which someone misrepresents the truth in a way that takes advantage of the other side. You know those emails telling you that the lovechild of a Third World dictator needs your help in getting $3 million out of his country—if you could, please, simply wire a processing fee of $379.95 immediately? That's a fraud, a scam. Investment advisers had better not defraud people like that. For example, if an adviser inflated client account balances in order to overcharge clients, that would be fraudulent. If an adviser sent out bogus account statements to conceal the fact that all client funds had long ago been turned into a Cadillac Escalade™, that would also be both fraudulent and frowned upon. Fraud can cause a person to end up losing his or her securities license (administrative action), getting sued (civil liability), and maybe even getting thrown in jail (criminal liability).

Let's take a look at a real-world example of an investment adviser who defrauded investors in the "Garden State" of New Jersey:

Office of The Attorney General

- Anne Milgram, Attorney General

Division of Criminal Justice

- Gregory Paw, Director

Jackson Woman Pleads Guilty to Defrauding Investors of $641,000

TRENTON – Attorney General Anne Milgram and Criminal Justice Director Gregory A. Paw announced that an Ocean County woman pleaded guilty today to defrauding investors of more than $600,000 through a false investment scheme.

According to Director Paw, Zina A. Martin, 43, of Jackson, pleaded guilty today to second-degree securities fraud before Superior Court Judge James Den Uyl in Ocean County. Under the plea agreement, Martin faces a sentence of three to five years in state prison. In addition, Martin must pay restitution to her victims of $641,000.

During the plea hearing, Martin admitted that she represented to investors that their money would be placed within certain investment vehicles but, in fact, she used the funds for other purposes. An investigation by the New Jersey Bureau of Securities determined that Martin used the funds to pay business expenses, make payments to other investors, and pay personal expenses, including mortgage payments, monthly living expenses and the purchase of a Cadillac Escalade.

Martin solicited $641,000 from about 25 investors as sole owner and president of Kairos Financial Corporation, which had offices at 331 Newman Springs Road in Red Bank. The Bureau of Securities investigation determined that Martin distributed a brochure to investors describing six different investment funds called the "Kairos Funds," including average yearly returns for some of the funds. She also issued monthly statements informing investors of the amounts they purportedly held in each of the funds. In reality, the Kairos Funds were fictitious and investor monies were commingled in a brokerage account of Kairos Financial.

The case was investigated for the Bureau of Securities by Supervising Investigator Michael McElgunn, Investigator Richard Smullen and Chief of Enforcement Richard Barry. Deputy Attorney General Patrick Flor is prosecuting the case for the Division of Criminal Justice - Major Crimes Bureau and handled today's plea hearing.

In October 2007, the Bureau of Securities revoked the investment adviser registrations of both Martin and Kairos Financial.

So in case you didn't already know, it's a violation to create little pretend mutual funds and send out bogus account statements in order to steal money from investors. I mean, it's creative. It's just, you know, not allowed. The securities regulators are not police officers, though—the regulators are administrative authorities concerned with granting, suspending, or revoking licenses in order to protect investors. When the activities go beyond unethical business practices and into the land of criminal offenses, the state securities regulators turn the case over to a criminal prosecutor. If you were to actually read the criminal code for your state, you would find fraud lumped in there with theft, burglary, and other felonies I don't want on *my* record. Nor do you—as we'll see, the regulators can keep people out of the business for at least 10 years based on felony convictions or even misdemeanors involving crimes of theft and/or deception. One little shoplifting conviction can keep someone out of the business a long time. Creating little pretend mutual funds—usually a career ender.

CONFLICTS OF INTEREST

Maybe the most important thing to know about investment advisers and their IARs is that they are considered "fiduciaries" who must avoid or at least disclose all conflicts of interest to clients. The SEC lays it all out at their excellent website www.sec.gov, which describes the fiduciary obligation like so:

> As an investment adviser, you are a "fiduciary" to your advisory clients. This means that you have a fundamental obligation to act in the best interests of your clients and to provide investment advice in your clients' best interests. You owe your clients a duty of undivided loyalty and utmost good faith. You should not engage in any activity in conflict with the interest of any client, and you should take steps reasonably necessary to fulfill your obligations. You must employ reasonable care to avoid misleading clients and you must provide full and fair disclosure of all material facts to your clients and prospective clients. Generally, facts are "material" if a reasonable investor would consider them to be important. You must eliminate, or at least disclose, all conflicts of interest that might incline you — consciously or unconsciously — to render advice that is not disinterested. If you do not avoid a conflict of interest that could impact the impartiality of your advice, you must make full and frank disclosure of the conflict. You cannot use your clients' assets for your own benefit or the benefit of other clients, at least without client consent. Departure from this fiduciary standard may constitute "fraud" upon your clients.

You may have noticed that regulators do enjoy double negatives such as the phrase, "to render advice that is not disinterested." As on the exam, you occasionally have to interpret such language back to a more natural form that you can work with. And this phrase is actually pretty simple—the advice needs to be disinterested, so anything that could make it "not disinterested" needs to be disclosed. If I'm buying a mutual fund for my advisory client because of the suitability and the excellent track record of performance and low expenses, I'm probably acting as a fiduciary. If I'm buying the mutual funds that pay me the best compensation as an agent or broker-dealer on the side without disclosing that to the client, my advice is "not disinterested," and I may be receiving some registered mail from the regulators very soon. Also notice the "consciously or unconsciously" phrase. An adviser may unconsciously favor advice and actions that benefit the adviser and must, therefore, be mindful of situations that may lead to that problem. He may be the most honest person in the world, but if he's getting a commission when putting his advisory clients' assets into particular securities, the advice is "not disinterested."

Some students in my classes seem to think they'll take care of such problems simply by continuing to be the same trustworthy, decent, hard-working sales professionals they've always been. No, the SEC is saying that you still have to consider, identify, and then disclose the *potential* conflict of interest, even if you think you're far too honest to stoop to such self-serving activities as overcharging clients or favoring mutual funds that pay the highest 12b-1 fees. Whether it is or not, you must tell your clients that this *may* be a conflict of interest or this *could potentially* lead to a conflict of interest. That is how advisers must communicate with their clients.

Clients of investment advisers have a right to expect all investment advice to be given objectively—the adviser doesn't stand to benefit when the client accepts the advice. Rather, the adviser is just giving the client the best advice they can and will charge the same amount whether the client buys a mutual fund, a stock, a bond, or even nothing at this time. We demand that investment advisers remain impartial, disinterested, objective advisers. They get compensated for doing just that. So, if a recommendation to a client would lead to a benefit to the adviser (on top of the advisory fee) if the client accepts it, we have a potential **conflict of interest**. The regulators and the courts have determined long ago that a failure to disclose any conflict of interest to an advisory client is a fraud/deceit, period. Therefore, the following conflicts—to name a few—must be carefully and clearly disclosed to advisory clients.

ACTING AS PRINCIPAL

Full-service firms often have an investment advisory business and a broker-dealer business. So, when the investment advisory business is trading client accounts for a percentage of assets, should they just go ahead and buy the securities directly from the affiliated broker-dealer? Does that sound objective? Any chance that some of the trades this month might have been executed to help the affiliated broker-dealer more than it helped the advisory client? Whose interests is the adviser looking out for here? As a seller of the securities, the broker-dealer wants to get the highest price possible, but as a buyer, you want to get the lowest price possible. Since they're supposed to put your needs first, we now have a major conflict of interest. That's why the adviser would have to disclose the fact that he/they will act as a **principal** in the transaction, and get the client's written consent before "completion of the transaction," which is the settlement of the trade. To act as a principal just means the adviser will either sell the security from the inventory of their related broker-dealer to the customer or buy it for inventory from the customer. It's okay to do it, as long as the potential conflict of interest is disclosed and the customer's written consent is given before the deal is completed.

Now, just in case the exam feels like turning up the heat, what I just told you only applies when the investment adviser is *recommending* the security. If this is an "unsolicited" order, then it was the client's idea, and now we have a completely different situation. It's when the investment adviser is recommending that you buy a security (or using discretion to buy it) that we need the disclosure. Also note that recommending a security and using discretion to purchase it on behalf of the client would be the same thing for the purposes of this rule.

AGENCY CROSS TRANSACTION

Another example of where the adviser will benefit as a result of the advice given is called an **agency cross transaction**. Here, the firm is advising you to buy 1,000 shares of ABC, and, as it turns out, their related/affiliated broker-dealer will act as a broker between you and the seller.

Excuse me? So, should you buy these 1,000 shares because they're a good investment, or because the adviser likes to help the affiliated broker-dealer pocket commissions in addition to the percentage-based advisory fee assessed on your account? That's what we mean by a "conflict of interest"—any situation where the adviser might be financially tempted to talk you into something that benefits the adviser, as opposed to giving objective advice. It might only be a potential conflict of interest, but the fact is that businesses like to make money, so there's just the slight chance that the advice to buy or sell the security might be tainted by the adviser's financial incentive to get the client to accept the advice. Now, the firm might not even charge the advisory client a commission, but if they're charging the other side (the brokerage client) a commission, that could be the incentive that makes their advice less than objective.

So, as usual, the adviser would need to disclose the potential conflict of interest in such a case, get the advisory client's written consent by completion/settlement of the trade, and at least once per year send a statement itemizing all the "agency cross transactions" effected on behalf of the client.

Notice that even though broker-dealers and investment advisers are different business models, most well-known financial services firms are both advisers and broker-dealers. They charge some clients commissions and markups when they broker and deal securities. They act as investment advisers for others, charging a percentage of assets or charging hourly rates for financial planning services. So, for these first two examples of potential conflicts of interest, we are saying, basically, that your investment adviser would also like to work the broker-dealer side of the business. If they act as a dealer/principal on the transaction, they benefit by either selling you a security at a high price (markup) or buying one of yours at a low price (markdown). If they act as a broker on the transaction, they benefit by charging you a commission. Either way, the financial benefit they receive when you accept their advice might be tainting their objectivity. Did your adviser buy 1,000 shares of ABC for your account because it's a good investment, or because he'd like to make a commission or markup for the affiliated broker-dealer? Very possibly the former, but how can you decide if you don't have all the facts?

ADDITIONAL COMPENSATION FOR DIRECTED BROKERAGE

So, as we just said, if the investment adviser, who is charging an asset-based fee on an account's value, is also a broker-dealer, they might want to act as a dealer/principal when the customer buys or sells a security, or they might want to act as an agent/broker when the customer does the trade either on his own or—more likely—because his IAR entered the order through the trading platform.

Many advisers are not broker-dealers, though. Rather, they are very independent types who manage the accounts but let a completely unaffiliated broker-dealer hold the clients' assets and execute all the trades. We could call these unaffiliated firms "custodial broker-dealers," and firms such as TD Ameritrade or Charles Schwab are quite willing and able to maintain custody of an independent investment adviser's client assets. I've passed the Series 65 recently, so if I wanted to, I could register as an investment adviser in any particular state. If so, I would get my clients to grant me the authority to place trades in their account (discretion), but TD Ameritrade, Charles

Schwab, or another broker-dealer would have custody of my client accounts. They would execute all the trades that I place on my clients' behalf and would send account statements to the clients. So, as a businessman, maybe I work out a deal with one of these custodial broker-dealers to receive some sort of economic benefit in exchange for letting them have custody of my client assets. Illegal? Hardly. But if the investment adviser is receiving any economic benefit from the broker-dealer in exchange for maintaining custody and/or executing securities transactions for the advisory clients, that needs to be disclosed. After all, it's only fair that the client be fully informed of all of the rules of the game in which her money is playing. Even if the economic benefit is considered **soft-dollar compensation** that comes in the form of research services or computer software aiding the adviser, it would have to be disclosed to clients as a potential conflict of interest.

12B-1 FEES

Investment advisers and their IARs often also have a Series 6 or 7 license, allowing them to get compensated for selling mutual funds and variable annuities. If an adviser or an IAR is recommending mutual funds and annuities to their clients, they need to disclose the conflict of interest here—what conflict? Their advice is not objective if it leads to extra compensation, right? A 12b-1 fee is a form of regular compensation that the salesperson receives as long as the client stays invested in the mutual fund, and some funds pay upfront based on the sales charge on a front-end loaded fund (A-share). So, as NASAA indicates on their website, an investment adviser must disclose the fact that "the adviser is receiving transaction-based compensation, including 12b-1 or other marketing fees, related to securities recommended to its clients."

Again, did they recommend that you purchase this particular growth-and-income fund because it's an excellent investment opportunity, because it's an excellent opportunity for them to make high 12b-1 fees, or maybe a little bit of both? See, when the adviser provides proper disclosure of potential conflicts of interest, the investor then has a chance to decide such important answers for herself.

ACTING CONTRARY TO RECOMMENDATIONS

If the adviser's recommendations to the client are in opposition with their own investment strategy, that needs to be disclosed. I mean, how would you feel if you found out that your adviser was recommending that you buy a risky tech stock while they are actually selling it short, profiting if it goes down? Shouldn't they at least disclose that they're telling you to do the exact opposite of what they're up to?

HOLDS A POSITION IN THE SECURITY RECOMMENDED

When a stock trades on the OTC market, it is called a NASDAQ stock if it's big and important enough to quote regularly over NASDAQ. The little, less important ones that aren't worth quoting all the time trade on the "OTC Bulletin Board" or "Pink Sheets." These are often illiquid markets, which means that any large buy or sell order tends to shoot the stock price way up or way down. Therefore, if the investment adviser happens to own, say, 10,000 shares of some thinly traded Bulletin Board stock, they would benefit if they could get about 100 clients to put in buy orders. In fact, that might be the main reason they recommend the stock, which would be in direct conflict to their "fiduciary duty" to the client—to put the client's needs first. The stock recommended should be recommended only because it benefits the client. If the purchase of the stock would also benefit the adviser, that potential conflict of interest needs to be disclosed ahead of time. So investment advisers have to disclose that they may buy and sell the same securities that are bought and sold for client accounts. Personally, I would *prefer* that my adviser had some skin in the game before putting me into a large stock position, but that's just me. The regulators, as always, demand full and fair disclosure of all the important/material facts.

Just the way they roll.

TRADE ALLOCATIONS

Portfolio managers aren't generally buying different stocks for different clients. Generally, a portfolio manager has a portfolio model that all clients go into, and the adviser purchases what are called "bunched trades" and then allocates the big bunch of, say, ORCL or IBM shares to various accounts. As the SEC says:

> An adviser may defraud its clients when it fails to use the average price paid when allocating securities to accounts participating in bunched trades and fails to adequately disclose its allocation policy. This practice violates the Advisers Act if securities that were purchased at the lowest price or sold at the highest price are allocated to favored clients without adequate disclosure.

The SEC also says:

> An adviser may defraud its clients by waiting to decide how to allocate a trade among its clients' accounts based on subsequent market movements. The concern is that the adviser could allocate the trade to favored clients if the price movement was favorable and allocate the trade to other accounts if the price movement was unfavorable. This practice is known as "cherry-picking," and violates the Advisers Act.

Also, there is nothing more exciting than an IPO of some company that most people are convinced is the new-new thing. But advisers need to make sure they have a policy on allocating IPO shares—especially "hot" ones, or those that are in great popular demand—and disclose any conflicts of interest here. As the SEC says:

> An adviser may defraud its clients when it disproportionately allocates hot initial public offerings (IPOs) to favored accounts, and does not adequately disclose this practice to all clients. For example, allocations of IPOs may be inequitable when the following types of accounts are favored: proprietary accounts; accounts that pay performance-based fees; accounts that have relatively

poor performance; and new investment companies (in order to boost performance to attract additional assets).

DISCLOSE OR ABSTAIN

Usually, disclosing potential conflicts of interest ahead of time and obtaining the client's consent will take care of the problem; however, sometimes the conflict is so great that the IA must simply abstain from action. What would be so bad that mere disclosure would not take care of the problem? How about if the portfolio manager manages the investment account (the proprietary accounts mentioned a few lines earlier) of the investment advisory business he works for? In this account there are 1 million shares of XYZ common stock. XYZ common stock has also been placed in many client accounts, based on the portfolio manager's discretion. Well, one morning the portfolio manager reads in *The Wall Street Journal* that XYZ's CEO is going to be indicted for fraud, and the company is also going to restate earnings for the past five years, so he unloads the 1 million shares the firm is holding before starting to sell the shares he's put in client portfolios.

Not a chance. Advisers are fiduciaries, who must put the needs of their clients <u>first</u>. This obvious conflict of interest is a no-no, and no amount of disclosure would make it okay. The adviser should have simply abstained from this self-serving activity. I mean, isn't the adviser the same genius who put XYZ stock in the client portfolios? Why should the captain of the ship get to be the one to bail out with the only lifeboat on board when the iceberg looms up out of the fog? You steered us into this mess, Captain, and you can go down with the rest of us.

Compensation Based on Capital Gains, Appreciation

Investment advisers performing "continuous, supervisory management services" get paid a flat fee. Maybe they charge 1% of the assets. That's a great incentive for the adviser, right? One percent of $150,000 is nice, but one percent of $200,000 is even nicer. So, the percentage stays flat and the adviser's compensation only grows if the customer's assets grow.

Sounds like a great way to compensate an investment adviser, right? Well, some advisers would prefer to just take a share of the paper gains or the actual profits made from trading. Every time the adviser buys at 10 and sells at 18, the adviser gets a piece of that capital gain. What about the rest of the stocks? Who cares? We had one big gain, and I, as your adviser, demand my cut. Those other stocks didn't work out the way we figured—what can I tell you?

See, if a client were to pay an adviser with a share of capital gains, the adviser could make a huge profit on one lucky stock pick even if the rest of the account goes down miserably. That might be hard to see, so let's drill down a bit. Say you invested $100,000 with an investment adviser who said he was not going to charge any ongoing fees; rather, he would just take half of any trading profits/capital gains. Sounds darned nice of him at first, but let's say he puts you into 10 stocks with $10,000 invested in each. One stock goes up from $10,000 to $18,000, and you sell it for an 80% profit. You make a short-term capital gain of $8,000, and the adviser takes $4,000. You get $4,000, which could be taxed somewhere between 25% and 35% at the federal level, plus a few more percentage points at the state level. Basically, your after-tax gain is going to be about $2,500. Now, the adviser tells you to just be patient, just wait until those 9 other stocks go up. Only, they never do. You wait and wait, and wait some more, but not only do the other stocks not begin to rise on cue, they also begin to spiral downward. The account drops from $90,000 to $60,000 in a hurry, then slowly drifts down to $36,000, at which point you tell him to sell everything and send you a check for what's left.

So, how did you do in this case? You put down $100,000 and are left with $36,000 plus an after-tax profit of about $2,500. You're down close to 62%! How did the adviser do? He made a fast profit of $4,000 with absolutely no risk to himself. Maybe it's not such a great way to compensate your adviser after all.

Or, maybe dependable, blue chip growth and income stocks are perfectly suitable for a client's portfolio. Unfortunately, if the investment adviser gets paid on a share of capital gains/appreciation, why bother with the slow-and-steady stocks that might not go anywhere for a while? Regardless of the client's risk tolerance, why not pick 20 of the most speculative stocks trading on the OTC Bulletin Board or Pink Sheets? So, offering to share the gains or just the capital appreciation (paper gains) with an investment adviser entices the adviser to take on much bigger risks and often puts the adviser's interests in conflict with those of the client.

And that's why advisers cannot be compensated as a share of capital gains as a general rule. Advisers managing a portfolio, as a general rule, should be compensated as a percentage of assets over a specified time period. If the portfolio manager bills 1% of assets annually, then at the end of each financial quarter, the asset value is multiplied by .25% and that is billed to the account. But investment advisers generally cannot be compensated as a share of capital gains or capital appreciation, or receive a bonus for performance.

The Uniform Securities Act then clarifies that this rule "does not prohibit an investment advisory contract which provides for compensation based upon the total value of a fund averaged over a definite period, or as of definite dates or taken as of a definite date." Maybe "clarifies" was an overstatement. The lawyers who drafted that simply mean that while an adviser can't share the gains on individual stocks or take a percentage of the amount that the account "went up," the firm can bill the client based on the average account balance over a certain period of time or bill a percentage of assets as of, say, the end of each financial quarter. Later, we'll see that this is the general rule, but that sophisticated clients actually can pay the adviser as a share of capital gains or pay a performance bonus to the adviser. But, let's save that excitement for later.

ASSIGNMENT OF CONTRACT

The prohibition against **assignment of contract** means that an adviser cannot sell or transfer a customer's contract to another party without the client's consent. Wouldn't you be ticked if you called up your advisory firm and found out that since your account balance fell below a certain minimum, they just sold it to a money manager in Missoula, Montana? That's why the contract between the investment advisor and the client can only be passed off or "assigned" to another party with the written consent of the client, and the contract must state that fact. Did you get that? Not only would the investment adviser get in trouble for assigning the contract to another party without the client's consent, but if their contract with the client forgot to stipulate that this is not allowed, that would also get them in trouble. The Uniform Securities Act states:

> no assignment of the contract may be made by the investment adviser
> without the consent of the other party to the contract

The Act also says:

> the investment adviser, if a partnership, shall notify the other party to the contract of any change in the membership of the partnership within a reasonable time after the change

NOTIFICATION OF CHANGE IN PARTNERSHIP STRUCTURE

The point directly above means that if the advisory firm is organized as a partnership, whenever one of the partners withdraws or dies—or a new partner is admitted—the firm must inform all clients in a reasonable time frame that the partnership structure has changed. Why? Maybe you're a client because of Jenkins and never particularly cared for Williams or Sonoma, so if Jenkins leaves Williams, Jenkins, and Sonoma Wealth Management Partners, LP, maybe it's time for you to go, too. It doesn't matter in this case if the change was due to a partner with a majority or minority interest.

A slightly different issue is that if a *minority* partner is admitted, withdraws, or dies, even though the partnership must inform its clients of that fact in a timely manner, that is not considered to be an "assignment of contract." In other words, your investment adviser has not changed so drastically that the account is now being handled by another party. The contract didn't get assigned by ABC to XYZ. It's just that ABC has a slightly different partnership structure now. On the other hand, if the change in partners involves a majority owner being admitted or withdrawing, that would require the clients to sign new advisory contracts. If the firm didn't do that, they would have assigned the clients' contracts in violation of securities law.

Before we move on, recall that both state and federal securities laws require advisory contracts to provide at least three things in writing:
- The adviser shall not be compensated for performance (except in certain cases)
- No assignment of contract is allowed without client consent
- If the adviser is a partnership, clients will be notified of any change in the partnership structure

CUSTODY OF CLIENT ASSETS

If fraud is the f-word, custody is the c-word. What's the big deal? Think "Bernie Madoff." How was he able to take clients' money—and I mean *take* clients' money? The clients, unfortunately, allowed him to maintain custody of their assets through an affiliated broker-dealer. Therefore, ole Bernie, the "investment adviser," was able to send out the account statements that showed his clients exactly what he felt they would believe, for years—even when it appears that no investing was ever actually taking place! So, it makes me real nervous when the adviser, who gets paid as a percentage of client assets, can determine or report what those assets are worth without any independent oversight. Some states don't allow it, and good for them. Much of the fraud that takes place in the advisory business could be avoided if investors simply refused to give their investment adviser custody/control of the account assets.

An investment adviser is considered to have **custody** of client assets if the adviser is either holding the funds/securities or has the ability to appropriate (get his hands on) them. If the adviser has the ability to automatically deduct money from the client's account or write checks out of the account, the adviser is considered to have custody of client assets. Or, if the adviser has an ownership stake in the broker-dealer who maintains custody, the adviser is also considered to have custody of client assets. Or, if the adviser is the general partner in a limited partnership or a managing member of an investment LLC, the adviser is considered to have custody. The Uniform Securities Act (state law) says that before taking custody, the adviser first has to check with the state securities Administrator to see if there is a rule prohibiting custody of client assets. If so, they don't take custody. If there's no rule against it, the adviser can take custody so long as they notify the Administrator in writing. So, what if there's no rule against taking custody, and the adviser, in fact, takes custody but fails to inform the Administrator?

The adviser screwed up.

Maintaining custody is an awesome responsibility, and it requires the adviser to maintain higher minimum net capital, to provide an audited balance sheet to the regulators and to clients, and the adviser even has to pay a CPA to come in and audit the books once a year in a surprise audit. If the CPA can't make sense of all the securities and cash positions on the "books and records," they have to notify the Administrator promptly in order to get the firm in trouble. So, the real point of "custody" is that most advisers avoid it like the plague. They're advisers, not banks, right?

The exam might ask what the adviser should do if he receives a check from a client payable to a third party and does not want to be considered to have custody of client assets. First, the "third party" had better truly be an independent party and not an affiliate of the adviser. Second, to avoid the adviser being deemed to have custody, the check must be forwarded to the third party within three business days of receipt, and the adviser must keep records of what happened. Also, if the adviser inadvertently receives client securities in the mail, they must be returned to the sender within three business days. As long as the adviser keeps records as to what happened with the check and/or the securities, they will avoid being deemed to have custody. Therefore, they don't need to maintain higher net capital, update their registration information (**Form ADV**), or have the annoying and expensive CPA audit.

Since few advisers want to keep books and records as accurate as a bank's, most use **qualified custodians** for their clients' funds and securities. If the exam asks about qualified custodians, remember this bullet-point list:

- Banks and Savings Associations
- Registered Broker-Dealers (Custodial Broker-Dealers)
- Registered Futures Commission Merchants
- Foreign Financial Institutions

And, if we're talking about mutual fund shares, the IA can simply use the transfer agent, which is the normal party holding custody of investors' mutual fund shares.

The NASAA website also states:

> NOTE: because the qualified custodian needs to be independent, there should not be any affiliation between the investment adviser and the qualified custodian through any direct or indirect common control relationship.

And then continues with:

> When the investment adviser uses a qualified custodian, the adviser must notify the client immediately in writing of the qualified custodian's name, address, and manner in which the funds or securities are maintained when the account is opened. If the adviser opens accounts for a client with more than one custodian, the client must be notified of all qualified custodian locations. Prompt notification to the client in writing following any changes to the client's account information also is required.

Advisers who automatically deduct management fees from the client account held by the custodian do have custody, but they can avoid maintaining higher net capital or having the CPA audit if they follow "certain safeguards." This means that the adviser must get the client's written authorization to bill the custodian directly, and the adviser must provide both the custodian and the client with an invoice/bill showing how the heck they arrived at their fee. Do they have custody? Yes. Do they have to deal with the higher net capital and the annual surprise audit, etc.? No. Will the exam get this technical and detailed? Maybe. Will I stop asking myself questions now? I will.

If the exam asks about **account statements**, those will be sent from the custodian to the client and must be sent at least quarterly; however, it is still up to the investment adviser to send *billing* statements to the client. Account statements show the securities positions in the account and their most recent market values, plus any dividends and interest received, purchases and sales of securities, deposits and withdrawals of cash over the period. A billing statement, on the other hand, is just an invoice showing the adviser's management fee and how they arrived at it. Since the adviser has a fiduciary duty to the client to make sure that those account statements are being sent by the custodian, it's a good idea to ask the custodian to send a duplicate to the adviser.

For more information on custody, visit www.nasaa.org and read the Q & A as well as the NASAA Model Rule on Custody.

DISCLOSING IDENTITY, AFFAIRS OF CLIENTS

If an advisory firm is trying to land new clients, it would probably be tempting to show prospects what the firm has done for existing clients, disclosing the identity, affairs, or investments of their clients, especially the rich and famous ones.

Yes, well, the existing clients—as well as the securities regulators—would probably have a problem with that. The only way the firm can disclose the identity or the financial matters of its clients is if the clients give permission, or if the firm is forced to turn over the information by court order or a subpoena from a securities regulator.

ADVERTISEMENTS

An advertisement for an investment adviser is defined by the federal government as

> any notice, circular, letter or other written communication addressed to more than one person, or any notice or other announcement in any publication or by radio or television, which offers (1) any analysis, report, or publication concerning securities, or which is to be used in making any determination as to when to buy or sell any security, or which security to buy or sell, or (2) any graph, chart, formula, or other device to be used in making any determination as to when to buy or sell any security, or which security to buy or sell, or (3) any other investment advisory service with regard to securities.

Okay, I promise not to do too much of that. Basically, whatever the media he uses, an adviser is creating an advertisement if he addresses more than one person concerning his advisory services. Advertisements for investment advisers must be fair and accurate. An adviser may not use testimonials from satisfied clients. I guess they can't use testimonials from *dissatisfied* clients, either, though, of course, they wouldn't want to pay somebody big money to go on television and rip the heck out of them. The adviser can list past stock picks provided they don't imply that future results are somehow guaranteed, and if the adviser lists past stock picks, they have to include ALL recommendations—winners and losers—over the same period, which must be at least one year. Because it would be real misleading to talk about your 100% winners over the past week, right? Especially if you conveniently failed to bring up the 100% losers. If the actual picks aren't provided, it needs to be clear that a list will be provided upon written request without charge or obligation. Also, if the adviser's stock picks are up 50%, how does that compare to the market in general? If the S&P gained 52% and this guy's stock picks gained 50%, I'd be better off knowing the *whole* story, right? If the recommendations listed pertain only to a select group of the adviser's clients, that needs to be made clear. It also needs to be clear whether the performance figures are including the IA's management fees (deducted from the returns, right?). "If the advertisement claims that any graph, chart, formula or other device being offered will assist any person in making his own decisions, the advertisement must prominently disclose the limitations thereof and the difficulties with respect to its use." If the adviser offers "free services with no obligation," those services had better actually be free, with, sure enough, no obligation. In general, IA advertisements need to go to great lengths to avoid misleading prospects and clients. And, any performance claims made by the adviser need to be backed up by the "books and records" required to be kept by the firm.

Now, as exciting as this chapter and book have been up to now, I would like to raise the excitement level even another notch by showing you that this stuff does not just exist in the so-called "test world." Most of what I'm telling you is as real-world as a heart attack. In fact, in my own fine state of Illinois, the securities Administrator recently cracked down on an investment adviser who was kind enough to exemplify many testable points that we just finished discussing. Let's take a look at how some of this regulatory stuff works out in the real world.

STATE OF ILLINOIS
SECRETARY OF STATE
SECURITIES DEPARTMENT

	)
IN THE MATTER OF: ROBERT WILLIAM ESCH	) No.
DBA WHITEMOUNTAIN FINANCIAL	) 0300042
	)

<u>CONSENT ORDER</u>

TO THE RESPONDENT: Robert William Esch
DBA WhiteMountain Financial
539 Troy Plaza
Troy, Illinois 62294

C/O Charles J. Northrup
Sorling, Northrup, Hanna,
Cullen & Cochran, Ltd
Attorneys at Law
607 East Adams Street, Suite 800
Springfield, Illinois 62705

WHEREAS, Robert William Esch DBA WhiteMountain Financial on January 12, 2005 executed a certain Stipulation To Entry Of Consent Order (the "Stipulation"), which hereby is incorporated by reference herein.

WHEREAS, by means of the Stipulation, the Respondent has admitted to the jurisdiction of the Secretary of State and service of the Notice of Hearing in this matter and the Respondent has consented to the entry of this Consent Order.

WHEREAS, the Secretary of State, by and through his designated representative, the Securities Director, has determined that the matter related to the aforesaid formal hearing may be dismissed without further proceeding.

WHEREAS, the Respondent has acknowledged that the allegations contained in paragraph seven (7) of the Stipulation shall be adopted as the Secretary of State's Findings of Fact as follows:

1. At all times relevant, the Respondent was an Illinois registered Investment Adviser and Investment Adviser Representative pursuant to Section 8 of the Illinois Securities Law of 1953, 815 ILCS 5/1 et seq. (the "Act").

2. That from on or about January 2003 to on or about July 15,

2004 the Respondent advertised, operated and managed an investment management system under the name of the Super T Asset Management System and had about 25 persons participating in the system including the Respondent and some of the Respondent's family members.

3. The Super T Asset Management System was advertised and described to clients and prospective clients ("clients") as an investment advisory program in which the client would invest a minimum of $25,000 to be managed by the Respondent for a management fee of .75% of assets under management or a minimum of $250 each half year. Additionally, clients were told that their investment would be invested all in cash or all in one stock of the Respondent's choice. In later contracts, the phrase "all one stock" was replaced with "all one security" or "all one investment."

4. As part of the Super T Asset Management System, clients entered into an investment advisory contract with the Respondent in which they agreed to open brokerage accounts with a third party discount brokerage firm and give authority to the Respondent to execute transactions in these accounts on their behalf. Pursuant to such authority the Respondent executed buy and sell transactions of the security SPY, an exchange traded fund in the form of a Unit Investment Trust listed on the American Stock Exchange.

5. The Respondent mailed, delivered or caused to be delivered to clients advertising material which included performance measurement figures and/or charts for the Super T Asset Management System.

6. The Respondent violated the Illinois Securities Act and its Rules and Regulations in the following matter.

7. The advertising material referenced in paragraph 5 above contained performance measurements without complying with United States Securities and Exchange Commission Rule 206(4)-1 of the Rules and Regulations Under the Investment Advisers Act of 1940.

8. Additionally, the advertising material was misleading or false because: (a) it did not disclose that the past performance measurements for the Super T Asset Management System were not based upon actual trades but were based solely upon hypothetical recommendations and transactions; (b) failed to disclose that the percentage returns quoted in the material

were before any fees paid or transactions costs and that actual returns would be lower; (c) failed to disclose that a quoted annualized rate of return was hypothetical and based upon a projection of a rate of return from 3-4 months and not upon an actual annualized rate of return; and (d) falsely misrepresented that the Super T Asset Management System was a registered or trademarked system when in fact it was not.

9. Failed to disclose material information to clients by: (a) failing to disclose that management fees were negotiable and that some clients were paying a reduced fee or had their fees waived by the Respondent; (b) failing to disclose that the minimum investment amount of $25,000 in the Super T Asset Management System was negotiable and some clients had invested less; (c) failing to disclose that the security SPY was an Exchange Traded Fund and a Unit Investment Trust and not a stock; and (d) failing to disclose that some participants in the Super T Asset Management System were relatives of the Respondent and were not paying advisory fees and/or had invested less than the minimum investment amount of $25,000.

10. Respondent entered into some investment advisory contracts with clients which: (a) did not include terms stating that the contract could not be assigned without the consent of the other party; (b) did not reflect that the minimum investment amount had been modified by previous agreement of the parties; and/or (c) identified the incorrect name of the client/party to the contract.

11. For some clients, the Respondent was accepting fees of over $500 and six or more months in advance but was not complying with Illinois Securities Department Rule 844 and in one case the Respondent billed the client an incorrect fee amount resulting in an overcharge to the client of 2.5 times the correct amount.

12. The Respondent provided to clients forms which he requested the client to fill out which stated at the bottom of the forms that: a) "This form is required by the Illinois Securities Department. Thank you for your cooperation."; or (b) "The information requested on this form is required by the Illinois Securities Department. Your cooperation is appreciated." When in fact neither the form nor the information was required by the Illinois Securities Department.

13. Filing a Form ADV with the Department which contained

misleading or inaccurate information or omitted material information.

14. That Rule 130.844 of the Rules and Regulations under the Illinois Securities Act, 14 Admin Code 130.100 et seq., provides, inter alia, that each registered investment adviser which accepts prepayment of fees in excess of $500.00 per client and six (6) or more months in advance shall file [with the Department] a statement of financial condition (balance sheet) and interim financial statement, in such detail as will disclose the nature and amounts of assets and liabilities and net worth of the investment adviser.

15. Section 8.E.1(b) of the Act provides, inter alia, that subject to the provisions of subsection F of Section 11 of the Act, the registration of an investment adviser or investment adviser representative may be suspended or revoked if the Secretary of State finds that the investment adviser or investment advisor representative has engaged in any unethical practice in the offer or sale of securities or in any fraudulent business practice.

16. Section 8.E.1(m) of the Act provides, inter alia, that subject to the provisions of subsection F of Section 11 of the Act, the registration of an investment adviser or investment adviser representative may be suspended or revoked if the Secretary of State finds that the investment adviser or investment advisor representative has conducted a continuing course of dealing of such nature as to demonstrate an inability to properly conduct the business of the dealer, limited Canadian dealer, salesperson, investment adviser or investment adviser representative.

17. Section 8.E.1(q) of the Act provides, inter alia, that subject to the provisions of subsection F of Section 11 of the Act, the registration of an investment adviser or investment adviser representative may be suspended or revoked if the Secretary of State finds that the investment adviser or investment adviser representative has failed to maintain the books and records required under this Act or regulations under this Act or under any requirements established by the Securities and Exchange Commission or self-regulatory organization.

WHEREAS, the Respondent has acknowledged that the allegation contained in paragraph eight (8) of the Stipulation shall be adopted as the Secretary of State's Conclusion of Law as follows:

By virtue of the foregoing, the Respondent is subject to the entry of an Order which revokes his investment adviser and investment adviser representative registrations in the State of Illinois pursuant to the authority provided under Section 8.E.1(b), (m) or (q) of the Act.

NOW THEREFORE IT IS HEREBY ORDERED THAT:

1. The allegations contained in paragraphs seven (7) and eight (8) of the Stipulation shall be and are hereby adopted as the Secretary of State's Findings of Fact and Conclusion of Law;

2. The Respondent's Investment Adviser and Investment Adviser Representative registrations in Illinois are revoked as of the last date that the registrations were effective;

3. The Respondent, Robert William Esch, shall pay a fine of $15,000 payable to the Secretary of State by certified check or money order within thirty days of the entry of the order;

4. The Respondent shall deliver a copy of this consent order, along with a cover letter stating that if the recipient has any questions regarding the consent order to contact the Illinois Securities Department, to all of his current and former investment advisory clients within 10 business days of the entry the consent order;

5. The Respondent shall not reapply for any registration under the Illinois Securities Act for two years from the date of entry of the consent order; and

6. The formal hearing scheduled on this matter is hereby dismissed without further proceeding.

ENTERED: This _____ day of _____, 2005.

_____

JESSE WHITE
Secretary of State

NOTICE: Failure to comply with the terms of this Order shall be a violation of Section 12.D of the Illinois Securities Law of 1953 [815 ILCS 5] (the "Act"). Any person or entity who fails to comply with the terms of this Order of the Secretary of State, having knowledge of the existence of this Order, shall be guilty of a Class 4 felony.

Attorney for the Secretary of State:
David Finnigan
Illinois Securities Department
Lincoln Tower, Suite 200
520 South Second Street
Springfield, Illinois 62701
Telephone: (217) 785-4947

Wow—where do we start? First, it is *not* okay to enter into advisory contracts with clients that state that the minimum investment is $25,000 and the management fees are a set amount, when, in fact, some clients don't have to meet the minimum and don't have to, like, pay. WTH? If the minimum investment and the fees charged are actually negotiable, it is a fraudulent business practice to sign contracts with clients that state or imply otherwise. Speaking of the advisory contracts, we notice that the adviser accepted prepayment of fees in excess of $500 six or more months in advance but did not comply with the Administrator's rules governing this practice—he needed to provide clients and the state securities Administrator an audited balance sheet. Oopsie. Also, his contracts failed to state that no assignment of contract was allowed without client consent—in other words, even though he didn't actually assign the contracts, he still screwed up by forgetting to insert that clause into the contract itself.

Okay, so his advisory contracts were sloppy and misleading, and he accidentally billed somebody 2.5 times the correct amount. Stuff happens, right? What really caught my attention was his advertising. Now, when the regulators use words such as "were not based upon actual trades but were based solely upon hypothetical recommendations and transactions," it's not always easy to see what they mean. What they mean is that the dude is showing us how wonderful his stock picks performed recently with one sort of important fact being omitted—dude never actually bought any of the stocks. I mean, come on, all I have to do is find the 10 best performing stocks of last year and put out an advertisement claiming that I was all over them. If I didn't mind getting busted, that is. So, not only did he not purchase the stocks he claimed to have picked, but the performance figures on the little pretend stock picks only covered a period of 3 or 4 months, which he then multiplied by 3 or 4 to get an annualized rate of return. Now, when we were calculating annualized rates of return in another section, we were partly just doing an academic exercise. No way can an investment adviser get a 10% return in one week and then advertise his 520% annualized rates of return. Remember that when an investment adviser puts out an advertisement listing stock picks, the period covered has to be *at least one year*. And, the regulators would be tickled to death if the adviser actually bought the stocks he claims to have bought and can back it all up with the "books and records required to be kept by the firm." I mean, if you say you picked all those wonderful stocks, what's the problem with pulling out the trade confirmations and account statements backing up your claims?

Finally, not only did he not pick any of the stocks he claimed to have bought; not only did the period used for his little pretend stock picks not cover a full year; but also the performance figures he quoted on the stocks he never picked failed to clarify that if management fees and transaction costs had been included, the numbers would have been lower.

Other than that, it was a great advertising piece.

Did you also notice a few things at the end of the consent order? First, there is a mandatory two-year sabbatical. Next, the dude has to deliver a copy of this consent order to each current and former client with a cover letter encouraging the customer to contact the state regulator if they have any questions. Third, the order states that any "willful violation" of this order is considered a Class 4 felony in Illinois. And, the penalties for a Class 4 felony in Illinois are very close to what the Uniform Securities Act uses with its "three years in prison, $5,000 fine, or both."

In other words, try not to commit any willful violations if you can help it. And please know that I just happened to use an Illinois enforcement order—the exam is *not* concerned with the specifics of the Illinois Securities Act. It's just that the Illinois, California, Missouri, or Oregon securities laws would be very close to one another, since they all follow the template called the Uniform Securities Act. And, you can see hundreds of these enforcement orders at the state regulatory websites for yourself. Do a Google search on something like "State of California Securities" or "Oklahoma Securities Administrator." Or, assuming they don't change the website, you can quickly find any state regulator by going to www.nasaa.org and clicking on "contact your regulator," which pulls up a list of regulators for all the states and Canada.

USE OF SOLICITORS

There is one main reason I have not opened my own advisory business: I hate to sell. I hate making the phone calls, leaving the voice mails, and—most of all—I hate driving out to some godforsaken place and finding the client is not actually there for the appointment he just scheduled two freaking hours ago. Since I hate to sell, I could hire some licensed individuals as my investment adviser representatives. I'd send the state a U4 form with their information, pay an annoying little fee, and then turn them loose on investing prospects. Or, I could just use the services of licensed individuals or firms on more of an independent contractor basis. Since the individual or firm would be going around soliciting new business, the regulators decided to call such people **solicitors**. Remember that to use a solicitor the <u>adviser</u> must be registered; there can be no outstanding order suspending, limiting, or barring the <u>solicitor's</u> activities; and there must be a written agreement between the solicitor and the adviser. Also, the following conditions must be met:

- The agreement between the adviser and the solicitor must describe the solicitation activities and the compensation arrangement.
- The solicitor must provide the client with the adviser's disclosure brochure and a separate solicitor disclosure document.
- The adviser must receive a signed acknowledgment from the client that he/she received both the IA's and the solicitor's disclosure documents.

As usual, the investment adviser has a lot of responsibility in this situation. Notice how the adviser needs a signed acknowledgment from the client that both disclosure brochures were received. Also, you can bet that if the solicitor were some shady character, the adviser would not be able to stand back shrugging off responsibility to the regulators with something like, "Hey, I ain't responsible for what that clown told them people. He's a big boy; he shoulda known better." That, of course, would not generally be a good response to a securities regulator, with or without the non-standard grammar.

The adviser would be expected to do some due diligence on this "clown" that they employ, and if an adviser knew the dude was, like, a convicted felon or somebody who's been popped for fraud, forgery, or embezzlement, for example, and hired him anyway...ooh, you wouldn't believe how upset the regulators get over that kind of stuff. Pretty soon they're spitting Latin phrases at you, sending requests for documents by registered mail, and doing everything in their power to make sure you don't have any good days for a long, long while.

And, let's see how closely you're reading this material—does the solicitor have to be registered? I never actually said that, did I? The important point is that the adviser has to be registered, has to oversee the solicitor, and the solicitor cannot be some walking regulatory nightmare. Most states would call a "solicitor" an "investment adviser representative" and make him register as such. But not all states feel that way.

USE OF REPORTS

If an adviser sells you a recommendation, plan, or analysis, you'd probably assume it was their work, right? To avoid misleading the client, then, if somebody else actually did the work, that would have to be disclosed by the adviser. However, if an adviser subscribes to a newsletter or buys reports that help them make recommendations to you, that's just fine and requires no disclosure. The adviser's disclosure brochure would already indicate in general what sources of information are used in determining recommendations (financial newspapers and magazines, research materials prepared by others, company press releases, annual reports filed with SEC, etc.). So, there's a big difference between passing off some other professional's work as the adviser's and using other professionals' work to *help* the IA make/render the investment advice to the client.

MISLEADING NAMES

Regulators register securities professionals. They never certify or approve them. A securities professional might earn credentials such as "Chartered Financial Analyst" or "Certified Financial Planner," but that means that an independent organization has decided to issue that designation. The securities regulators don't certify or approve the professionals. To indicate that you have been "certified" or "approved" by the securities regulators will get you into all kinds of trouble. Section 208 of the Investment Advisers Act of 1940 makes this very clear with the following statement:

> **Representations of sponsorship by United States or agency thereof. It shall be unlawful for any person registered under section 203 to represent or imply in any manner whatsoever that such person has been sponsored, recommended, or approved, or that his abilities or qualifications have in any respect been passed upon by the United States or any agency or any officer thereof.**

The title "investment counsel" may only be used by those advisers deemed to be performing "supervisory services." In other words, to call yourself an "investment counsel," you have to be actively managing money/affairs for particular clients, not just writing newsletters to a group of subscribers or performing annual reviews of their financial plans.

And that same Section 208 of the Investment Advisers Act of 1940 makes this point quite clearly for us, as well, when it states:

> Use of name "investment counsel" as descriptive of business. It shall be unlawful for any person registered under section 203 to represent that he is an investment counsel or to use the name "investment counsel" as descriptive of his business unless (1) his or its principal business consists of acting as investment adviser, and (2) a substantial part of his or its business consists of rendering investment supervisory services.

Securities regulators are currently making a coordinated effort to crack down on financial services professionals who use special designations to mislead senior citizens. While some of the credentials are legitimate, many make the regulators nervous, including the ever-popular "Certified Financial Gerontologist." Regulators recently performed a survey that showed that one-quarter of all senior investors were told that the financial professionals they were talking to were specially certified or qualified to help senior citizens, and half of those investors said they were more likely to listen to the advice because of that. Unfortunately, designations are often obtained simply by paying a fee to the organization that prints you up an official-looking certificate. NASAA has written a model rule for states trying to deal with this hot regulatory topic, and I recommend that you read it. You do plan to spend some serious time at the NASAA website, right? It is their exam, remember.

CODE OF ETHICS

Investment advisers are responsible for the activities of their employees and, therefore, the SEC requires that advisers "establish, maintain, and enforce a written **code of ethics**." If you are an investment adviser, your code of ethics needs to include:

- A standard of business conduct that you require of your supervised persons reflecting your fiduciary obligations and those of your supervised persons
- Provisions requiring your supervised persons to comply with applicable federal securities laws
- Provisions that require all of your access persons to report, and you to review, their personal securities transactions and holdings periodically
- Provisions requiring supervised persons to report any violations of your code of ethics promptly to your chief compliance officer
- Provisions requiring you to provide each of your supervised persons with a copy of your code of ethics and any amendments, and requiring your supervised persons to provide you with a written acknowledgment of their receipt of the code and any amendments

For purposes of this rule, the SEC uses the term "access persons" and then defines them as

> any supervised person who has access to nonpublic information
> regarding any clients' purchase or sale of securities, or nonpublic
> information regarding the portfolio holdings of any reportable fund,
> or who is involved in making securities recommendations to clients,
> or who has access to such recommendations that are nonpublic.

In other words, if you are making recommendations to clients, managing their portfolios, or simply know what securities are inside those client portfolios, you are an access person. If your firm manages mutual funds, and you know what they're buying before the public does, you are clearly an "access person." Directors, officers, and partners are presumed to be access persons, as well. Under this code of ethics, the adviser needs to keep records of their access persons' securities holdings (what they own) and transactions (what they buy and sell). The holding reports must include:

- The title and type of security, and as applicable the exchange ticker symbol or CUSIP number, number of shares, and principal amount of each reportable security in which the access person has any direct or indirect beneficial ownership
- The name of any broker, dealer or bank with which the access person maintains an account in which any securities are held for the access person's direct or indirect benefit; and
- The date the access person submits the report

These reports must be filed with the chief compliance officer no later than 10 days after becoming an "access person," and once a year an updated report must be filed. The information must be accurate as of no more than 45 days prior to filing the report.

The transaction reports that "access persons" must file with the chief compliance officer have to include at a minimum:

- The date of the transaction, the title, and as applicable the exchange ticker symbol or CUSIP number, interest rate and maturity date, number of shares, and principal amount of each reportable security involved
- The nature of the transaction (e.g., purchase, sale or any other type of acquisition or disposition)
- The price of the security at which the transaction was effected
- The name of the broker, dealer or bank with or through which the transaction was effected; and
- The date the access person submits the report

These transaction reports need to be submitted for each financial quarter and no more than 30 days after the end of the quarter. The simplest way to comply with the code of ethics requirement is for the adviser to require their "access persons" to have copies of their brokerage statements and trade confirmations sent to the firm.

The rule also states that before an access person buys into an IPO or limited offering, he/she must receive pre-approval from the chief compliance officer. And, lest we think the SEC lacks a sense of humor, the rule actually states, "if you have only one access person (i.e., yourself), you are not required to submit reports to yourself or to obtain your own approval for investments in any security in an initial public offering or in a limited offering, if you maintain records of all of your holdings and transactions that this section would otherwise require you to report."

Since every rule has to have exceptions, an investment made through an "automatic investment plan" is not a transaction that has to be reported. In other words, if you are set up for a DRIP (dividend reinvestment program), in which your dividends regularly purchase more shares of stock, that is, by definition, not a suspicious purchase of securities since it's happening on autopilot. Or, if you're doing a systematic withdrawal plan out of a mutual fund, same deal. Finally, investments in the following are not reportable:

- Direct obligations of the government of the United States
- Banker's acceptances, bank certificates of deposit, commercial paper and high-quality short-term debt instruments, including repurchase agreements
- Shares issued by money market funds
- Shares issued by open-end funds other than reportable funds (you're not an adviser to this fund, and neither is the firm that controls you)
- Shares issued by unit investment trusts that are invested exclusively in one or more open-end funds, none of which are reportable funds

NASAA MODEL RULE ON BUSINESS PRACTICES FOR ADVISERS

The organization of state and Canadian provincial securities regulators is called **NASAA**, which stands for the **North American Securities Administrators Association.** They're not a regulatory body themselves; they are the organization of state securities regulators that attempts to keep all the regulators on top of important issues and working from more or less the same page when writing and rewriting rules for their various states. NASAA is in charge of the Series 63, 65, and 66 exams, so you can maybe send them a thank-you note when you're done with your test. Either way, their model rules and statements of policy are highly testable on your exam, so let's take a look at them in extreme detail.

The following is the actual model rule telling investment advisers, investment adviser representatives, and federal covered advisers what's what. It is followed by my own plain-English translation of the legalese. No matter how dense this document is, try to hang with it. These are among the most testable pages of material related to the exam.

Model Rule 102(a)(4)-1
Adopted 4/27/97, amended 4/18/04, 9/11/05

Rule 102(a)(4)-1 Unethical Business Practices
  Of Investment Advisers, Investment Adviser
  Representatives, And Federal Covered Advisers

[Introduction] A person who is an investment adviser, an investment adviser representative or a federal covered adviser is a fiduciary and has a duty to act primarily for the benefit of its clients. The provisions of this subsection apply to federal covered advisers to the extent that the conduct alleged is fraudulent, deceptive, or as otherwise permitted by the National Securities Markets Improvement Act of 1996 (Pub. L. No. 104-290). While the extent and nature of this duty varies according to the nature of the relationship between an investment adviser or an investment adviser representative and its clients and the circumstances of each case, an investment adviser, an investment adviser representative or a federal covered adviser shall not engage in unethical business practices, including the following:

(a) Recommending to a client to whom investment supervisory, management or consulting services are provided the purchase, sale or exchange of any security without reasonable grounds to believe that the recommendation is suitable for the client on the basis of information furnished by the client after reasonable inquiry concerning the client's investment objectives, financial situation and needs, and any other information known by the investment adviser.

(b) Exercising any discretionary power in placing an order for the purchase or sale of securities for a client without obtaining written discretionary authority from the client within ten (10) business days after the date of the first transaction placed pursuant to oral discretionary authority, unless the discretionary power relates solely to the price at which, or the time when, an order involving a definite amount of a specified security shall be executed, or both.

(c) Inducing trading in a client's account that is excessive in size or frequency in view of the financial resources, investment objectives and character of the account in light of the fact that an investment adviser or an investment adviser representative in such situations can directly benefit from the number of securities transactions effected in a client's account. The rule appropriately forbids an excessive number of transaction orders to be induced by an adviser for a "customer's account."

(d) Placing an order to purchase or sell a security for the account of a client without authority to do so.

(e) Placing an order to purchase or sell a security for the account of a client upon instruction of a third party without first having obtained a written third-party trading authorization from the client.

(f) Borrowing money or securities from a client unless the client is a broker-dealer, an affiliate of the investment adviser, or a financial institution engaged in the business of loaning funds.

(g) Loaning money to a client unless the investment adviser is a financial institution engaged in the business of loaning funds or the client is an affiliate of the investment adviser.

(h) Misrepresenting to any advisory client, or prospective advisory client, the qualifications of the investment adviser or any employee of the investment adviser, or misrepresenting the nature of the advisory services being offered or fees to be charged for such service, or to omit to state a material fact necessary to make the statements made regarding qualifications, services or fees, in light of the circumstances under which they are made, not misleading.

(i) Providing a report or recommendation to any advisory client prepared by someone other than the adviser without disclosing that fact. (This prohibition does not apply to a situation where the adviser uses published research reports or statistical analyses to render advice or where an adviser orders such a report in the normal course of providing service.)

(j) Charging a client an unreasonable advisory fee.

(k) Failing to disclose to clients in writing before any advice is rendered any material conflict of interest relating to the adviser, or any of its employees which could reasonably be expected to impair the rendering of unbiased and objective advice including:

(1.) Compensation arrangements connected with advisory services to clients which are in addition to compensation from such clients for such services; and

(2.) Charging a client an advisory fee for rendering advice when a commission for executing securities transactions pursuant to such advice will be received by the adviser or its employees.

(l) Guaranteeing a client that a specific result will be achieved (gain or no loss) with advice which will be rendered.

(m) [Alternative 1] Publishing, circulating or distributing any advertisement which does not comply with Rule 206(4)-1 under the Investment Advisers Act of 1940.

(m) [Alternative 2] (1.) Except as otherwise provided in subsection (2.), it shall constitute a dishonest or unethical practice within the meaning of [Uniform Act Sec. 102(a)(4)] for any investment adviser or investment adviser representative, directly or indirectly, to use any advertisement that does any one of the following:

(i.) Refers to any testimonial of any kind concerning the investment adviser or investment adviser representative or concerning any advice, analysis, report, or other service rendered by such investment adviser or investment adviser representative.

(ii.) Refers to past specific recommendations of the investment adviser or investment adviser representative that were or would have been profitable to any person; except that an investment adviser or investment adviser representative may furnish or offer to furnish a list of all recommendations made by the investment adviser or investment adviser representative within the immediately preceding period of not less than one year if the advertisement or list also includes both of the following:

(A) The name of each security recommended, the date and nature of each recommendation, the market price at that time, the price at which the recommendation was to be acted upon, and the most recently available market price of each such security.

(B) A legend on the first page in prominent print or type that states that the reader should not assume that recommendations made in the future will be profitable or will equal the performance of the securities in the list.

(iii.) Represents that any graph, chart, formula, or other device being offered can in and of itself be used to determine which securities to buy or sell, or when to buy or sell them; or which represents, directly or indirectly, that any graph, chart, formula, or other device being offered will assist any person in making that person's own decisions as to which securities to buy or sell, or when to buy or sell them, without prominently disclosing in such advertisement the limitations thereof and the difficulties with respect to its use.

(iv.) Represents that any report, analysis, or other service will be furnished for free or without charge, unless such report, analysis, or other service actually is or will be furnished entirely free and without any direct or indirect condition or obligation.

(v.) Represents that the [Administrator] has approved any advertisement.

(vi.) Contains any untrue statement of a material fact, or that is otherwise false or misleading.

(2.) With respect to federal covered advisers, the provisions of this section only apply to the extent permitted by Section 203A of the Investment Advisers Act of 1940.

(3.) For the purposes of this section, the term "advertisement" shall include any notice, circular, letter, or other written communication addressed to more than one person, or any notice or other announcement in any electronic or paper publication, by radio or television, or by any medium, that offers any one of the following:

(i.) Any analysis, report, or publication concerning securities.

(ii.) Any analysis, report, or publication that is to be used in making any determination as to when to buy or sell any security or which security to buy or sell

(iii.) Any graph, chart, formula, or other device to be used in making any determination as to when to buy or sell any security, or which security to buy or sell.

(iv.) Any other investment advisory service with regard to securities.

(n) Disclosing the identity, affairs, or investments of any client unless required by law to do so, or unless consented to by the client.

(o) Taking any action, directly or indirectly, with respect to those securities or funds in which any client has any beneficial interest, where the investment adviser has custody or possession of such securities or funds when the advisor's action is subject to and does not comply with the requirements of Rule 102e(1)-1. and any subsequent amendments.

(p) Entering into, extending or renewing any investment advisory contract, unless such contract is in writing and discloses, in substance, the services to be provided, the term of the contract, the advisory fee, the formula for computing the fee, the amount of prepaid fee to be returned in the event of contract termination or non-performance, whether the contract grants discretionary power to the adviser and that no assignment of such contract shall be made by the investment adviser without the consent of the other party to the contract.

(q) Failing to establish, maintain, and enforce written policies and procedures reasonably designed to prevent the misuse of material nonpublic information contrary to the provisions of Section 204A of the Investment Advisers Act of 1940.

(r) Entering into, extending, or renewing any advisory contract contrary to the provisions of Section 205 of the Investment Advisers Act of 1940. This provision shall apply to all advisers and investment adviser representatives registered or required to be registered under this Act, notwithstanding whether such adviser or representative would be exempt from federal registration pursuant to Section 203(b) of the Investment Advisers Act of 1940.

(s) To indicate, in an advisory contract, any condition, stipulation, or provisions binding any person to waive compliance with any provision of this act or of the Investment Advisers Act of

1940, or any other practice contrary to the provisions of Section 215 of the Investment Advisers Act of 1940.

(t) Engaging in any act, practice, or course of business which is fraudulent, deceptive, or manipulative in contrary to the provisions of Section 206(4) of the Investment Advisers Act of 1940, notwithstanding the fact that such investment adviser or investment adviser representative is not registered or required to be registered under Section 203 of the Investment Advisers Act of 1940.

(u) Engaging in conduct or any act, indirectly or through or by any other person, which would be unlawful for such person to do directly under the provisions of this act or any rule or regulation thereunder.

The conduct set forth above is not inclusive. Engaging in other conduct such as non-disclosure, incomplete disclosure, or deceptive practices shall be deemed an unethical business practice. The federal statutory and regulatory provisions referenced herein shall apply to investment advisers, investment adviser representatives and federal covered advisers to the extent permitted by the National Securities Markets Improvement Act of 1996 (Pub. L. No. 104-290).

ONCE MORE, IN ENGLISH...

The first point this model rule makes is that an investment adviser, investment adviser representative, or federal covered adviser is a fiduciary and has a duty to act primarily for the benefit of its clients. Of course, we've already mentioned that, but notice how NASAA mentions it right off the bat in this model rule. It's that important. Also, by listing all three terms (investment adviser, investment adviser representative, federal covered adviser), the document reminds us that each term is related yet different. The investment adviser and federal covered adviser are business entities, while the investment adviser representative is the individual who represents one of those business entities. Also, there is a difference between an "investment adviser" and a "federal covered adviser." The difference is simply that the federal covered adviser is registered with the SEC, while the "investment adviser" is subject to the state's registration. Notice how the provisions laid out in this document (written by a group of *state* regulators) "apply to federal covered advisers to the extent that the conduct alleged is fraudulent, deceptive, or as otherwise permitted by [**NSMIA**]."

Please make sure you understand the rather nuanced concepts surrounding a "federal covered adviser." A federal covered adviser could have an office in the state of California and have 7.5 bazillion dollars under management. Clearly, they register with the SEC and are federal covered. But, this model rule is also making clear that the big, bad advisory firm is still subject to the state's powers to enforce anti-fraud rules. In other words, the federal covered adviser sends Form ADV to the SEC, and tells the SEC to send a copy to the State of California. This is called a "notice filing." As long as they do that, this adviser will not have to hear from the State of California again, unless "the conduct alleged is fraudulent, deceptive, or as otherwise permitted by NSMIA." So, a federal covered adviser registers only with the SEC, but the adviser is still subject to both the SEC's and the state's ability to protect investors from fraudulent, deceptive practices in the securities business. And, really, how could it be any other way? Since we had so much fun dissecting the *introduction* to this NASAA model rule, let's now have some fun looking at the specifics.

Item (a) reminds investment advisers not to recommend the purchase or sale of any security unless they have reasonable grounds to believe it's a suitable recommendation. Notice how the item specifically mentions clients "to whom supervisory, management or consulting services are provided." Another type of advisory service is called "impersonal advice," and this advice does not even purport/claim to be specific for the individual client. There is a world of difference between delivering the same advice to a group that is generally interested in, say, value investing, and providing "supervisory, management or consulting services" to a specific client. If I'm supervising your investment activities, actually managing your portfolio, or getting paid a big hourly rate as a consultant, the regulators would be tickled to death if I actually knew something about your situation before I start running my mouth or running the meter.

The second item is a little surprising to me. I would have figured the adviser needs written discretionary authority from the client *before* using discretionary power, but it turns out the client can give oral authorization to get the discretionary nature of the account going. The adviser then has 10 business days after the first discretionary order is placed to obtain written authorization.

Actually, this makes perfect sense. Broker-dealers need written discretionary authority before making any discretionary trades because they get compensated per transaction and the temptation to just start buying stuff on their client's behalf would be overwhelming, like asking my two cats to baby-sit your pet hamster for a couple of days. I mean, after a while, what are you gonna do? It's a hamster—we're hungry predators with sharp claws. But an investment adviser gets compensated by charging a percentage of the assets, so if he makes some dumb purchases he'll not only not gain from it, but also his fee will start going down with the assets. One percent of $100,000 is better than 1% of $80,000, right? Discretion allows a broker-dealer or adviser to enter transactions on behalf of a client without first talking to the client. If they can choose which security is to be bought or sold and how many shares, they are using discretion.

Item (c) simply says that advisers should not try to induce their clients to become frantic traders, especially if the adviser is getting compensated for those transactions. So, churning is always a bad idea, and an even worse idea if the adviser is also getting paid to broker the trades.

Item (d) reminds advisers and their reps not to purchase or sell securities when they have no authorization from the client to do so. I can't imagine trying to manage a client's portfolio unless I had the discretion to make trades as I saw fit, but that doesn't mean that all investment advisers have been granted that discretion. If the adviser or IAR is unauthorized to execute transactions without talking to the client, doing so would be a violation known, surprisingly, as an "unauthorized transaction."

Item (e) is basically saying that if your client's husband calls up and says his wife wants you to sell 1,000 shares of MSFT, you can only do so if the client has given her husband written trading authorization and you have that on file. Otherwise, you have to talk to your customer, the wife. Don't take orders from anybody but your client, unless the third party has been granted written third-party trading authorization.

Items (f) and (g) address borrowing and lending. Borrowing money from clients is a practice that makes regulators really nervous. An investment adviser can only borrow money from a client if the client is a broker-dealer, an affiliate of the adviser, or a financial institution in the business of making loans (Bank, Savings & Loan, Thrift, etc.). So, don't borrow from customers unless the customer is in the business of loaning money. And, don't lend money to a customer unless your advisory firm is in the business of making loans, or the customer is an affiliate of your advisory firm. One example of an "affiliate" of an investment adviser would be the investment adviser representatives and their supervisors. Another example would be a business entity affiliated with the adviser.

Item (h) really takes the fun out of being an adviser. These heavy-handed regulators insist that I not lie about my qualifications, the qualifications of my employees, or the services we will provide through our contract with the client and the fees we will charge for performing those services. And, remember, the state regulators are convinced that advisers and their reps can commit fraud even when just soliciting clients, so lying about credentials would be a really bad idea.

Item (i) is a little tricky and, therefore, fertile ground for harvesting exam questions. If I provide a report or a recommendation to a client when, in fact, that report or recommendation was actually prepared by someone else, I have to disclose the fact and tell you who provided it. However, if I order prepared reports or use published research/statistical analyses to come up with my recommendations, that's different. No disclosure there. I'm just doing my homework to come up with a better plan for my customer. So, if you get a tricky question on this, try to determine if the adviser is trying to pass off somebody else's work as their own, or if they order reports and analyses to help them come up with better recommendations. I mean, I'd kind of like to think my adviser is constantly poring over published reports, just crunching data with his nose to the grindstone and shoulder to the wheel 10–12 hours a day, and I do not really care which websites or newsletters or reports he subscribes to. On the other hand, if he's paying another firm to come up with the recommendations for my portfolio, I want to know that rather than find out my adviser was just trying to make it *look* like he actually knew something about investing himself.

Item (j) also takes all the fun out of the business by prohibiting advisers from gouging their clients. What would make the fee "unreasonable"? The regulators are indicating that you and your firm have two options here: 1) you can charge fees that are reasonable or 2) we can have ourselves a hearing.

The next item, (k), would probably produce a test question. Basically, it's just saying that if the advice being given will also lead to the advisory firm or any of its employees receiving a commission or any other compensation should the client act on the advice, that potential conflict of interest must be disclosed in writing. In other words, wouldn't you feel better about paying for investment advice knowing that the advice is being given by a totally objective professional, rather than someone who will make a big commission check if you take the advice? For example, if the IAR or adviser receives 12b-1 fees on the mutual funds recommended or purchased for the client, that needs to be disclosed.

Item (l) is the very familiar prohibition against guarantees. Don't guarantee a profit. Don't guarantee against a loss. I have recently seen many instances at the state regulatory websites of representatives who have horribly dropped the ball and then tried to appease the client by cutting a personal check. You know, maybe after you accidentally sell 1,000 of the client's B-shares three years after purchase when you were sure they were A-shares, costing her $3,500 by your little gaffe, you invite her to lunch, slip her a check for $3,500, pick up the tab, and everybody's happy.

Not a good idea. In another instance, a shady operator sold an Illinois resident shares of stock in a company that was not even public yet, telling her that when the company did their IPO, she would make "a return at least equal to her original investment" and that by investing in said stock "she would become a millionaire." Of course, the stock never went public, the investor never made a return *on* her original investment, and can't seem to get a return *of* her original investment.

Item (m) probably threw you for a loop, what with the whole "[Alternative 1], [Alternative 2]" thing. Either way, the item is telling advisers to be careful about the advertisements they put out. If you have a photographic memory, perhaps you recalled that in that consent order against the adviser with the sloppy advertising the Illinois Administrator's office referred to the advertisement's not being in accordance with the rule under the Investment Advisers Act of 1940. Believe it or not, when I showed that consent order to a different state securities regulator, the folks at the table were a little baffled as to why anything about the Investment Advisers Act of 1940 had been referenced in a state regulatory action. In fact, they said they would not have written it that way themselves. In other words, there was a disagreement among lawyers, if you can believe such a thing. Well, NASAA is a group of lawyers, basically, and they know that some state regulators would rather not refer to the federal legislation, while some are quite comfortable not reinventing the wheel. I mean, if those high-energy types in Washington DC have already exhausted all kinds of time and effort laying out a set of perfectly good stipulations, why not use them? This way, we don't even have to go to the trouble of copying and pasting them into our own rules. Instead, we can just refer to the rule spelled out in the Investment Advisers Act of 1940 and call it a day.

In any case, whether we just point the adviser to the federal rule or kind of spell the same thing out for him in our own words, as state regulators we want advisers to know that their advertising had better not be misleading in any way. Of course, our buddy from Illinois provided a textbook definition of how not to do things. You can't list stock picks that you didn't actually pick. And when you do actually pick the stocks you claim to have picked, the period covered has to be at least one year, and all types of disclosures have to be provided, too. Also notice that testimonials from clients are not allowed.

> Investment Advisers Act of 1940, Rule 206(4)-1…It shall constitute a fraudulent, deceptive, or manipulative act, practice, or course of business for any investment adviser to publish, circulate, or distribute any advertisement…which refers, directly or indirectly, to any testimonial of any kind concerning the investment adviser or concerning any advice, analysis, report or other service rendered by such investment adviser…

Item (n) is a likely testable point: don't divulge the identity, affairs, or investments of your client to anyone else without the client's written permission or some sort of legal order to turn the information over to a court or the police. Might be tempting to show prospects what you've done for, say, Oprah Winfrey's account, but both Ms. Winfrey and the state securities Administrator would probably have a real problem with that.

Item (o) basically boils down to, "Be real careful what you do with client funds/securities under custody." The Rule 102e(1)-1 referenced in this item is also currently viewable at the NASAA website and could easily help you snag a test question or two. We'll be looking at custody issues in more detail in a while. Try not to get too excited just yet.

Item (p) looks like a test question waiting to be written. It reminds us that all advisory contracts must be in writing and must stipulate all the terms of the contract: services provided, term of the contract, advisory fees, formula for computing the fees, the amount of prepaid fees that are refundable, whether the adviser has discretion, and that no assignment of contract can occur without client consent. Also note that even if the adviser did not end up assigning a client's contract to another party without consent, the fact that their contract with the client failed to state that provision could lead to problems with the regulators. So, before an advisory firm can sell a majority ownership position to a new entity, all client contracts would have to be re-executed with the new entity. Otherwise, the contracts would have been improperly "assigned" without client consent.

Item (q) is talking about the adviser's code of ethics policy. Any "access person" or individual at the firm who could easily see what the portfolio managers are up to is required to report his/her holdings to the advisory firm. We cover this in more detail elsewhere. Item (r) reminds us that state regulators often use SEC rules as their own—if the advisory firm has contracts that conflict with SEC rules under the "Act of 1940," the state Administrator has a real problem with that.

Item (s) reminds us that no waivers of any provision are allowed. So, if the adviser wants to charge a client in a way that's not allowed, he and the client cannot just draw up a waiver indicating that they both mutually agree to violate the laws and rules governing the industry. Any such "waiver of compliance" would be considered null and void in an Administrative or court proceeding, anyway, which means it would not be worth the paper it's printed on, much less the legal fees foolishly spent having the thing drawn up.

Item (t) points out that whether an adviser or IAR is subject to state registration, federal-only, or exempted from registration at the federal level, they can still get busted for fraudulent, deceptive practices by the state Administrator. Item (u) points out that beyond fraudulent/manipulative practices, an investment adviser or IAR can get in trouble for engaging in any conduct that is a violation of the securities laws of the state and the rules thereunder.

And the final blurb is very typical of these detailed lists. It reminds us that this list is "not inclusive," meaning this is just *some* of the stuff we felt like talking about in THIS particular publication. It does not represent ALL of the stuff that can get you in trouble.

So be on your best behavior.

BUSINESS PRACTICES FOR BROKER-DEALERS AND AGENTS

NASAA's Policy Statement for Broker-Dealers and Agents is fertile ground for test questions, so let's have a crack at it. First, we'll read it in the native legalese. Then, I'll break it down for you in a language you're likely more familiar with. English.

Dishonest or Unethical Business Practices
of Broker-Dealers and Agents

Each broker-dealer and agent shall observe high standards of commercial honor and just and equitable principles of trade in the conduct of their business. Acts and practices, including but not limited to the following, are considered contrary to such standards and may constitute grounds for denial, suspension or revocation of registration or such other action authorized by statute.

1. BROKER-DEALERS

a. Engaging in a pattern of unreasonable and unjustifiable delays in the delivery of securities purchased by any of its customers and/or in the payment upon request of free credit balances reflecting completed transactions of any of its customers;

b. Inducing trading in a customer's account which is excessive in size or frequency in view of the financial resources and character of the account;

c. Recommending to a customer the purchase, sale or exchange of any security without reasonable grounds to believe that such transaction or recommendation is suitable for the customer based upon reasonable inquiry concerning the customer's investment objectives, financial situation and needs, and any other relevant information known by the broker-dealer;

d. Executing a transaction on behalf of a customer without authorization to do so;

e. Exercising any discretionary power in effecting a transaction for a customer's account without first obtaining written discretionary authority from the customer, unless the discretionary power relates solely to the time and/or price for the executing of orders;

f. Executing any transaction in a margin account without securing from the customer a properly executed written margin agreement promptly after the initial transaction in the account;

g. Failing to segregate customers' free securities or securities held in safekeeping;

h. Hypothecating a customer's securities without having a lien thereon unless the broker-dealer secures from the customer a properly executed written consent promptly after the initial transaction, except as permitted by Rules of the Securities and Exchange Commission;

i. Entering into a transaction with or for a customer at a price not reasonably related to the current market price of the security or receiving an unreasonable commission or profit;

j. Failing to furnish to a customer purchasing securities in an offering, no later than the due date of confirmation of the transaction, either a final prospectus or a preliminary prospectus and an additional document, which together include all information set forth in the final prospectus;

k. Charging unreasonable and inequitable fees for services performed, including miscellaneous services such as collection of monies due for principal, dividends or interest, exchange or transfer of securities, appraisals, safekeeping, or custody of securities and other services related to its securities business;

l. Offering to buy from or sell to any person any security at a stated price unless such broker-dealer is prepared to purchase or sell, as the case may be, at such price and under such conditions as are stated at the time of such offer to buy or sell;

m. Representing that a security is being offered to a customer "at the market" or a price relevant to the market price unless such broker-dealer knows or has reasonable grounds to believe that a market for such security exists other than that made, created or controlled by such broker-dealer;

n. Effecting any transaction in, or inducing the purchase or sale of, any security by means of any manipulative, deceptive or fraudulent device, practice, plan, program, design or contrivance, which may include but not be limited to;

(1) Effecting any transaction in a security which involves no change in the beneficial ownership thereof;

(2) Entering an order or orders for the purchase or sale of any security with the knowledge that an order or orders of substantially the same size, at substantially the same time and substantially the same price, for the sale of any such security, has been or will be entered by or for the same or different parties for the purpose of creating a false or misleading appearance of active trading in the security or a false or misleading appearance with respect to the market for the security;

(3) Effecting, alone or with one or more other persons, a series

of transactions in any security creating actual or apparent active trading in such security or raising or depressing the price of such security, for the purpose of inducing the purchase or sale of such security by others;

o. Guaranteeing a customer against loss in any securities account of such customer carried by the broker-dealer or in any securities transaction effected by the broker-dealer or in any securities transaction effected by the broker-dealer with or for such customer;

p. Publishing or circulating, or causing to be published or circulated, any notice, circular, advertisement, newspaper article, investment service, or communication of any kind which purports to report any transaction as a purchase or sale of any security unless such broker-dealer believes that such transaction was a bona fide purchase or sale of such security; or which purports to quote the bid price or asked price for any security, unless such broker-dealer believes that such quotation represents a bona fide bid for, or offer of, such security;

q. Using any advertising or sales presentation in such a fashion as to be deceptive or misleading; or

r. Failing to disclose that the broker-dealer is controlled by, controlling, affiliated with or under common control with the issuer of any security before entering into any contract with or for a customer for the purchase or sale of such security, the existence of such control to such customer, and if such disclosure is not made in writing, it shall be supplemented by the giving or sending of written disclosure at or before the completion of the transaction;

s. Failing to make a bona fide public offering of all of the securities allotted to a broker-dealer for distribution, whether acquired as an underwriter, a selling group member, or from a member participating in the distribution as an underwriter or selling group member; or

t. Failure or refusal to furnish a customer, upon reasonable request, information to which he is entitled, or to respond to a formal written request or complaint.

2. AGENTS

a. Engaging in the practice of lending or borrowing money or securities from a customer, or acting as a custodian for money, securities or an executed stock power of a customer;

b. Effecting securities transactions not recorded on the regular books or records of the broker-dealer which the agent represents, unless the transactions are authorized in writing by the broker-dealer prior to execution of the transaction;

c. Establishing or maintaining an account containing fictitious information in order to execute transactions which would otherwise be prohibited;

d. Sharing directly or indirectly in profits or losses in the account of any customer without the written authorization of the customer and the broker-dealer which the agent represents;

e. Dividing or otherwise splitting the agent's commissions, profits or other compensation from the purchase or sale of securities with any person not also registered as an agent for the same broker-dealer, or for a broker-dealer under direct or indirect common control; or

f. Engaging in conduct specified in Subsection 1.b, c, d, e, f, i, j, n, o, p, or q.

[CONDUCT NOT INCLUSIVE.] The conduct set forth above is not inclusive. Engaging in other conduct such as forgery, embezzlement, nondisclosure, incomplete disclosure or misstatement of material facts, or manipulative or deceptive practices shall also be grounds for denial, suspension or revocation of registration.

PLAIN-ENGLISH VERSION

As you saw, the policy statement starts with the conduct of broker-dealers and then moves on to

the agents who represent them. Item A prohibits unreasonable and unjustifiable delays in delivering securities that customers have purchased or in paying out a request from the cash balance. Broker-dealers earn interest on their clients' uninvested cash, so they would probably prefer to sit on that client cash as long as possible. However, if the client has $2,000 of "cash" in her account, the firm has to pay her promptly upon request. Regular-way settlement is "T + 3," so once that trade is completed on the third business day, the customer can request a check for that amount. Also, stocks that pay dividends and bonds that pay interest will build up the cash balance in the investor's account. NASAA is just reminding broker-dealers that if their customers want their cash paid out to them, or their stock certificates shipped to them, the firms cannot unreasonably delay these requests.

Item B is the legalistic definition for **churning**. Notice how churning involves excessive size as well as frequency of trading. Remember that suitability is the name of the game, and frequent trading is unsuitable for the vast majority of investors working with a registered representative. Of course, frequent trading does seem to help the registered rep's paycheck, and broker-dealers do know who their "big producers" are, but NASAA is reminding broker-dealers not to let registered reps encourage frequent trading or the trading of huge positions relative to the account balance. Administrators in the real world frequently write orders to revoke a license that explain how a particular rep was engaging in a "turnover ratio" of, say, 15, or possibly higher. A "turnover rate/ratio of 15" would indicate that if the customer's average account balance is $20,000, the registered rep somehow talked the guy into executing $300,000 worth of trades over the year. Frequent trading might be suitable if the client is a former commodities trader and a multimillionaire who knows what he's doing, but given the character of the account, if the rep is encouraging trading that is too frequent, the Administrator can definitely move to suspend or revoke the license. Often, FINRA would catch it first and then just forward the information on over to the state—either way, regulators hate churning. It's an obvious way in which a registered rep can put the client's entire life savings at extreme risk while the registered rep faces no financial risk himself and, in fact, benefits on every trade whether the client wins or loses. That's okay for Vegas casinos, but broker-dealers are in a slightly different offshoot of the "financial services" industry.

Item C is a reminder that when the firm recommends the purchase, sale, or exchange of a security, they have to have reasonable grounds to make the recommendation based on an investigation of the client's situation. This brings up many important concepts. First, if the customer calls the firm to place an order, that's an unsolicited transaction in which the broker-dealer has no suitability requirements. But, if the broker-dealer recommends a transaction, they have to know that it's suitable. If the client is "unsophisticated," the firm has to know that the client understands the complexities or risks of products such as collateralized mortgage obligations, variable annuities, or securitized viatical settlements (death bonds). Older investors generally have a major need for liquidity—even if the broker-dealer gets compensated handsomely for selling deferred variable annuities, that fact, in and of itself, doesn't mean they should sell them to a lot of 75-year-old investors unless the firm knows for sure that the investors don't need any of this money during the surrender period, and that they all understand that "subaccounts" are just a fancy term for "stock and bond markets," both of which can be a little, well, unpredictable from time to time. FINRA inserts a few phrases into their suitability rule that NASAA leaves out here. FINRA uses the word "non-institutional" so that we understand the firm doesn't have to hand-hold with the big institutional investors. And, they insert the notion that to recommend a security, the firm needs the customer's financial information and profile, but that the firm could recommend a money market mutual fund even without having the client's information. That makes perfect sense, actually. A money market mutual fund…if that's too hot for an investor to handle, she isn't an investor. She's a bank customer who took a wrong turn somewhere—somebody please point her back toward the large FDIC signs before anyone gets hurt. But if the question says, "according to the NASAA policy statement…" answer it accordingly.

Item D reminds the firm not to buy or sell securities for a customer if the customer hasn't authorized the broker-dealer to do so. You might be shocked to see how many firms seem to forget this idea, but if the customer hasn't talked to anyone about buying or selling securities, the customer should *never* end up seeing that purchases or sales have been taking place in the account, right?

If your roommate came home one night and said, "I bought you the nicest pair of shoes for $1,200—here's your credit card back," how would you feel? Would you be thankful that someone had the good sense to spend your money on something you didn't even know you needed? Of course not. That's why unauthorized transactions are a very serious violation. Spending clients' money without their knowledge has gotten many broker-dealers in hot water with the regulators, as it should. Broker-dealers make recommendations to clients, and as long as those recommendations are suitable, the broker-dealer isn't responsible for the outcome of the investment. However, if they're placing orders that no one actually gave, their license could certainly end up being suspended or revoked before or after FINRA disciplines them.

Item E is very closely related. Before a broker-dealer can choose to enter purchase or sale orders on behalf of a client, without first talking to the client and getting his okay, the customer must grant written discretionary authorization. So, if the firm does not have written discretionary authorization from the customer before making any of those choices, they've made a big mistake. A Series 63 question might ask what the broker-dealer can do once the client informs the firm that the discretionary authorization form is in the mail. Not much at this point—the broker-dealer needs it signed, in writing, on file, before they choose the asset, the activity, or the amount of shares. The time and price at which an order is executed is not considered such a major aspect, so the firm could take a market order from a customer and then have the "time and price discretion" to enter it later, when they're convinced the customer can get a better price—those are called "market not held" orders, by the way, in case you don't have enough to remember at this point. The firm does not need written discretionary authority to choose time/price for a customer order. So, to make sure we have a good grasp on this highly testable concept, if the customer says, "Buy 1,000 shares of a software company," the firm would need written discretionary authority to insert the name of a particular company into that order, e.g., Oracle, Microsoft, or Computer Associates. But, if the customer said, "Buy 1,000 shares of MSFT at a good price today," the broker-dealer does not need written discretionary authority to execute that as a "market not held" order that will be executed when they think they can get a better price. Also, remember that *investment advisers* can place trades that they feel are suitable, without first talking to the client, after receiving oral authorization from the client for 10 days before getting the authorization in writing. Broker-dealers need it in writing *before* placing *any* discretionary orders for the customer. Why? Broker-dealers get paid per transaction, regardless of how the trade works out for the client, while advisers have no such incentive to enter lots of trades.

Item F reminds the firm not to let a customer start trading on margin unless the firm gets a signed margin agreement promptly *after* the initial transaction. I would have expected the rule to require the agreement ahead of time, but nobody asked my opinion. And, you can see why the Series 63 has such a nasty reputation—you have to remember that the firm needs discretionary authorization signed before using discretion, but they can execute a margin transaction and *then* get the signed margin agreement. And, trust me, the Series 63 will try to trick you on these points—it could easily ask you which of the following four is a violation and make it look like the firm is screwing up by executing the margin transaction and then promptly getting the signed margin agreement. Most people who kind of half-studied will grab that answer choice as a violation and somehow overlook some obvious example of churning or unauthorized transactions.

Item G speaks to the bookkeeping requirements for broker-dealers holding customer securities, some of which have been pledged as collateral for the loan in a margin account. NASAA is reminding broker-dealers to keep the customers' fully paid securities separate from the firm's securities or securities pledged as collateral. Item H reminds broker-dealers not to pledge customer securities as collateral unless they have written authorization from the customer. In other words, in a margin account, the customer signs a hypothecation agreement, giving the broker-dealer the authority to pledge the securities as collateral. But, if a broker-dealer just started pledging the securities that customers thought were in "safekeeping" as collateral for loans to the firm, we would have a very ugly situation on our hands. It would be like finding out that a neighbor just borrowed $300,000 and put *your* house up as collateral. Even funnier, he can't repay the loan, so the bank is foreclosing on *your* property. To protect customer assets, broker-dealers need to keep their books stringently so that it's crystal clear that these shares belong to the firm's account, and those belong to the customers.

Item I is pretty straightforward. Let's say that a municipal bond issued by a small school district seldom trades. A customer comes in and wants to liquidate 100 of these bonds. There isn't much of a secondary market for these things, but if the firm knows that the most recent transactions occurred yesterday at $1,100 per bond, they can't give this guy $900 apiece for those same bonds. That's not reasonably related to the market price. The firm also can't charge commissions that are way out of line with the industry norms.

Item J requires underwriters to deliver a prospectus "no later than the due date for confirmation." Sometimes, rather than a final prospectus, a final statement is sent out that completes any information not already covered in the preliminary prospectus. Either way, NASAA is reminding firms to deliver a prospectus in a new offering. Why wouldn't a firm always want to deliver a prospectus? Because those things lay out a lot of gloom-and-doom scenarios that can easily scare an investor away from the table. One minute the investor is ready to buy an additional offering of Starbucks common stock, the next minute she's reading about the risk of a "global pandemic" or "possible negative health effects associated with the company's products" and padlocking her purse. Oh, well. Investors have to be fully informed of all the important risks—otherwise, the broker-dealer would be selling securities fraudulently.

Item K reminds firms not to charge unreasonable or inequitable fees for services performed, including a host of various services that broker-dealers provide. The regulators don't spell out maximum fees, but they expect firms to keep their charges reasonable and fair among their various customers. If not, the Administrator can always schedule a hearing at the firm's earliest convenience.

Point L is talking about a violation called "backing away." If a broker-dealer puts out a firm quote, they had better be prepared to trade at the price they indicate. Point M is admonishing broker-dealers not to mislead customers by saying that a security is being offered "at the market" if there is really no secondary market out there for the security. I have seen several examples of investors getting duped into buying "preferred stock" in some shaky company and then finding out later that the stock isn't listed or traded anywhere. Maybe one of those investors wants to liquidate and get some of her money back—the broker-dealer can't say that they're offering to buy those shares "at the market" unless they know an actual secondary market for the security exists. If they're the only firm willing or crazy enough to buy that preferred stock, they need to be clear about that.

Item N goes into great detail in explaining that market manipulation will get you into all kinds of trouble. We can't just get together with another firm and buy a huge block of thinly traded stock, then start creating the illusion of an active market for it, so that we can later dump our stock at a much higher price, all based on our deception and manipulation of the market. The process might make for some entertaining scenes in *The Sopranos* or *Boiler Room*, but we should probably not model our business conduct after any of the characters represented in either work—especially Ben Affleck's character in *Boiler Room*, who committed the worst violation of all: loaning out Series 7 books for free. Bastard.

Item O reminds the firm not to guarantee the customer against a loss. Broker-dealers make suitable recommendations, but they don't protect customers from market losses. If the word "guaranteed" is used, it has to be explained clearly to the investor to avoid misleading him. A US Treasury security is definitely guaranteed as to interest and principal by the US Treasury, but it still has interest rate and market risk. A corporate bond could be "guaranteed" if a third party promised to pay interest and/or principal in the event of a default, but that also needs to be explained clearly to an investor. A broker-dealer could sell someone a "put-able bond" or a bond with a "put option" that gives the investor the right to sell the bond back for a set price in exchange for some kind of premium. In this case, there would be a written agreement, and it would be clear what the customer paid and what the customer would get. But a broker-dealer doesn't tell a customer that if the trade they're recommending goes sour, the broker-dealer will eat the losses for them. They're not insurance companies accepting premiums in exchange for protection against market loss. And, if they tell an investor her money is "guaranteed" when, in fact, it isn't, that would be a very serious violation. If they told her that a Fannie Mae mortgage-backed security is guaranteed by the US Treasury—which it isn't—the firm would be in big trouble, no matter how safe the security might be or how *close* Fannie and Freddie really are to being guaranteed. "Close" doesn't count—the regulators want *full* disclosure of *all* material facts.

Item P reminds broker-dealers not to publish that a transaction has occurred unless they actually know it occurred. Otherwise the firm might be engaging in market manipulation, or being used as pawns by those who are.

Item Q reminds the firm not to circulate material that is misleading or deceptive. For example, it might be tempting to put out a flyer that shows how much Company XYZ would be worth if over the next 6 months they simply eliminated $5 billion in debt, increased revenues 10,000%, and slashed costs 89% without resorting to layoffs or pay cuts. You could even show graphs of this wonderful turnaround effort. Trouble is, it's all based on wild conjecture, is so improbable as to be nearly impossible and, therefore, should not be circulated at all. It is "nonfactual," misleading, and probably deceptive.

Don't do that.

If the broker-dealer is owned by the issuer of the stock that the firm is selling to investors, that's kind of an important detail that should be disclosed, as Point R reminds us. Right? The broker-dealer is recommending that you buy stock, bonds, or commercial paper in the parent company? Doesn't that sort of directly benefit the broker-dealer even beyond the typical commissions earned? Item S reminds underwriters not to get greedy when they realize that the stock they're bringing to the primary market is likely to take off like a rocket ship. Might be tempting to hang onto the stock for their own accounts and cancel all the indications of interest, but that would be "failure to make a bona fide offering" and would get the firm into all kinds of trouble.

Item T is a very clear reminder to give customers the information they are entitled to. Customers are certainly entitled to trade confirmations, account statements, mutual fund prospectuses, etc. They are even entitled to independent research on companies generated by other firms. Broker-dealers have to respond to written customer complaints, as well. And, they have to keep detailed records on how the complaint was handled.

And then the policy statement addresses agents specifically.

Item A reminds agents not to borrow money from customers unless the customer happens to be a lending institution: bank, savings & loan, thrift, credit union, building & loan, etc. If an agent wants to borrow from a customer who is a human being, the agent needs to check the broker-dealer's policy on this. Maybe it's okay to borrow money from a client if the client is an immediate family member or a business partner. But many agents out there try to borrow money from clients under the table, promising to "pay it right back." Maybe the agent borrows $100,000 from a client and then goes bankrupt, gets fired, or dies…then what is the client supposed to do about the hundred grand he foolishly lent to his former agent?

That's basically the situation the regulators are hoping to avoid.

An agent cannot "act as a custodian for" customer money or securities. Once the client's money goes into the agent's bank or brokerage account, it has no chance of survival. Many investors have been swindled by cutting personal checks to their sales agent or by handing him cash. I recall an enforcement action in Arkansas in which an investor gave an agent over $50,000 cash money, and the agent gave the investor a personal check "as a receipt for the cash," instructing the customer not to try and cash the check or anything, but to, instead, hang onto it as a, you know, receipt for the cash. The most shocking part was that *most* of the investor's money did eventually make it into his brokerage account. Well, all but six grand, but now we're just being fussy.

Item B warns against executing transactions not recorded on the books and records of your firm unless you have written authorization from the firm to do so, and it's slightly hard to picture how you'd get that. An official order to deny an agent's license in the State of Washington told the sad story of an agent who got an elderly investor to cut him three personal checks for $50,000, all of which ended up in his brokerage account. So, right there, he has "acted as a custodian for client money" and "commingled client funds with his own," which is, to say the least, ill-advised. But then when he started executing trades, the Administrator could also add item B to the list of allegations, since those transactions were certainly *not* recorded on the regular books or records of the broker-dealer, who knew nothing about the little scheme.

Item C is pretty clear. If there is an offering of stock open only to accredited investors, and your customer isn't close to meeting the net worth and income requirements, would it be okay to indicate a higher net worth and income on the required paperwork in order to allow him to buy the limited offering?

No. Not if there were any chance of getting caught, anyway.

Item D reminds us that, basically, you shouldn't be sharing profits and/or losses with a customer. The only exception is when you're in a joint account with the customer and you've received the customer's authorization as well as your broker-dealer's. If you get any test question on the sharing arrangement, remember that you must share in proportion to your investment in the account. Unless it's an immediate family member and then nobody cares how you share.

Item E makes it clear that you can only split commissions with registered agents at your firm or a firm directly related to your firm—such as a subsidiary, for example. So, you can split commissions, as long as the agent is registered and works for your firm directly or indirectly. Many agents' assistants get their licenses in order to take client orders and share commissions with their agents. That's fine. But it wouldn't be fine for an agent to tell 20 of his friends that he'll split commissions with them in exchange for referrals. Refer me a new client with $1 million net worth, and I'll give you 1/3 of the commissions I make off them for the first year—what do you say?

The regulators say, "Don't do it."

The policy statement then tells the agent not to do the stuff it told broker-dealers not to do, except for the stuff that would only relate to the firm.

And then the policy statement ends with a reminder that these prohibited activities are not inclusive, meaning there's still plenty of other stuff that could get you in hot water with the regulators. They just felt like pointing out *some* of the things not to do in this policy statement.

MORE NASAA CONCERNS

Since no one can actually know how deep the questions will go on your Series 63, and since we're still having so much fun admit it, let's go ahead and add a few more concerns right here.

RESEARCH REPORTS

First, it is a major violation for broker-dealers to compensate their research analysts, who publish reports on the merits of particular stocks, based on the amount of investment banking they can drum up by making certain companies happy with said research reports. In other words, a broker-dealer can't offer a bonus to the research analyst who just wrote a positive report on, say, GE when GE then hires the firm to help with a merger/acquisition as a thank-you for helping to push the price of the stock up, that inflated stock now being used to acquire the target company. I know that concept is a little hard to follow, and that's the nature of most industry violations—the average Joe and Joann don't even understand what the heck the firms are doing or why that would be, like, bad. Well, in the situation we're explaining here, the average Joe and Joann are being defrauded—how? They're being sent research reports to help guide their investment selection…only these "research reports" are not objective in the least. Rather, they are tools used to inflate the market price of the stock just so the firm can make money helping the issuer do some investment banking down the road—that issuer often using the inflated stock price as the currency used to buy the other company. Talk about an unholy mess!

So, there had better not be any funny business going on between the broker-dealer's research analysts and their investment bankers. The investment banking division cannot set the compensation of research analysts, and there can be no link between the research analysts and the investment banking division. If you look at a research report these days, you'll see lots of disclosure on the front cover that the broker-dealer may do underwriting business for the issuers whose stock they are promoting—I mean, researching. Due to a settlement with the New York State Attorney General's office, the disclosure also mentions that readers should consult other sources before making decisions and can request free independent research reports from the broker-dealer.

HOLDING SEMINARS

Whenever the regulators hear that financial services professionals are holding seminars, their ears perk up just like my cat's do at the sound of an electric can opener. *Holding seminars, are we? Senior citizens? Oh, they get a free hot lunch, and there's no pressure to invest. Tell us more. No, we insist.*

There is just something at least mildly dangerous about combining the following words in any order:

- Senior citizens
- Investment seminar
- Free hot lunch

In other words, things might turn out okay here, but we certainly do want to take a much closer look. For example, are you holding yourself out as being an objective adviser when, in fact, you're just trying to scare these senior citizens out of perfectly safe bank accounts and into some fixed annuity products that pay you HUGE commissions? The State of Massachusetts had a recent action against some folks doing exactly that, and it would be hard to find any state that wasn't showing increased concern over the increased use of senior seminars and annuity sales. Not that annuities are inherently evil (they aren't), but if they carry a long surrender period and a big surrender charge, that would make them almost inherently unsuitable for senior citizens. And if the seminar somehow failed to disclose such facts, we'd be talking about securities fraud.

Also, the seminar might be perfectly legitimate and otherwise compliant except for one problem—the agent forgot to tell his compliance principal about the seminar and forgot to show him the invitations, handouts, and PowerPoint slides. Those communications need to be either monitored or pre-approved by a principal, so holding seminars without your firm's knowledge would be a violation of industry rules. When FINRA finds out, they'll fine and suspend/bar the agent and then send notice to the state regulators, because getting in trouble with an SRO (self-regulatory organization) is also a violation of state securities law

Using the Internet

The statements on research reports and seminars apply to the broker-dealer side of the industry, but using the Internet applies equally to the brokerage and the investment advisory side of the financial services industry. NASAA has a policy statement on the use of the internet for "general dissemination of information on products and services." Basically, it comes down to this: if you're putting up a website discussing your services and products, anyone with a web connection can see it, which might include people in states where you and the broker-dealer are not registered. If you are deemed to be transacting securities business in a state where you're not registered, well, your life is going to become very complicated. So, NASAA is putting out the uniform idea for state regulators that an agent or broker-dealer using a website is not considered to be transacting business in states where they're not registered if the following bullet points are taken into account:

- The Internet Communication contains a legend in which it is clearly stated that the broker-dealer, investment adviser, BD agent or IA rep in question may only transact business in this state if first registered, excluded or exempted from registration requirements, and follow-up, individualized responses to persons in this state that involve either the effecting or attempting to effect transactions in securities, or the rendering of person-alized investment advice for compensation, will not be made

> absent compliance with state registration requirements, or an
> applicable exemption or exclusion

In other words, your website needs some text clearly explaining that you're not trying to offer securities or investment advice through the website and would only do so if registered or excused from registration in the web visitor's state.

Also:

- The Internet Communication does not involve either effecting or attempting to effect transactions in securities, or the rendering of personalized investment advice for compensation in this state over the Internet, but is limited to the dissemination of general information on products and services

That means that the website had better not involve effecting or attempting to effect purchases/sales of securities or the delivery of personalized investment advice for compensation.

Now, when this statement of policy first went out, not that many agents had the time or technical savvy to build an actual "website." But nowadays, with Facebook, Twitter, blogs, etc. imagine how easy it is for a securities agent to open up Facebook and accidentally post something about the benefits of variable annuities or the superiority of the mutual funds she sells. Oopsie. As many readers have already been told by a supervisor or two, be very careful what you post on Facebook and other social media. You might think it's "just your opinion" or that you're speaking your mind "on your own time," but that's not the case. Whatever you post concerning securities would have to first be cleared by a compliance principal as advertising. Most firms are probably telling their agents and IARs right now something like the following: don't talk about securities or your practice on Facebook or other social media, and only post what we give you to post.

I shudder to think how many agents will end up getting fired and regulated right out of the business due to an inability to keep their opinions in check, but I predict that by the time this book goes to press we will be seeing the first round of let's-make-an-example-out-of-these-clowns disciplinary actions by the securities regulators. So, just to make sure you don't end up in that crowd, let's clarify that I, the guy who writes the textbook, can say whatever the heck I want on my Facebook wall and my company's fan page. You, the person with the securities license, you can't say squat on Facebook about securities, your firm, or your practice, unless your firm says it's okay.

REGULATORY AUTHORITIES

Okay, so those are statements from NASAA designed to guide actual state securities regulators. NASAA is not a regulator, remember—it is an organization of state securities regulators. So, let's talk about the actual regulators that you and your firm must answer to. The **Financial Industry Regulatory Authority (FINRA)** is a self-regulatory organization (SRO) with authority over member broker-dealers and their associated persons. This is how they explain themselves to the public at their website link http://www.finra.org/AboutFINRA/.

About the Financial Industry Regulatory Authority

The Financial Industry Regulatory Authority (FINRA) is the largest independent regulator for all securities firms doing business in the United States. FINRA's mission is to protect America's investors by making sure the securities industry operates fairly and honestly. All told, FINRA oversees nearly 4,540 brokerage firms, about 163,675 branch offices and approximately 631,725 registered securities representatives.

FINRA touches virtually every aspect of the securities business—from registering and educating industry participants to examining securities firms; writing rules; enforcing those rules and the federal securities laws; informing and educating the investing public; providing trade reporting and other industry utilities; and administering the largest dispute resolution forum for investors and registered firms. We also perform market regulation under contract for the major US stock markets, including the New York Stock Exchange, NYSE Arca, NYSE Amex, The NASDAQ Stock Market and the International Securities Exchange.

FINRA has approximately 3,000 employees and operates from Washington, DC, and New York, NY, with 20 regional offices around the country.

So, those 4,500 brokerage firms, with their 163,000 branch offices and over 630,000 registered representatives, are all regulated by FINRA. FINRA handles violations of the **member conduct rules** through their **Code of Procedure.** For example, if a broker-dealer is not delivering mutual fund prospectuses to their investing customers, FINRA can fine the firm and make them promise to improve their supervisory system. If an agent is churning accounts or making unsuitable recommendations, they can suspend him (temporarily) or even bar him (permanently). What is the maximum monetary fine that FINRA can impose?

Trick question—they've never set a maximum. They simply have the authority to set fines that seem to fit the violation. What if you were barred from associating with any member firm and fined $250,000? If you didn't pay the fine, would they come after your house and other possessions? No, but unless you paid that fine they would never let you back into the brokerage industry. They're not a court of law; they're just a self-regulatory organization with lots of power over broker-dealers and their associated persons. If an agent, a principal, or the firm itself gets in hot water with FINRA, they do get a chance to tell their side. But if FINRA still thinks a disciplinary action is in order, they can suspend or expel a member firm, and they can suspend or bar an individual from associating with his member firm or *any* member firm for x-amount of time. Monetary fines, as we mentioned, are also frequently used to get people's attention. For a highly educational and surprisingly interesting read, go to the FINRA website sometime at www.finra.org and look up recent disciplinary actions. They usually have them for the month and/or the financial quarter. You will see quickly that people in the brokerage business find many, many ways to run afoul of FINRA regulations and securities law.

FINRA doesn't want member firms and their associated persons suing each other all the time. To avoid the time-consuming and costly process of civil court, FINRA insists that virtually all disputes in the industry are handled by their **Code of Arbitration.** If one broker-dealer says another broker-dealer owes them money, they can't sue them endlessly in civil court. Rather, they submit the claim to arbitration, and an arbitration panel makes a final decision to resolve the matter. Period. No appeals.

Customers of a broker-dealer are only forced to use arbitration if and when they sign an arbitration agreement. The arbitration agreement has to be very clear what the process is and what it involves. Customers need to understand that arbitrators often come from the industry, that there are generally no appeals to their decisions, and that the arbitration panel does not have to explain how they reached their decision. As we mention elsewhere, when an individual wants to associate with a broker-dealer as a registered representative, the firm and he complete a Form U4. If there are any arbitration awards above a certain amount of money, they must be disclosed here. Also, when an agent/registered representative leaves the firm, the firm files a Form U5. Here, they have to list the reason for the agent's termination. Often, the agent is terminated for violating firm policies, breaking industry rules, and/or having to pay out an arbitration award to some very upset former customers. If so, that's all disclosed on Form U5.

FINRA is then nice enough to make the relevant sections of an agent's U4 and U5 information open to the public through a handy service called "Broker Check." For fun, go to www.finra.org and find this part of the site. You can then type in the name of your firm, your principal, your coworkers, etc., to see if they've all actually passed their exams and if anybody has gotten into hot water before. It's all public information, just the way FINRA likes it.

The system that broker-dealers use to register themselves and their employees is called the **Central Registration Depository (CRD),** by the way. FINRA opens up the regulatory and disclosure reporting sections to the public through "Broker Check," so that investors can say no-thanks to certain bad boys out there and also feel more confident about the good guys after doing a quick background check. After all, if you saw that the guy planning to come to your house to sell you a mutual fund had been busted for signing customer signatures to documents, wouldn't you cancel that appointment? Or at least ask him to explain what the heck he was thinking at the time before cutting a check and handing it to him.

Broker-dealers, principals, and agents are regulated by FINRA, then, and also the SEC. You have a place of business in at least one state, so you will also have to register with at least one state securities Administrator. Therefore, the brokerage side of the industry is regulated by the state securities Administrators, the SRO known as FINRA, and also the SEC or Securities and Exchange Commission.

The investment advisory business, on the other hand, does not have an SRO. Why not? Unlike broker-dealers, who are trading partners with one another and work together as syndicates bringing securities to the primary market, investment advisers do not work cooperatively. They manage their clients' portfolios, period. No cooperation required between one adviser and another.

Investment advisers—the firms—are either registered with the state securities Administrators or with the SEC (Securities and Exchange Commission). While the firm might be registered with the SEC, all investment adviser representatives are subject to state registration only. Remember, there is not a Self-Regulatory Organization (SRO) for the investment advisory business. So, an RIA or an IAR is regulated *either* by the SEC (federal covered advisers) or the states (all IARs and also state-registered investment advisers). Just as an investor can find out about a broker-dealer or agent through "Broker Check," the SEC has a site called "IAPD" for Investment Adviser Public Disclosure. With a few keystrokes and clicks, the public can find information on investment advisers and/or their IARs. For example, before allowing you to come to my house for our first meeting, I might want to verify that you do work for the firm you said, that you have been in the business 10 years, and that there are no regulatory problems. If there are events to disclose, that first meeting may end up being very interesting...or canceled.

FEDERAL SECURITIES ACTS

SECURITIES ACT OF 1933

The Securities Act of 1933—sometimes referred to as the "Paper Act"—involves registering the security (the paper) with the SEC before the issuer is allowed to sell or "issue" their securities to the public. As an investor, before you buy a brand-new share of stock, you have to be provided with a **prospectus** that discloses everything you might want to know about the company issuing the paper. You can read about its history, its board of directors, its products and services, its chances for success, and its chances for failure. You can look at the balance sheet and the income statement. You'll still be taking a risk if you buy—because all securities carry risk—but at least you'll be able to make an informed decision because of this full and fair disclosure.

When a corporation wants to raise cash by selling securities, they have to get a group of **underwriters** together and fill out paperwork for the federal government in the form of a registration statement, or "S1." Part of this information will become the prospectus, which is the disclosure brochure that the public will be provided with. An "underwriter" is just a broker-dealer that likes to take companies public, remember. Another name for an underwriter is **investment banker**, but they don't act like a traditional bank. No deposits or checking offered here. They're just salesmen who like to play a high-risk game known as securities underwriting or investment banking. Part of the reason they like it is because it can pay very well.

Anyway, once the underwriters and the issuer file the registration papers, they go into a **cooling-off period**, which will last a minimum of 20 days. This process can drag on and on, as the SEC reviews the paperwork, but no matter how long it takes, the issuer and underwriters can only do certain things during this "cooling-off" period. Number one, they can't sell anything. They can't even advertise. They can announce that a sale is going to take place by publishing a **tombstone** ad in the financial press. A tombstone ad is just a boring rectangle with some text—looks like a tombstone. It announces that a sale of securities will take place at particular offering price (or yield) and informs the reader how he/she can obtain a prospectus. But it is neither an offer nor a solicitation. The underwriters can find out if anyone wants to give an "indication of interest," but those aren't sales. Just names on a list. If someone gives an indication of interest, they have to receive a preliminary prospectus, which contains everything that the final prospectus will contain except for the effective date and the final/public offering price or "POP." The registered rep may NOT send a research report along with the preliminary prospectus and may not highlight or alter it in any way. A research report is considered sales literature and, remember, during the cooling-off period no sales or advertising are allowed. As you may know, the **preliminary prospectus** is also referred to as a "red herring," due to the red-text warning that information may be added or altered. The release date and the final public offering price are two pieces of information yet to be added to what's in the red herring in order to make it a final prospectus.

The issuer and the underwriters attend a due diligence meeting toward the end of the cooling-off period to try and make sure they provided the SEC and the public with accurate and full disclosure. Nothing gets sold until the SEC "releases" the security on the **release date/effective date**. Starting on that date, the prospectus will have to be delivered to all buyers of these new securities for a certain length of time. And, even though the SEC makes issuers jump through all kinds of hoops, once it's all done, the SEC pretty much washes its hands of the whole affair. The SEC doesn't approve or disapprove of the security. They don't guarantee accuracy or adequacy of the information provided by the issuer and its underwriters. In other words, if this whole thing goes horribly wrong, the liability still rests squarely on the shoulders of the issuers and under-writers, not on the SEC. For that reason, there has to be a disclaimer saying basically that on the prospectus. It usually looks like this:

> The Securities and Exchange Commission has not approved or disapproved of these securities. Further, it has not determined that this prospectus is accurate or complete. Any representation to the contrary is a criminal offense.

So, how does the SEC feel about the investment merits of the security? No opinion whatsoever. They just want to make sure you receive full and fair disclosure in order to make an informed decision to invest or to take a pass.

EXEMPT ISSUERS/SECURITIES

The Securities Act of 1933 is a piece of federal legislation, so it's not surprising that the folks who passed it gave themselves an exemption from the rule. That's right; US government securities are exempt from this act. They don't have to be registered in this way. Neither do municipal securities. Charitable organization securities, such as church bonds, are exempt from the act. So are bank securities, which are already regulated by bank regulators. Securities that mature in 270 days or less—commercial paper, banker's acceptances—are also exempt from this arduous registration process. An exempt security simply does not have to register. It's still a security, so if anybody offers or sells it deceptively, that is considered fraud, which is always a bad idea. People can get sued and thrown in jail for fraudulent offers/sales of securities, and registered representatives have been known to lose their registration.

Exempt Transactions

There are exempt securities, and there are also *transactions* that qualify for exemptions. Believe it or not, the transactions that qualify for exemptions are called **exempt transactions**. In other words, there's absolutely nothing special about the security being offered here—it's the way it's being offered and sold that makes it exempt from the typical registration process. Under a Reg A exemption, an issuer can sell a small offering of securities without going through the full registration process. Or, if the issuer agrees to sell the stock to residents of only one state, they will qualify for a Rule 147 exemption. This only works if the issuer's main business is located in that state and 80% of its assets are located there. Also, the buyers can't sell the security to a <u>non</u>-resident for 9 months after the close of the offering period. The issuer registers with the state, rather than the SEC, since it's all taking place in that one state. Intr<u>A</u>state. All in <u>A</u> state. When we get down to the state (Uniform Securities Act) level, we'll see that the issuer would most likely use "registration by qualification" to do the intra-state IPO. The SEC is federal, in charge of INTERstate commerce. So if it's all within a state, it's that state's concern.

Sometimes issuers offer their shares primarily to "accredited investors." These are sophisticated investors, often with millions of dollars at their disposal. If the individual has a certain amount of net worth or income, he/she is accredited, and presumed to be able to look after him- or herself. So, an issuer can place their securities under a **Reg D** transaction with as many of these folks as they want. This "private placement" is, by definition, not being offered to the general public, so the SEC eases up a bit—as much as the SEC ever eases up, anyway. Besides wealthy individuals, the issuer can place these unregistered securities with as many institutional investors—mutual funds, pension plans, insurance companies—as they want, again on the assumption that they can tell a loser from a winner. They can also sell to insiders of the corporation, which would include officers, directors, and large shareholders. So, a Reg D/private placement transaction is exempt from the Act of 1933 because it is offered to an exclusive group of investors. No more than 35 non-accredited investors can buy these securities, and everybody has to hold the stock for the first year before selling it. That's a restriction—having to hold the stock fully paid for at least one year—so they often call stock purchased in a private placement "restricted stock." There is a legend printed on the certificates indicating when the shares may be transferred, and the transfer agent won't allow the transfer to happen until that date. Because of the little legend, the securities are sometimes referred to as "legend stock."

Seriously. I'm not saying it's *likely* you'll have to recall the phrase "legend stock," or even "restricted stock," but I am saying it *could* show up. Also know that the Administrator has the authority to get a copy of whatever paperwork the issuer is filing with the SEC when claiming this exemption at the federal level.

SECURITIES EXCHANGE ACT OF 1934

The **Securities Exchange Act of 1934** is often referred to as the "People Act," which is easy to remember, because it dictates how people may act in the securities markets. Some securities are excused from having to register under the Securities Act of 1933, but that is all that it means to be an "exempt security." You don't have to be registered? Big deal. You're still a security, and the Securities Exchange Act of 1934 says that *any* person in connection with the offer, sale, or purchase of *any* security can get into huge trouble for making material misstatements of fact or omitting material facts in a way that is misleading. For example, church bonds do not have to be registered. But in order to sell, say, $200 million worth of church bonds, the church would still put together a very detailed offering circular. At the top of this offering document, we would see that these securities have not been registered with the SEC in reliance upon a specific exemption available under the Securities Act of 1933. And that saves the issuer lots of time, which can also save them lots of money. But it doesn't save them from the Securities Exchange Act of 1934's anti-fraud provision.

What they're offering and selling definitely meets the definition of a "security," so if there are bogus financial reports or misleading statements designed to trick the investor into thinking the bonds are much safer than they really are, we're talking about securities fraud.

Which is bad. The Act of 1934 talked about insider trading, warning investors not to pass around or use non-public information. If you knew that your sister's company was going to be purchased by Google, it would be very tempting to buy a bunch of calls on her company's stock and tell your clients to do the same. Unfortunately, the SEC would sue you for "treble damages," meaning they would try to extract three times the amount of your benefit in civil court.

The "Act of '34" gave the Federal Reserve Board the power to regulate margin. It also requires public companies to file quarterly and annual reports with the SEC. And it sort of prefers that these quarterly and annual reports are accurate.

The Securities Exchange Act of 1934 gives federal prosecutors the authority to prosecute criminal violations. So, if the insider trading activity is handled in civil court, the SEC will try to extract three times your benefit. If they turn it over to the US Attorney's office for criminal prosecution, God help you. I would really hate to have to meet with a federal prosecutor who smirks as she offers me a deal of $3 million and five years or the chance of taking it to trial and maybe getting $5 million and 20 years. Then again, I have no plans to become the CFO of a major corporation, let alone one smart enough to cook the books yet dumb enough to think he won't get caught.

Finally, the exam could mention that the "Exchange Act" also wrote rules on short sales in an attempt to prevent short sellers from piling onto a dying stock. The "plus tick rule" or "uptick rule" based on this has actually been rewritten again as "regulation SHO," but there are just so many bits of minutiae that one mind can possibly recall for one exam, so let's keep moving.

TRUST INDENTURE ACT OF 1939

To protect bondholders, Congress passed the **Trust Indenture Act of 1939**. If a corporation wants to sell $5,000,000 or more worth of bonds that mature outside of one year, they have to do it under a contract or indenture with a trustee, who will enforce the terms of the indenture to the benefit of the bondholders. In other words, if the issuer stiffs the bondholders, the trustee can get a bankruptcy court to sell off the assets of the company so that bondholders can recover some of their hard-earned money. Sometimes corporations secure the bonds with specific assets like airplanes, securities, or real estate. Maybe even nice oil paintings. If so, they pledge title of the assets to the trustee, who just might end up selling them off if the issuer gets behind on its interest payments. So just remember that an indenture is a contract with a trustee, who looks out for the bondholders.

INVESTMENT COMPANY ACT OF 1940

The **Investment Company Act of 1940** classified investment companies as face amount certificate companies, unit investment trusts, or management companies. As we saw, the management companies are either open-end or closed-end funds. The distinguishing factor is that the open-end funds are redeemable, while the closed-end shares trade on the secondary market among investors. The unit investment trust is usually linked with "having no board of directors," so maybe that will show up in a test question. To fit the definition of "investment company," the shares must be able to easily be sold and the number of shareholders must exceed 100. Hedge funds go the other way to avoid fitting the definition of "investment company." That is, they don't let people sell their investment freely and they keep the number of investors under 100, because if you can escape the definition of "investment company," you can escape the hassle of registering the investments and providing lots of disclosure to the SEC and the public markets. As usual, under the Act of 1940 the average investor is protected more than the sophisticated investor. Mutual funds and variable annuities are for the average investor; therefore, they need to be registered and watched closely by the SEC. Hedge funds are for the sophisticated investor primarily, so maybe things don't need to be watched so closely with them.

INVESTMENT ADVISERS ACT OF 1940

If you want to give people your expert advice on their specific investment situation and receive compensation for doing so, you have to register under the **Investment Advisers Act of 1940** or under your state securities law. Portfolio managers, financial planners, pension fund consultants, and even many sports and entertainment agents end up having to register in order to give investment advice to their clients. All open- and closed-end funds are managed by registered investment advisers, and pension funds typically farm out their assets to many different investment advisory firms. Because the role they play is so important and so potentially dangerous, all investment advisers have to be registered unless they can qualify for some type of exemption.

INSIDER TRADING AND SECURITIES FRAUD ENFORCEMENT ACT

Although the Securities Exchange Act of 1934 talked plenty about insider trading, apparently it didn't quite get the message across. So in 1988 Congress raised the penalties for insider trading by passing the **Insider Trading and Securities Fraud Enforcement Act (ITSFEA)**. If your brother-in-law happens to be the Chief Financial Officer of a public company and over a few too many martinis lets it slip that his company is going to miss earnings estimates badly this quarter, just pretend like you didn't hear it. In fact, don't pretend. You did NOT, in fact, hear it. Because if you start passing out that information, or if you—God forbid—buy a bunch of puts on the stock, you could and probably will have yourself all kinds of problems. The SEC could fine you three times the amount of your profit (or even your loss avoided). In other words, if you made (or avoided losing) $800,000, they could fine you 2.4 million bucks in a civil suit. And, as you may have noticed from all the CEO-in-handcuffs footage in the news a few years ago, the US Attorney's office might also pursue you in criminal court, which is never a good place to be, from what I understand.

Sure, but how the heck would they ever catch me?

Interestingly enough, those words have been carved into many federal prison cell walls since they passed the Insider Trading and Securities Fraud Enforcement Act in 1988. Any material information the public doesn't have, that's inside information. Don't pass it around, don't use it. Wait until it's disclosed, then do whatever you want with it.

Lots of students ask, "But what's the big deal? If you know something, why not trade on it?"

The way the regulators see things, trading on inside information is a manipulative and deceptive device (fraudulent) under the Securities Exchange Act of 1934 because a fiduciary relationship exists between the shareholders of a corporation and the insiders who have obtained confidential information through their position with that corporation. This fiduciary relationship that we have discussed to death in terms of investment advisers implies a duty on the insider to either disclose information or refrain from trading on that information—the "disclose or abstain" thing we mentioned a while back. Since disclosure of the information isn't practical, that leaves the "informed" insider with only one option: to abstain from trading on it. Or hope he doesn't get caught.

CHAPTER 4 REVIEW QUIZ

1. **As part of its fiduciary duty to clients, an adviser has an obligation of full and fair disclosure of all material facts to clients. Examples of failure to disclose material information to clients would include:**

    I.   An adviser clearly discloses all fees that a client would pay in connection with the advisory contract

    II. An adviser fails to disclose its affiliation with a broker-dealer providing custodial services only to advisory clients

    III. An adviser with discretionary assets under management fails to disclose that it is in a precarious financial condition that is likely to impair its ability to meet contractual commitments to clients

    A. I
    B. II, III
    C. II
    D. III

2. **An investment adviser owes all of the following duties to its clients except**
    A. a duty to seek to obtain the best net price reasonably available under the circumstances for client transactions
    B. a duty to obtain the lowest possible price for all securities transactions
    C. a duty to disclose that directed client brokerage leads to client referrals from certain broker-dealers
    D. a duty to disclose that directed client brokerage leads only to free research from certain broker-dealers

3. **A broker-dealer was recently suspended by FINRA and fined $80,000 for failure to pay an arbitration award. Therefore, the Administrator of the state where the firm maintains its principal office**

    A. has no authority to take disciplinary action

    B. may revoke the firm's license, even before providing prior notice, an opportunity for a hearing, and written findings of fact/conclusions of law

    C. may institute disciplinary proceedings based on FINRA's actions

    D. would not consider a development under FINRA's Code of Arbitration relevant to the firm's registration

4. **All of the following are prohibited activities except**

    A. selling away

    B. selling dividends

    C. breakpoint selling

    D. selling short without first buying the stock

5. **As an investment adviser representative with discretion over a client account, you are about to purchase 500 shares of ORCL through your firm's related broker-dealer, who makes a market in the stock. Therefore all of the following are accurate statements except:**

    A. This is a principal transaction

    B. This is an agency cross transaction

    C. Your firm must receive the client's acknowledgment by settlement of the trade

    D. This represents a conflict of interest subject to disclosure by the investment adviser

6. **Under the Uniform Securities Act, which of the following situations require(s) that the investment adviser maintain a specified minimum net capital?**

    A. The adviser maintains custody of client funds/securities

    B. The adviser has discretion over the account(s)

    C. The adviser accepts prepayment of >$500 six or more months in advance

    D. All of the choices listed

7. **An investment adviser registered in five states announces its services through a website. The website is, of course, accessible in all 50 states. Therefore:**

    I.   The adviser is in violation of advertising rules for investment advisers

    II. As long as the website contains a legend clearly stating that the investment adviser may only transact business in those states where they are registered or not required to be registered, no violation has occurred

    III. As long as the website does not involve the rendering of investment advice for compensation but merely disseminates information about the adviser's services, no violation has occurred

    IV. Since the Internet clearly involves interstate commerce, only the SEC has jurisdiction over any Internet-based advertisements or advisory activities

    A.   I only

    B.   IV only

    C.   II, III only

    D.   II, III, IV only

8. **A firm with a place of business in the state advises corporate clients on mergers & acquisitions and helps them structure and sell their initial equity offerings to institutional and retail investors. The firm must register as**

    A.   An investment adviser

    B.   A broker-dealer

    C.   A broker-dealer and an investment adviser

    D.   A research analyst

9. **An agent has been holding investing seminars for senior citizens. As an agent with 10 years' experience, she is well qualified to speak on the topics of annuities and wealth preservation and has earned her CFP distinction. The Administrator discovers that the agent has not informed her supervisor of the seminars and that she made several statements at the seminars that were misleading and deceptive. Therefore, which of the following represent(s) true statements of this situation?**

    I.   As an expert, the agent was not obligated to inform her firm of the seminars

    II. As a representative of the broker-dealer, the agent was obligated to inform her firm of the seminars and have the compliance department review and/or approve all invitations, handouts, computer slide shows, etc.

    III. As long as no money was collected and no contracts were signed at the seminars, no fraud could have taken place, as no offers of securities could, therefore, have occurred

    IV. The agent will likely be the subject of an Administrative proceeding for her conduct

    A.   I

    B.   I, III

    C.   II

    D.   II, IV

10. **Which of the following represent(s) a true statement concerning the powers of the Administrator?**

    A. If a self-regulatory organization expels a member firm, the state may use that as a reason to take action against the firm

    B. If a national exchange registered under the Securities Exchange Act of 1934 expels a member, that fact may be used by the Administrator against the party

    C. Both A and B

    D. Neither A nor B

11. **Melissa meets with a 73-year-old widow who collects $20,000 a year from her deceased husband's pension. Melissa recommends that her client purchase a deferred variable annuity. Six months after selling the annuity, Melissa recommends that her client invest the value of her annuity into a safe, income-producing intermediate-term Treasury mutual fund that her firm is rolling out. The client surrenders the annuity, paying a 7% surrender charge, and transfers the money into the mutual fund that pays income monthly. Which of the following statements best addresses this situation?**

    A. Melissa made a suitable recommendation when selling the variable annuity

    B. Melissa made a suitable recommendation when converting the annuity

    C. Because of the surrender charges and the client's life expectancy, the deferred annuity was a suitable recommendation

    D. Recommending the deferred annuity and recommending the surrender, in light of the contingent deferred sales charges, are both grounds for potential regulatory action against Melissa

12. **An agent may offer or sell a security in a state if the security is**

    A. federal covered

    B. exempt from registration

    C. registered under the Uniform Securities Act

    D. all choices listed

13. **Which of the following transactions is/are exempt from the state's filing requirements and anti-fraud rules?**

    A. isolated non-issuer transactions in outstanding securities

    B. transactions between an issuer and an institutional investor

    C. both A and B

    D. neither A nor B

14. **When a FINRA-member broker-dealer acts as a "market maker," the firm is involved with which of the following activities?**
    A.   executing transactions in exchange-listed securities on an agency basis
    B.   publishing and honoring firm two-sided quotes for stocks trading OTC
    C.   bringing new issues of stock to public investors on the primary market
    D.   bringing new issues of stock to private investors on the secondary market

15. **Which of the following is an accurate statement?**
    A.   all fraudulent practices are also prohibited
    B.   all prohibited practices are also fraudulent
    C.   fraud occurs if the state can prove that the violator knew he was misleading the other side of the transaction
    D.   fraudulent sales practices are unethical but not inherently prohibited by law

16. **Which of the following would allow a security to be sold in a state without registration?**
    A.   The selling agents represent the issuer of the securities
    B.   The security is common stock trading on the non-NASDAQ OTC market
    C.   The firm selling the security is excluded from the definition of a broker-dealer
    D.   The security is sold in a private placement

17. **An investment adviser would not be deemed to have custody of client assets in which of the following cases?**
    A.   An adviser places client assets in custody of a financial institution in which he is merely a limited partner
    B.   An adviser automatically deducts management fees, sending a billing statement to the custodian and the client
    C.   An adviser accepts client securities from a client in the adviser's office and promptly forwards them to the custodian
    D.   An adviser inadvertently receives client securities in the mail and returns them to the sender 2 days later

18. **Which federal act requires that public companies report to the SEC and shareholders?**
    A.   Sarbanes-Oxley
    B.   Securities Exchange Act of 1934
    C.   Securities Act of 1933
    D.   USA Patriot Act

19. **Under the Uniform Securities Act, violators are subject to**
    A. criminal sanctions
    B. civil liability
    C. administrative hearings
    D. all choices listed

20. **Fraud is an essential element in all of the following industry violations except**
    A. breach of fiduciary duty
    B. unauthorized transactions
    C. omitting material facts in the offer/sale of securities
    D. charging unreasonable markups/markdowns

21. **Which of the following is a true statement concerning the personal trading of investment adviser representatives?**
    A. There are no restrictions provided the IARs are properly licensed/registered
    B. The firm may prevent IARs from buying but not selling any security
    C. The adviser may restrict personal trading as it sees fit
    D. There are no restrictions provided the IARs are properly supervised

22. **Which federal act requires that a prospectus be registered with the SEC?**
    A. Sarbanes-Oxley
    B. Securities Exchange Act of 1934
    C. Securities Act of 1933
    D. USA Patriot Act

23. **A Unit Investment Trust is most closely associated with**
    A. Investment Advisers Act of 1940
    B. Securities Exchange Act of 1934
    C. Securities Act of 1933
    D. Investment Company Act of 1940

24. **Selling away is a violation in which**
    A. a securities agent offers investments to clients of her broker-dealer that are unsuitable
    B. a securities agent offers investments to investors that her employer knows nothing about
    C. a mutual fund investor does not receive the breakpoint she is entitled to
    D. a securities agent buys stock before placing a large customer order, hoping to benefit from the uptick

CHAPTER 4 REVIEW
QUIZ ANSWERS

1. **ANSWER:** B

    WHY: there is no problem with disclosing all fees that a client would pay, of course, so don't let yourself misread an answer choice like Choice I.

2. **ANSWER:** B

    WHY: advisers must seek the "best execution" of client transactions, but "lowest possible price" goes too far. Where does this regulatory concern come from? Many advisers are in cahoots with broker-dealers; the regulators don't like to see broker-dealers receive inflated profits and advisers receive kickbacks for the favor of running client transactions through the firm, all at the expense of investors. Remember, the Administrator protects investors, not broker-dealers and investment advisers.

3. **ANSWER:** C

    WHY: if the firm is suspended by FINRA, the Administrator can definitely use that as grounds to take action. How else would it work? FINRA suspends the firm, but they can go on operating, anyway?

4. **ANSWER:** D

    WHY: when selling short, by definition the trader is not buying the stock. Rather, he is selling borrowed shares, with the obligation to replace them—at a lower price, he hopes. Selling away involves selling securities your broker-dealer knows nothing about. Selling dividends is misleading and fraudulent, as is refusing to help a client achieve the next breakpoint on a mutual fund purchase.

5. **ANSWER:** B

    WHY: an agency cross transaction is also a conflict of interest subject to disclosure, but the transaction in this question is done on a principal basis. For principal transactions, the firm must get the client's signed acknowledgment by "completion of the transaction."

6. **ANSWER:** D

    WHY: these are the three situations spelled out in the NASAA Model Rule on Minimum Financial Requirements. For custody, the minimum net worth/net capital is $35,000. For discretion-only, $10,000. For the prepayment situation, the adviser must maintain positive net worth at all times.

7. **ANSWER:** C

    WHY: the adviser is not considered to be doing business in the other states as long as it's clear he isn't trying to do business in any state where he's not registered or exempt. Also know that agents and IARs have to show their affiliation with their employing firms and must have compliance approve all communications on the website.

8. **ANSWER:** B

    WHY: the word "advises" is not proof that the firm is an investment adviser. In fact, they are not providing investment advice at all—are they helping clients invest their money in securities? No, they're acting as investment bankers/broker-dealers by raising capital for their clients. Note, even when an investment banker "advises" on a merger or an IPO, the firm is still a broker-dealer. Investment bankers help clients raise capital from investors. Investment advisers help investors invest the capital they already have among various securities.

9. **ANSWER:** D

    WHY: FINRA rules required the agent to inform the broker-dealer and have compliance review and/or approve all communications. Breaking FINRA—or any SRO rules—gives the Administrator grounds to take disciplinary action. Why not?

10. **ANSWER:** C

    WHY: remember, if any regulator has a problem with someone, so does the state securities Administrator.

11. **ANSWER:** D

    WHY: a deferred variable annuity with a steep surrender charge for a client with large needs for liquidity? Totally unsuitable. Talking the client into then pulling money out and suffering a surrender charge just so the agent can make another commission—also a problem.

12. **ANSWER:** D

    WHY: this question serves as a reminder of some very important concepts. First, if it is a security, it is subject to anti-fraud rules. Then, it either needs to be registered, or exempted from registration as an exempt security or through a transactional exemption. One example of an exempt security is a federal covered security, so choices A and B are sort of redundant.

13. **ANSWER:** D

    WHY: a true "trick question." Yes, both are exempt from the first part (filing requirements) but no <u>security</u> is exempt from the second part (anti-fraud rules).

14. **ANSWER:** B

    WHY: market makers don't act as agents; two different things. New issues don't come to market on the secondary market. And bringing new issues/IPOs to the primary market = investment banking. Always use test-taking skills, even when you think you know the answer. BTW, a "two-sided quote" is just a Bid and an Ask price, e.g., Bid-10, Ask-10.05.

15. **ANSWER:** A

    WHY: the Uniform Securities Act begins with a section called "Fraud and OTHER Prohibited

Practices." So fraud is definitely prohibited, too. Fraud is often handled in a civil action in which the buyers seek to get their money back plus interest. Occasionally, the fraud is a criminal operation that leads to jail time. The criminal prosecutors for the state would have to prove the defendant intended to defraud investors…but that's not so hard. If he issued little pretend "mutual funds" to investors and sent out bogus monthly account statements reflecting made-up balances? Yeah—that's some jail time right there.

16. **ANSWER:** D

   WHY: there are only two ways a security can be sold in the state without being registered: 1) it's an exempt security or 2) it's sold in an exempt transaction, for example, a "private placement."

17. **ANSWER:** D

   WHY: if the adviser has an ownership stake in the custodial institution, the adviser has custody. If the adviser can appropriate money from the client's account without going through the client, that also = custody. And, if the adviser *accepts* the securities in the office, they take custody of them right then and there. Remember that the securities sent inadvertently to the adviser need to be returned within 3 days, with the adviser keeping records as to what was received and sent and when it was received and sent.

18. **ANSWER:** B

   WHY: pull up a 10-K on any public company. Right at the top of the front cover, you will find your answer. Go ahead, we'll wait.

19. **ANSWER:** D

   WHY: the Uniform Securities Act in your state is part of your state's civil and criminal codes—the fact that the Administrator's authority stops before things cross into civil and criminal actions is a separate matter. The Administrator has sole authority over the Administrative hearings and enforcement actions. The Attorney General of your state/commonwealth would usually handle any criminal actions and—in some states—take civil action trying to return money to investors.

20. **ANSWER:** D

   WHY: fraud involves deceit, either through false statements or the omission of really important facts. You bought stock in an oil & gas drilling company, and they forgot to tell you the EPA is already leaning on them in federal court, no actual oil or gas reserves are proven, and the guy running the program has over 300 lawsuits against him? Yeah, that's fraud. The regulators have defined breach of fiduciary duty to be fraud, and spending money without your client's knowledge—also fraudulent, deceptive. If a firm is charging high markups, that's just a prohibited practice. No deceit is taking place. What if they're concealing the excessive markups from clients? Bingo—back to fraud again.

21. **ANSWER:** C

   WHY: as I recently confirmed with the SEC myself, their rule is merely the minimum standard for advisers to use in their code of ethics policies. If the adviser wants to say that all employees are banned from buying anything but Treasury securities and Exchange Traded Funds, then so be it. If employees don't like the policy, they can work somewhere else is how the regulators see it. The regulators themselves are usually precluded from investing/trading in securities, themselves, so you won't get much sympathy from an SEC attorney. Trust me.

22. **ANSWER:** C

WHY: the Securities Act of 1933 is only about new issues of securities and how they are registered. The prospectus is part of the registration statement. Registration statements, of course, are available online to the curious pre-license exam candidate with a little patience and savvy.

23. **ANSWER:** D

WHY: a Unit Investment Trust (UIT) is one of the three types of investment companies, classified under the Investment Company Act of 1940 as one of the following: unit investment trust, face-amount certificate company, or management company.

24. **ANSWER:** B

WHY: agents can only offer investments approved by their employing broker-dealer, with the broker-dealer overseeing their sales activities very closely. Other choices are examples of violations, but different types. For example, Choice A is an "unsuitable recommendation," believe it or not. Choice C is called "breakpoint selling," a major no-no. And Choice D is an example of frontrunning, also frowned upon.

Practice Final

1. **According to the Uniform Securities Act, what is the difference between an offer to sell and a sale of a security?**
    A.   an offer comes from the customer; a sale from the registered representative
    B.   an offer is the attempt to sell; a sale is a contract to dispose of a security for value
    C.   an offer to sell a security includes stock dividends in most cases
    D.   a reclassification of securities pursuant to bankruptcy proceedings is an offer to sell and an offer to buy simultaneously

2. **All of the following are "securities" except**
    A.   Investment contract
    B.   Commodity futures contract
    C.   Variable Life Insurance contract
    D.   Unit Investment Trust

3. **Under the Uniform Securities Act, which of the following investment advisers would most likely not have to register in the state?**
    A.   adviser with no office in the state who advises 7 high net-worth individuals who are residents of the state
    B.   adviser with an office in the state who advises 5 non-institutional clients who are residents of the state
    C.   adviser with an office in the state who advises 11 multimillion-dollar pension funds located in the state
    D.   adviser with no office in the state who advises 11 multimillion-dollar pension funds located in the state

4. **Which of the following persons are excluded from the definition of "investment adviser" under the Uniform Securities Act?**
    A.   securities agents
    B.   sports agents
    C.   banks
    D.   broker-dealers

5. **All of the following are investment adviser representatives except**

    A. individual hired by an Investment Adviser to help determine recommendations to clients

    B. individual hired by an Investment Adviser to sell the advisory services

    C. individual hired by an Investment Adviser to do filing and clerical work

    D. individual who supervises a staff of solicitors for the firm

6. **All of the following are exempt transactions under the Uniform Securities Act except**

    A. A sheriff liquidates securities at auction

    B. A receiver in bankruptcy liquidates securities to pay creditors

    C. A manufacturing company offers shares to public investors

    D. An issuer offers securities to 9 investors in the state

7. **A person in the business of effecting transactions in securities for the accounts of others or its own account is defined as a(an)**

    A. agent

    B. broker

    C. investment adviser

    D. broker-dealer

8. **All of the following professionals are excluded from the definition of "investment adviser" provided their advice is solely incidental except a/an:**

    A. lawyer

    B. accountant

    C. teacher

    D. economist

9. **Mary Ellen terminates her employment as an agent with Broker Dealer A in order to take a position at Broker Dealer B—also located in the state—as a registered representative. Who must notify the Administrator?**

    A. Mary Ellen only

    B. Mary Ellen, Broker Dealer A, Broker Dealer B

    C. Broker Dealer A

    D. Broker Dealer B

10. **Which of the following are required "books and records" to be kept by investment advisers?**

    A. records of all transactions by IARs

    B. records of all performance claims of the adviser's recommendations

    C. records of all advertising materials

    D. all choices listed

11. In which case would the Administrator most likely cancel a person's registration?

A. it is in the public interest to do so

B. the individual cannot be located

C. the individual lied on an initial application

D. the individual lied on a renewal application

12. If a security is "guaranteed," an investor may conclude that

A. there is no chance of sustaining an investment loss

B. a third party promises to pay if the issuer cannot

C. the security has been approved by the SEC

D. the security is a relatively safe investment

13. Which of the following is a true statement concerning registration of a successor firm?

A. this practice is illegal in a majority of states

B. the successor firm's registration is good for the unexpired portion of the year

C. this practice is illegal in a plurality of states

D. the successor firm must be in existence at the time of registration

14. Which of the following is a true statement concerning minimum financial requirements?

A. the Administrator must require minimum net capital at least as high as the federal requirement

B. the Administrator may require net capital requirements in excess of federal requirements for federal covered advisers notice filing in the state

C. rather than using a fixed dollar amount, some states use the ratio of net capital to aggregate indebtedness when determining minimum net capital requirements

D. minimum net capital requirements are only for those firms with discretion or custody

15. Under the Uniform Securities Act, a security must be registered in a state if it is

A. issued by a credit union

B. issued by a Canadian government

C. offered to existing shareholders of the issuer

D. offered to more than 10 persons in the state

16. Which of the following best describes the activities of an investment adviser?

A. individual charging commissions when selling non-exempt securities

B. firm charging commissions when selling exempt securities

C. firm dispensing specific investment advice on securities for a flat fee

D. firm dispensing advice on real estate purchases

17. **A customer of Q & R Investment Advisers calls an adviser representative to inquire what the "wrap fee" charged on her account represents. Which of the following represents the best response from the IA representative?**
    A.   A wrap fee is the same thing as a commission
    B.   A wrap fee is just like a sales load
    C.   A wrap fee is charged when the account achieves a certain level of return
    D.   A wrap fee combines charges for advice as well as execution of a transaction

18. **Janice is an IAR properly registered in State A and working for a federally registered investment adviser. Once a month Janice meets with clients in State B at the federal covered adviser's office. What is true about Janice's registration requirements?**
    A.   because she represents a federal covered adviser, she does not register in any state
    B.   because she has clients in State B, she must register there
    C.   because she has a place of business in State B, she must register there
    D.   because she represents a federal covered adviser, her registration in State B is automatic

19. **Which of the following is true concerning criminal penalties under the Uniform Securities Act?**
    A.   there is no statute of limitations
    B.   the statute of limitations is 7 years
    C.   the maximum penalty is 3 years in jail, $5,000 fine or both
    D.   ignorance of the law/rule has no bearing in criminal proceedings

20. **Before the Administrator enters an order to deny, suspend, or revoke a license, the affected party must be provided with all of the following EXCEPT:**
    A.   consent to service of process
    B.   prior notice
    C.   opportunity for a hearing
    D.   written finding of fact, conclusions of law

21. **A customer is sold an unregistered, non-exempt security in violation of the Uniform Securities Act. What is the customer entitled to receive?**
    A.   three times the amount paid for the security
    B.   original purchase price, plus interest, less income received
    C.   original purchase price, plus unspecified damages for pain and suffering
    D.   contumacy

22. **Which TWO of the following are accurate concerning Administrative orders to deny, suspend, or revoke a registration?**

    I.   be in the public interest

    II. provide necessary protection to investors

    III. be approved by the state legislature

    IV. be approved by the Securities and Exchange Commission

    A. I, III

    B. II, III

    C. I, II

    D. II, IV

23. **All of the following Administrative orders generally stem from violations in the securities industry except**

    A. suspension

    B. revocation

    C. withdrawal

    D. denial

24. **What must an investment adviser established as a partnership do if one or more members are admitted to the partnership?**

    A. incorporate

    B. notify all clients promptly

    C. notify all institutional clients promptly

    D. nothing

25. **A company invests, reinvests, and purchases shares of stock. What type of company is this?**

    A. A broker/dealer

    B. An investment company

    C. An investment banking company

    D. A company composed of investment advisers

26. **Which of the following statements is correct concerning securities registrations under the Uniform Securities Act?**

    A. a stop order issued by the state of Kansas may not affect the effectiveness of the securities' registration in Oklahoma

    B. the Administrator may not initiate a proceeding to deny a security's registration based on a fact known to him for more than 30 days

    C. all securities registered with the SEC must also be registered with the states

    D. all securities registered with the SEC are automatically registered with the states

27. All of the following statements are true of investment advisory contracts except

A. they must be filed with FINRA within ten business days of execution

B. they must contain a non-assignability clause

C. they must explain the basis for compensation

D. exculpatory provisions and waivers of compliance are prohibited

28. Which of the following represents an advantage of owning common stock compared to corporate bonds?

A. stock values are easier to ascertain than the proper price of debt instruments

B. stocks typically experience lower volatility

C. corporate bonds mature or are often forcibly redeemed, while common stockholders retain control over selling their investment and taking capital gains and losses

D. stocks provide higher after-tax yields

29. All of the following are prohibited activities except

A. painting the tape

B. arbitrage

C. selling away

D. frontrunning

30. One of your investing clients is 68 years old and works five days a month as a substitute teacher after retiring from full-time teaching three years ago. With her husband in a nursing home, you suggest that she purchase a single premium deferred variable annuity as it will provide her with dependable, guaranteed income when she stops teaching entirely in the next two years or so. If the annuity has an 8-year surrender period, what is true of this recommendation?

I. it could be considered deceptive and misleading

II. it is unsuitable given the client's needs and objectives

III. a periodic deferred variable annuity would have been suitable

A. I

B. II

C. I, II

D. I, II, III

31. **One of your customers is a retired widow living on a modest fixed income. She calls one afternoon and insists that she needs to sell her government bonds and put the money into small-cap technology stocks trading on the OTC Bulletin Board. What should you do?**
    A. inform the SEC or state securities Administrator within 48 hours
    B. petition the appropriate court to schedule a hearing to determine mental competence
    C. tell the customer you feel the action is unsuitable
    D. apply to the appropriate court for a temporary restraining order

32. **Which of the following investments of money is LEAST likely defined as a "security"?**
    A. viatical investment
    B. 9% profit interest in a prize-winning race horse
    C. investment program funding the purchase and sale for profit of rare and valuable baseball cards
    D. extremely rare and valuable baseball card

33. **Just before placing a large buy order for your customer on a thinly traded Bulletin Board stock, you buy calls on the stock yourself. This is an example of**
    A. market timing
    B. frontrunning, a violation
    C. an exempt transaction
    D. hedging against systematic risk

34. **Which of the following is not a legal person?**
    A. child
    B. S-corp
    C. estate
    D. LLC

35. **All of the following are considered securities except**
    A. Investment contract
    B. Profit-sharing agreement for a business in which the investor plays no active or managerial role
    C. Indexed annuity tied to the S&P 500
    D. Variable annuity

36. **All of the following are considered securities except**
    A. government bond
    B. passive interest in an oil-drilling operation
    C. ownership interests in prize-winning thoroughbreds
    D. S&P 500

37. **When a public company offers additional shares of stock to investors several years after the IPO, this is known as a**
    A. private placement
    B. initial public offering
    C. secondary offering
    D. subsequent primary distribution

38. **The CFO of an issuer represents the company in selling short-term debt securities to banks and S&L's. If he receives no special compensation for the sales, he**
    A. must register as a broker-dealer
    B. must register as an investment adviser
    C. is an agent but need not register
    D. is not an agent and need not register

39. **In which of the following cases would the Administrator most likely cancel a person's registration?**
    A. the individual has engaged in dishonest, unethical practices
    B. the individual cannot be located
    C. the individual lied on an initial application
    D. the individual lied on a renewal application

40. **Broker-dealers, investment advisers, and registered representatives share all of the following requirements for registration except**
    A. consent to service of process
    B. surety bonds
    C. minimum net capital
    D. criminal disclosure reporting

41. **Offerings of which of the following securities may be subject to the filing of sales literature/advertising with the state Administrator?**
    A. Indianapolis General Obligation Bond
    B. Microsoft° common stock
    C. IBM° preferred stock
    D. Stock trading regularly on the OTC Bulletin Board

42. **The Administrator has the power under the Uniform Securities Act to do all of the following EXCEPT:**
    A. issue rules and orders
    B. publish violations
    C. impose fines
    D. require federal covered advisers to pay fees to the state

43. **The Administrator may deny the registration of a security for all the following reasons except**
    A. underwriting compensation appears excessive
    B. the order is in the public interest
    C. the order provides protection to investors
    D. the issuing company has failed to pay dividends

44. **What is true of the difference between "BID" and "ASK"?**
    A. market makers sell at the bid, buy at the ask
    B. market makers buy at the bid, sell at the ask
    C. customers buy at the bid, sell at the ask
    D. the terms are synonymous

45. **What is true of mutual fund sales charges and 12b-1 fees?**
    A. 12b-1 fees are included in the expense ratio
    B. sales charges are not included in the expense ratio
    C. management fees may not be covered by 12b-1 fees
    D. all choices listed

46. **Dale has a life & health license. Peter, who also works at the firm, has both a life & health license and a Series 6. Therefore, when Dale refers clients who purchase variable annuities and mutual funds from Peter, Dale**
    A. may share in the commissions, since he and Peter share a common employer
    B. may not share in the commissions, since he is not securities licensed
    C. may share in the commissions if a principal approves it
    D. is guilty of a fraudulent securities transaction

47. **All of the following statements concerning securities registrations are true except**
    A. The registration statement must specify the amount of securities, states in which the offering is to be made, and any adverse order or judgment by a regulatory authority
    B. The Administrator may rule that the securities registered by coordination or qualification may only be sold on a specified form of subscription
    C. The Administrator may not deny the registration due to excessive underwriter compensation
    D. The Administrator may by rule permit omission of any item of information or document from any registration statement

48. **Securities of all the following issuers are exempt under the Uniform Securities Act except securities issued by**
    A. state banks
    B. national banks
    C. savings institutions
    D. bank holding companies

49. **Which of the following best represents a non-issuer transaction?**
    A. private placement
    B. secondary offering
    C. provides capital to an expanding corporation
    D. provides capital to an issuer and certain large shareholders

50. **What is true of a broker-dealer offering wrap accounts?**
    A. broker-dealers may not offer wrap accounts
    B. since the firm is a registered broker-dealer it need not register as an investment adviser
    C. broker-dealers may not also register as investment advisers
    D. the broker-dealer must also register as an investment adviser

51. **Under the Investment Company Act of 1940, which of the following represents a true statement?**
    A. open-end funds issue shares traded on the secondary market
    B. a diversified fund is one which holds securities issued by companies operating in at least 10 distinct industries
    C. closed-end shares are redeemable
    D. open-end and closed-end funds are management companies

52. **Which of the following investments is NOT subject to anti-fraud rules under the Uniform Securities Act?**
    A. certificate evidencing a 10% ownership of a prize-winning racehorse
    B. 5% ownership of five ATM machines
    C. fixed annuity
    D. none of these choices

53. **Which of the following issues represent items subject to voting by common stockholders?**
    I. mergers
    II. stock dividends
    III. acquisitions
    IV. stock splits

    A. I, III
    B. II, IV
    C. I, III, IV
    D. I, II, III

54. **Investment Advisers register with either the state securities Administrator(s) or the Securities and Exchange Commission by using an electronic**
    A. Form BD
    B. Form ADV
    C. Form U4
    D. Form 8-K

55. **The term "hypothecation" has to do with which of the following?**
    A. Options accounts only
    B. Margin accounts
    C. Derivatives trading accounts only
    D. Corporate and municipal bonds

56. **Which of the following facts would require that a broker-dealer register with the state securities Administrator?**
    A. All clients are institutions, e.g., insurance companies and pension funds
    B. The broker-dealer does not maintain a physical presence in the state
    C. The broker dealer has a small number of non-institutional clients in the state
    D. The broker-dealer is not also registered as an investment adviser

57. **When a market maker sells a security to an investor, the firm is compensated**
    A. By adding a small commission
    B. With a markdown
    C. Directly by the exchange the security is listed/trades upon
    D. With a markup

58. **An investor received an offer of rescission on the letterhead of the issuer of the convertible preferred stock. Forty-five days later, the investor signs the acceptance form and returns evidence of securities ownership to the address indicated on the letter. Therefore,**
    A. The investor will receive treble damages
    B. The investor has missed the deadline to accept the offer, and her right to recover has been lost
    C. The investor has the balance of two years to initiate a lawsuit against the plaintiff
    D. The investor will receive the price paid for the securities only

59. **Self-Regulatory Organizations (SROs) include all of the following EXCEPT:**
    A. SEC
    B. FINRA
    C. MSRB
    D. CBOE

60. **When an individual offering securities in violation of the Uniform Securities Act ignores the Administrator's cease & desist, the Administrator has the authority to**
    A. Issue a restraining order against the individual
    B. Impound the individual's assets
    C. Request injunctive relief from the appropriate court of law
    D. Fine the individual and revoke any licenses summarily

Answers to Practice Final

1. **B,** choices C and D are specifically not offers under the Uniform Securities Act.

2. **B,** commodity futures contracts are regulated by commodities regulators and are not considered to be "securities."

3. **D,** when looking for an exemption for a state-registered investment adviser look for the investment adviser with no office in the state first. Then, choose the one with only institutional clients.

4. **C,** an investment adviser is simply not a bank, ever, and vice versa.

5. **C,** these "ministerial employees" are not required to register as IARs, since they don't really impact the investments of the firm's clients.

6. **C,** no exemption for companies offering shares to investors. Choice D could be a private placement, which is an exempt transaction.

7. **D,** remember that broker-dealers are in the transaction business.

8. **D,** there is no exclusion for economists. The other professionals may need to discuss securities to an extent, but only to the extent their profession requires.

9. **B,** Mary Ellen and the former BD will file a U5; the new firm and Mary Ellen will file a U4.

10. **D,** three good things to know for the exam. There are other required books and records, of course, as mentioned in the textbook.

11. **B,** remember that a cancellation does not result from a violation. The registrant simply no longer needs the license because he has died, or the business has gone belly-up, for example.

12. **B,** there are no guarantees against a loss in the securities industry.

13. **B,** if the firm is changing from a partnership to a corporation, for example, it may register the successor firm before the year is up and use the unexpired portion (rest of the year) on the existing registration.

14. **C,** the liabilities-to-assets ratio is often used rather than stipulating that all advisers with custody have the same dollar amount for their net capital requirement.

15. **D,** if it were offered to more than 10 persons, the issuer could not claim an exempt transaction (private placement), so the security would have to be registered.

16. **C,** we're not saying that commissions and investment advisers never go together, but of these choices the firm selling advice on securities is clearly the best choice.

17. **D,** a wrap fee wraps it all together.

18. **C,** she has a place of business in the state, so she must register there.

19. **C,** if the person can prove he had no way to know what he did was a crime, he can keep himself out of prison, actually.

20. **A,** remember that the consent to service of process is filed by agents, broker-dealers, investment advisers, and investment adviser representatives when they first register with the state.

21. **B,** no pain and suffering offered here. Just make the investor whole, plus interest, and cover the expense of going after the person who sold the securities in violation of the Act.

22. **C,** the Administrator doesn't wait to have his decisions approved by other governmental departments

23. **C,** a withdrawal is filed when someone registered under the Uniform Securities Act will no longer be registered with a particular state securities Administrator.

24. **B,** this is considered material information, and clients must be informed promptly of any change in ownership to an investment adviser organized as a partnership or an LLC.

25. **B,** just a definitional question based on the Investment Company Act of 1940.

26. **B,** remember that federal covered securities are registered only at the SEC level, and securities registered by qualification are registered at the state level only.

27. **A,** FINRA does not regulate investment advisers. They regulate broker-dealers.

28. **C,** bonds are often called when interest rates drop; common stock ownership is indefinite.

29. **B,** arbitrage is a trading strategy, not a violation.

30. **C,** a deferred annuity is for someone putting away extra money, with no need to touch the money for a long, long time.

31. **C,** tell the client you think it's an unsuitable trade, but if she really wants to buy the stock, you can execute an order with the ticket marked "unsolicited" to relieve yourself of suitability issues.

32. **D,** the baseball card itself is not a security, but if some collectors devise a program whereby they use investor money to scout the country for rare and valuable baseball cards, with investors receiving their share of any profits, that program is an investment contract, which is a security.

33. **B,** taking advantage of the market moves your customer orders are likely to cause is called front-running, a major violation.

34. **A,** remember that the following are not legal "persons": minor child, deceased individual, individual declared mentally incompetent.

35. **C,** indexed annuities are still considered to be fixed annuities, which are not securities.

36. **D,** the S&P 500 is just an index, a piece of intellectual property. Securities have been created based on it, but that's a different question.

37. **D,** if capital goes to the issuer, you must have the word "primary" in there somewhere and you cannot have the word "secondary" in there.

38. **D,** he is not functioning as an agent.

39. **B,** a license is canceled when the registrant goes out of business, dies, moves, or cannot be located.

40. **C,** minimum net capital requirements are for broker-dealers and investment advisers, not agents.

41. **D,** nothing special about non-NASDAQ OTC securities. The federal covered securities—exempt at state level—trade on big, recognized exchanges with higher listing criteria, e.g., NYSE, AMEX, NASDAQ Global Select.

42. **C,** the Uniform Securities Act does not authorize the Administrator to impose fines. Federal covered advisers pay notice filing fees each year.

43. **D,** paying dividends or not paying them is a business decision made by the board of directors for the issuing corporation. There are pros and cons to paying out profits as dividends or reinvesting them back into the business, and this is simply not a concern for a securities regulator.

44. **B,** a market maker is a broker-dealer willing to buy a security from you at the BID or sell you the same security at the higher ASK price.

45. **D,** this is based on NASAA's Model Rule on sales of investment company shares. Remember that a 12b-1 fee is an ongoing operating expense, while a sales charge is a one-time event. Management fees are always separated out, not buried under other fees.

46. **B,** a pretty straightforward question—you have to be securities licensed to be compensated for sales of securities.

47. **C,** excessive underwriter compensation—whether in the form of money or unreasonable warrants/options—will definitely lead to problems with the Administrator.

48. **D,** bank holding companies are corporations that own banks. They get no exemption from registration requirements. Bank stock is regulated by bank regulators and is exempt from registration under the Uniform Securities Act.

49. **B,** associate "secondary" with "non-issuer," and you will likely get a question right on the Series 63 right there. Issuers, remember, receive the proceeds in a primary market transaction.

50. **D,** a wrap account includes a fee for advice (and commissions), so the BD would also have to be an investment adviser to be compensated that way.

51. **D,** open-end funds are redeemed as opposed to being traded on the secondary market. Closed-end funds do trade on the secondary market/are not redeemable.

52. **C,** only the fixed annuity escapes the definition of a security here. The investment contracts tied to a potential income stream from a prize-winning horse or ATM machines are most likely considered to be "securities." Variable contracts—annuities and insurance—are both insurance products and securities, but not fixed contracts backed by the insurance company's claims paying ability (general account).

53. **C,** remember that common stockholders do not vote on dividends. The board of directors makes that decision all by themselves.

54. **B,** if you aren't sure on a question like this, go with the most likely answer—Form ADV…for an <u>adv</u>iser. Right? BTW, the form used by broker-dealers is Form BD.

55. **B,** in a margin account the customer pledges the securities purchased on margin as collateral—that's known by a fancy phrase called hypothecation.

56. **C,** if the broker-dealer has non-institutional clients in a state, they must register there, whether they have a place of business there or not.

57. **D,** market makers earn markups when they sell and markdowns when they buy. When a firm acts as an agent/broker, they simply add a commission for executing/completing the trade.

58. **B,** the buyer had only 30 days to accept the offer of rescission or not. Looks like she chose not.

59. **A,** the SEC is the federal government. The other organizations are "SROs" or "Self-Regulatory Organizations" who regulate firms and exchanges but, in turn, answer to the SEC or Securities and Exchange Commission.

60. **C,** the Administrator can seek an injunction/restraining order from a court but has no power to issue one. Don't confuse the subpoena—which the Administrator does issue—with an injunction, which only a court/judge may issue.

Background

Most people taking the Series 63 exam have recently taken the Series 7 or Series 6 and, therefore, have some background knowledge of common stock, preferred stock, corporate bonds, etc. Then again, a certain percentage of candidates are taking the Series 63 all by itself. If you belong to the second group, this part of the book is written especially for you. If you belong to the first group, you still might want to read this section as a review of what you learned while studying for your Series 6 or Series 7 exam.

INVESTMENT SECURITIES

Investments come in three main categories: equity, fixed income, and money market. Your portfolio is probably allocated so that a certain percentage is devoted to equity investments, a percentage to fixed-income investments, and a percentage to money market or "cash" investments. The money you invest in equity securities is generally the money you don't need to touch for a while, the money that is supposed to grow into a pile large enough to achieve some long-term goal such as retirement, education, or, perhaps, world travel. Fixed-income securities are generally less volatile and provide a more dependable stream of income than equity. The money market component of your portfolio is for the money you might need to spend at a moment's notice. Liquidity and safety of principal are the main advantages of money market securities. That means that your account tends to be worth at least what you invested, and you can make a withdrawal without taking a hit if you need to.

CASH EQUIVALENTS (MONEY MARKET)

Money market securities are simply debt securities maturing in one year or less. Safe, liquid investments. Money market securities are called "cash equivalents" because, basically, they are just as good as cash. Better, actually, because unlike cash sitting in a drawer somewhere, money market instruments are earning interest. It's not necessarily a high *rate* of interest, but at least you're putting your cash to work and you're not risking it in the stock market where anything can happen, or the bond market, where interest rates could rise and knock down the value of your holdings. From a money market mutual fund account, investors can actually write checks—that's how stable the value of the investment is. On the other hand, a retiree making withdrawals from an account holding stocks, bonds, and most types of mutual funds can end up selling her holdings at a loss. So, if the investor will need to make frequent withdrawals from the account, that account needs to hold a money market mutual fund or money market securities. The problem with investing too much of your money into cash equivalents is that you will miss out on the big growth opportunities that arise when the stock or bond markets decide to go off on a tear, which is known as "opportunity cost." Also, short-term debt securities do not keep pace with inflation very well, leaving the investor with purchasing power or inflation risk.

T-BILLS

Buying T-bills is about as safe as it gets. Remember that the "T" is for "Treasury," and T-bills are guaranteed by the United States Treasury. That's right, the interest and principal are guaranteed, and the US Treasury has never stiffed anyone. So, if you don't need to withdraw a certain amount of money for several months or longer, you can buy the 3-month or 6-month T-bill and usually earn higher yields than you'd earn in a savings account. T-bills don't pay regular interest checks. Instead, investors buy them at a discount from their face value. In a high interest rate environment, a 6-month $100,000 T-bill might sell for just $97,000, allowing the investor to keep the $3,000 difference at maturity. When interest rates are low, the 6-month T-bill might sell for only a slight discount below the face amount. Suddenly, we're all paying $99,000 for a $100,000 T-bill, making just $1,000 over that 6-month period. In either case, though, we are buying high credit quality securities that leave us with virtually no default risk.

Bank CDs usually yield about the same as T-bills, but the bank's FDIC insurance usually stops at $250,000 per account. T-bills, on the other hand, are simply guaranteed no matter how large the denomination. Any given Monday T-bills are available by auction from as small as $100 par value and as large as $5 million. No matter how big your bill, it's insured/guaranteed by the US Treasury.

NEGOTIABLE/JUMBO CDS

Some people like to step outside the realm of FDIC insurance and purchase "jumbo" or "negotiable" CDs. The denominations here are at least $250,000 and often several millions of dollars. Therefore, jumbo CDs are often not fully insured by the FDIC but are, rather, backed by the issuer. That makes their yields higher. Also, if you've ever pulled out of a bank CD early, you know how painful that can be. With a jumbo CD you have a negotiable/marketable security that you can sell to someone else. That's what the word "negotiable" means. CDs do make interest payments, unlike T-bills, which are purchased at a discount from their face value.

BANKER'S ACCEPTANCE

When an American company imports, say, computer parts from Japan, they typically "pay" for the shipment by presenting a letter of credit from a bank. If the shipment is worth $10 million, maybe it would be better to get most of that cash right now. So, a "banker's acceptance" is created whereby a pension or mutual fund buys the $10 million banker's acceptance for, say, $9.9 million. In other words, they'll make the $100,000 difference in a few weeks or months. Not a ton of money to make, but there's also not much risk. As with a T-bill, banker's acceptances are so short-term that it would make no sense to send interest checks to the buyer. Instead, these short-term debt securities are purchased at a discount from their face value. The difference between what you pay and what you receive *is* your interest income.

COMMERCIAL PAPER

Commercial paper is a major component of money market mutual funds. In order to build an $800 million factory, it probably makes more sense to issue bonds and pay the lenders back slowly, as you are currently paying off the mortgage on your house. But if GE needs a mere $50 million to tide them over for a few months, they would probably prefer to borrow it short-term at the lowest possible interest rate. If so, they issue a piece of commercial paper with a $50 million face amount, selling it to a pension or mutual fund for, say, $49.8 million. Again, the difference between the discounted price and the face amount *is* the interest earned by the investor.

REPURCHASE AGREEMENTS

Large financial institutions borrow money at low interest rates over the short term by taking your money and paying whatever a savings account or CD currently offers. They then lend your money out to someone else long-term at a higher interest rate. As long as they're able to borrow at a lower rate than they lend, they're fine. But, the business model also puts them at risk in terms of fluctuating interest rates. In order to shield themselves from interest-rate risk over the next 30, 60, or 90 days, large financial institutions engage in repurchase and reverse repurchase agreements. Basically, one party sells the other party something today with the agreement to repurchase it at a set price in the near future. The difference between what you pay today and receive in the near future would be your fixed rate of return over that time frame. So, if one bank calls another one to propose the arrangement, that's a repurchase agreement. If they call the other bank and ask to do it the other way around, that's a reverse repurchase agreement. Although definitely part of the money market, they're more of a private arrangement than a piece of paper that gets bought and sold.

TAX-EXEMPT MUNICIPAL NOTES

We'll look at municipal securities in a moment, but for now just know that cities, counties, school districts, etc., can borrow money long-term by issuing bonds, and they can borrow short-term by issuing notes. Anticipation notes are very common, and their name tells you exactly what's going on—there is money coming into the city's coffers in the near future, but there are some bills due *right now*. For example, property taxes are collected twice a year. If the city wants some of that money now, they can issue a tax anticipation note or TAN. If it's backed up by revenues, from sewer and water services for example, it's a revenue anticipation note or RAN. If the note is backed up by both taxes and revenues, they call it a "tax *and* revenue anticipation note" or TRAN. But, my personal favorite of these short-term municipal notes has to be the "bond anticipation note" or BAN. In this case, the issuer borrows money from somebody now and backs it up with part of the money they're going to borrow in the near future when they issue more bonds.

Seriously.

The interest paid on these municipal notes is lower than the nominal rates paid on a corporation's commercial paper, but that's okay—the interest paid is also tax-exempt at the federal level. So, if an investor or an institution is looking for safety, liquidity, and dependable, tax-exempt interest over the short-term, they purchase these anticipation notes directly or through a tax-exempt money market mutual fund.

LAST WORD

While the textbook definition of a money market security is a debt security maturing in one year or less, the usual maturity is a maximum of 270 days. There is an exemption to registration under the Securities Act of 1933 and the Uniform Securities Act for short-term debt securities based on that 270 days, and no one wants to register a short-term debt security, since by the time they got it through registration interest rates would have changed. Also, if the test writers want to make you sweat, they might ask if a T-bond could be a money market security. At first glance you think, no, a T-bond matures in 10 to 30 years, so there's no way it could be in a money market portfolio. Well, when it's issued the thing might have a 10-year maturity. The next year it would be nine years from maturity. Eventually, it would be one year or less from maturity, so, yes, *any* debt security one year or less from maturity is a money market instrument, regardless of the original maturity.

DEBT SECURITIES (FIXED INCOME)

Even though money market securities are also fixed-income securities, the phrase "fixed-income" generally refers to longer-term debt securities. These longer-term debt securities go by many names, but whether we're calling them bonds, debentures, notes, or certificates, we're just talking about debt securities. Stockholders are part owners of the corporation. Bond holders are not owners of the corporation—they are lenders *to* the corporation. Debt securities (bonds) are loans that investors make to the corporation. The corporation, in other words, goes into debt when they issue debt securities (bonds) to investors. The debt securities pay regular interest to investors and return the principal of the loan at the end of the term. These loans that investors make have a liquid secondary market, so investors can sell their bonds and get some or all of their money back whenever the markets are open. Bond market prices do fluctuate, but, generally bond prices are not as volatile as stock prices. So, a bond mutual fund is more volatile than a money market mutual fund, but still not in the same category of risk with equity (stock) mutual funds. If your daughter were already 15 years old and headed to college, you'd probably be a lot more comfortable putting your money into investment-grade bonds than in the stock market. Over a 3–5-year period, it's a pretty sure bet that stock prices will fluctuate much more than bond prices. Also, bonds pay a stated rate of interest; with stocks, we assume the dividends will continue and we hope that the market price will go up in our favor. But assumptions and hope are not much good at paying tuition bills, so if the investor has a shorter time horizon or a major need to protect her invested principal, bonds (fixed income) would be much more suitable than stocks or stock mutual funds.

Bonds have a par value of $1,000. This is the amount an investor will receive with the very last interest payment from the issuer. Up to that point, the investor has only been receiving interest payments against the money he loaned to the corporation by purchasing their bond certificates. So the bond certificate has "$1,000" printed on the face, along with the interest rate the issuer will pay the investor every year. This interest rate could be referred to as the coupon rate or "nominal yield." We have to pick a number for an example, so let's use 8%:

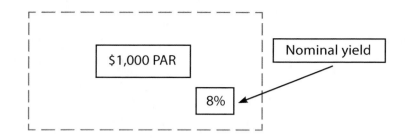

This bond would pay 8% of $1,000 in income to the investor every year, and then return the $1,000 with the final payment—end of story. This one pays $80 a year. A 5% bond would pay $50 a year. An 18% bond would pay $180 a year, and I sure hope somebody checked the credit rating on that one.

How often does this nominal yield change?

It doesn't. This nominal yield is what is paid to the investor every year. It represents a fixed payment, similar to a fixed-rate mortgage. Since the investor's income is fixed, they got all creative and decided to call bonds "fixed-income securities." The exam might also point out that borrowing money from investors or other lenders is called using "leverage," so a company that has issued a lot of debt securities and/or done a lot of long-term borrowing from banks is a "highly leveraged" company.

US GOVERNMENT DEBT

As we mentioned briefly in the money market section, some of the safest debt on earth is US Government debt, also called "Treasury" securities. This stuff is produced by the United States Treasury, the same folks who issue the ten-dollar bills in your wallet. Therefore, if you've never doubted the ability of the US Treasury to back up a ten-dollar bill, you have no reason to doubt their ability to back up the T-bills, T-notes, and T-bonds we're about to look at in some detail.

So, the US Treasury borrows money and also happens to have the ability to print more money to pay back the lenders. This "national debt" you've no doubt heard of from the chattering media is the amount of debt that has been issued by the US Treasury and still needs to be paid off. So, whenever the federal government wants to spend billions of dollars they don't actually have, they simply issue more of these debt securities and leave it to future administrations and taxpayers to either pay it off or pass it on to future generations.

Amazingly, the US Treasury has *always* managed to pay investors back plus interest, end of story. So, if you buy a bill, note, bond, or STRIP from the United States Treasury, you do not have to worry about default risk. You're going to get your interest checks on time, and you're going to get your money back. You just aren't going to get rich in the process. In fact, you usually need to be rich already to get excited about US Government debt, but that's another matter. For the test, just remember that US Government/Treasury debt is safe and liquid. If you can't stand the "risk" presented by owning Treasuries, you must drive to work in an armored vehicle and chew your food 29 times before swallowing.

Not that there's anything wrong with that.

T-bills

As we saw, T-bills are short-term debt securities issued by the US Treasury. T-bills pay the face amount at maturity, and investors try to buy them for the steepest discount possible. If the T-bill pays out $1,000, you'd rather get it for $950 than $965, right? In the first case you make $50 interest; in the second case you make only $35. It's tough to get excited about making $35 or $50 in interest, but if you add some zeros to your investment, things get a bit more interesting.

These bills mature in one year or less—4 weeks, 13 weeks, 26 weeks, 52 weeks—so there are no coupon payments. As we just saw, you buy the T-bill at a discount and receive the full face amount when it matures—the difference is your interest income. T-bills are the shortest maturity of the Treasuries, and they are offered in minimum denominations of $100. Every Monday excluding federal holidays, T-bills are offered at auction, allowing regular folks to buy a T-bill as small as $100 or as big as $5 million by putting in a "non-competitive tender." For further information on T-bills and auctions, please visit www.treasurydirect.gov. You might be shocked at how simply the federal government explains these things on their helpful website.

T-notes, T-bonds

So, T-bills do not pay interest per se—rather, they pay back more than they took from you a few weeks or months ago. If you want regular interest checks, you buy a T-note or T-bond. T-notes are offered with 2–10-year maturities. T-bonds go from 10 to 30 years.

T-notes and bonds both make semi-annual interest payments, and are both quoted in 32^{nds}. A quote of 98.16 means $980 plus $16/32^{nds}$ or ½. So a T-bond priced at 98.16 costs $985. It's not worth delving into—trust me.

T-notes and T-bonds would generally offer higher yields than T-bills, with the bonds offering slightly higher yields than the notes. Of course, that's when we have a normal yield curve. With any luck, the Series 63 will not sweat you on yield curves, which usually come up on the Series 65 or Series 7 exam, if at all.

STRIPS

Anyway, the Treasury Department can also take T-notes and T-bonds and "strip" them into their various interest and principal components. Once they "strip" the securities into components, they can sell interest-only or principal-only zero coupon bonds to investors. We call these STRIPS, which stands for the "separate trading of registered interest and principal of securities." For the test, if an investor needs to send kids to college and needs to have an exact amount of money available on a future date, put him into STRIPS, especially if the question says he wants to avoid reinvestment risk. This way, he'll pay a known amount and receive a known amount on a future date, without having to reinvest coupon payments every six months at varying interest rates. He won't get rich, necessarily, but he won't lose the kid's college fund in the stock market, either.

Treasury Receipts

Broker-dealers sell the same basic product, only they call them Treasury Receipts. Even though they have the word "Treasury" in their name, Treasury Receipts are not direct obligations of the US Government. Rather, they are backed up by the Treasury securities the broker-dealer holds in escrow. Close, but yet so far from being a *direct* obligation of the US Treasury. So, STRIPS are direct obligations; receipts are not. For both receipts and STRIPS, remember that they are purchased at a discount and mature at the face value. The interest earned by investors on T-bills, T-notes, T-bonds, STRIPS, and even Treasury Receipts is all taxable only at the federal level.

TIPS

As if Treasury securities weren't already safe enough, the government created TIPS, which stands for "Treasury Inflation Protected Securities." When inflation rises, the payout increases, and when inflation drops, the payout goes down. As usual, we use the CPI to measure the rate of inflation.

Mortgage-backed Securities

The US Government also has agencies that issue debt securities. The Farm Credit System and Federal Land Bank help farmers finance equipment and land purchases. Like a bank, they also issue debt securities in order to borrow money from one party and lend it to somebody else at a higher interest rate. These debt securities are not a direct obligation of the US Treasury, so they're not as safe as the T-bills, T-notes, T-bonds, and STRIPS we just looked at. Then again, if these things scare some investors, I'm not sure how they manage to get out of bed in the morning. But, a testable point could be that agencies are not direct obligations of the US Treasury.

I would expect the exam to focus more on the mortgage-backed securities guaranteed by Ginnie Mae, or issued by Fannie Mae and Freddie Mac. Those are the nicknames for the Government National Mortgage Association (GNMA), the Federal National Mortgage Association (FNMA), and the Federal Home Loan Mortgage Corporation (FHLMC).

To create a mortgage-backed security, some really smart people take a pool of mortgages and then create debt securities out of the money paid into this pool so that the investors who buy the funky things will receive most of the interest and principal that is being paid by the homeowners in the pool. When will all of this principal be paid off? Ask yourself that question—when will you have all of your principal paid off? As soon as you pay it off or refinance your mortgage. When will you refinance? Whenever rates drop again. Since we can't predict when homeowners will pay off their mortgages, mortgage-backed securities carry "prepayment risk." When rates drop, the homeowners refinance, and all of the principal is returned to the investors at once. The investors go to reinvest the proceeds, but rates are now lower upon reinvestment.

GNMA or "Ginnie Mae" is special. Although we said that agency securities are not a direct obligation of the US Treasury, Ginnie Mae actually is because she guarantees all the mortgages in the pool with Uncle Sam's full faith and credit. Most of the mortgages guaranteed by Ginnie Mae are FHA loans, and some are VA (Veterans Administration) and RHA (Rural Housing Authority) loans. But, Ginnie is the only one backed by the full faith and credit of the US Government. Fannie and Freddie are public companies now, sometimes called "quasi-agencies" or "government-sponsored enterprises" (GSEs). They have a line of credit with the US Treasury allowing them to borrow money at lower rates than their competitors, but the US Treasury would not have to bail out Fannie or Freddie if they got themselves into trouble. Would they let them fail? Probably not. Could they let them fail? Absolutely. Since Fannie and Freddie are public companies or "quasi-agencies," you can buy stock in them. There is no stock in Ginnie Mae because it's not a company—it's purely a government agency. Fannie and Freddie promote home ownership by providing a liquid secondary market allowing lenders to sell their mortgages and, therefore, make more mortgages at perhaps lower rates. They guarantee the mortgages, but, again, Fannie and Freddie securities are not a *direct* obligation of the US Government.

Agency securities are taxable at the federal, state, and local levels.

CMOs

CMOs are sold by companies who buy up mortgage-backed securities and create a fancy product called a collateralized mortgage obligation, or CMO. This is how a very simple CMO would function: the investors in the CMO are divided up into three classes or "tranches." They are called class A, B or C. Each class differs in the order they receive principal payments, but receives interest payments as long as the principal is not completely paid off. Class A investors are paid principal first with prepayments and repayments until they are fully repaid. Then class B investors are paid off, followed by class C investors. In a situation like this, class A investors bear most of the prepayment risk, while class C investors bear the least. Prepayment risk is the risk that mortgages will be repaid more quickly than expected when rates drop. It seems unlikely, but the exam could bring up some of the following bullet points. It seems a waste of time to delve into this topic, but it also seems foolish to ignore it, since the Series 63 has a habit of bringing up some very surprising topics from time to time:

- Backed by agency pass-through securities
- CMOs usually offer low returns because they are very low risk and are sometimes backed by government securities.
- Most rated AAA
- They do not have a liquid secondary market, due to their complexities
- Brokers must use extra care to determine suitability due to the complex nature of the product
- CMOs are derivatives (as are options)
- PAC stands for "planned amortization class"
- PACs are protected from prepayment risk and extension risk
- TAC stands for "targeted amortization class"
- TACs present more extension risk, the risk that principal will be paid back too slowly
- TACs generally yield more than PACs

MUNICIPAL BONDS

When the US Government wants to borrow money, they issue Treasury Securities and pay folks back out of taxes. When states, counties, cities, school districts, etc., borrow money, they issue municipal bonds and pay investors back either out of taxes or out of the revenues generated by the project being financed with the bonds. If the municipal bonds are paid off through sales, income, or property taxes, we call these general obligation bonds, backed by the "full faith and credit" of the issuer. Maybe you've voted on the issuance of school bonds used to improve your local schools. Those are general obligation bonds. They had to ask your permission to hike your property taxes in order to pay back the buyers of the bonds used to improve the schools. Your community might also want to build fun stuff like a water park, museum, or convention center. Those projects generate revenue in the form of parking fees, entrance fees, and concession sales, so the issuer can borrow the money through a "revenue bond." Remember that the revenue generated (they hope) by the facility represents all that the issuer has to pay the bond interest and retire the principal to the bondholders. So, which bond typically yields more, revenue or "G.O."? In other words, which one carries more risk to the bond holder, the one backed by the full faith and credit/taxing power of the issuer, or the one that is only as solid as the revenues we *hope* are generated?

The revenue bond is riskier, so it yields more.

Municipal bonds generally pay tax-exempt interest at the federal level. See, the federal government wants states/counties/cities to have good schools, roads, sewers, etc. If they don't tax the interest the issuer pays on the bonds, the issuer can pay lower nominal yields to investors, meaning the issuer can borrow money on the cheap. Why would investors take lower coupon payments? Because the coupon payments aren't taxed by the federal government. Therefore, if you're in the 30% tax bracket, a municipal bond could pay you 5%, and you'd still come out better than if you'd bought a corporate bond paying 7%. Just take the .05 the municipal bond pays and divide by the "other side" of your tax bracket (.70) to get the municipal bond's tax-equivalent yield of 7.14%. The corporate bond would have to yield 7.14% to be equivalent to the municipal bond paying just 5%.

So, a municipal bond investment is tax-exempt, right?

Careful now. Depends on what your meaning of the word *is* is.

First, the only thing that could be tax-free is the interest payment; capital gains are fully taxable, so if you buy a municipal bond at $908 and sell it at $950, you pay a capital gain on the $42 difference. Second, if the municipal bond pays tax-free interest, that's at the federal level. Your state and local government could tax the interest if you buy the bond from an issuer outside the state or locality. If you live in Mississippi and buy a bond issued by Birmingham, Alabama, the state of Mississippi can tax the interest, as can your local government.

So, if you buy a municipal bond that qualifies for tax-exempt interest at the federal level, you'll only get a break at the state level if the bond is issued inside your home state, and your local government can tax the interest in any case, unless they happen to be the issuer of the bond. So a New York City resident who buys a general obligation bond issued by New York City gets a break from the federal government, the state of New York, and the government of NYC.

Third, not *all* municipal bonds are tax-exempt or "tax qualified." The ones that provide an essential service (schools, for example) tend to get the break. But Industrial Development Revenue (IDR) bonds are often fully taxed. And any municipal bond that provides what the IRS considers an inessential service (private purpose) is subject to AMT taxes. Milwaukee's third convention center or first domed sports stadium might not seem as essential to the IRS as it does to the mayor and the city council. In that dispute, guess who generally wins the argument?

The IRS, who, as always, is here to help.

Therefore, all municipal bonds pay tax-free interest at the federal level, except all the municipal bonds that don't. Bonds issued to fund schools and necessary infrastructure get the break; those that build parking garages and convention centers often don't. And, that's not even taking the state/local tax into consideration. The official statement for a municipal bond offering would specify whether the bonds will subject investors to AMT, or will provide tax-exempt interest or—sometimes—fully taxable interest.

Who buys municipal bonds? Investors looking for income, safety, and tax advantages. You need those objectives plus their state of residence before making recommendations, and—most of all—you need their tax bracket. Low-bracket investors do not buy municipal bonds.

CORPORATE BONDS

When the US Treasury or a local government borrows money, they have the ability to pay back the lenders with taxes. When a corporation borrows money, they have to pay back the lenders either with profits, or by borrowing more money from other lenders. To protect the folks buying corporate bonds, Congress passed the Trust Indenture Act of 1939. If a corporation wants to sell $5,000,000 or more worth of bonds with a maturity of more than one year, they have to do it under a contract or "indenture" with a trustee, who will enforce the terms of the indenture to the benefit of the bondholders. In other words, if the issuer stiffs the bondholders, the trustee can get a bankruptcy court to forcibly sell off the assets of the company so that bondholders can recover some of their hard-earned money.

Secured Bonds

Sometimes corporations secure the bonds with specific assets like airplanes, government securities, or real estate. If so, they pledge title of the assets to the trustee, who just might end up selling them off if the issuer gets behind on its interest payments. Investors who buy bonds attached to specific collateral are secured creditors, the most likely investors to get paid should the company go belly up. If the collateral used is real estate, we call it a mortgage bond. If the collateral is securities, we call it a collateral trust certificate. And if the collateral is equipment, such as airplanes or railroad cars, we call it an equipment trust certificate. Since these bonds are probably more secure than other bonds issued by the same company, they offer the lowest coupon payment, too. Remember, if you take a small risk, you usually only get a small reward.

Unsecured Bonds

Most corporate bonds are backed only by a promise known as the "full faith and credit" of the issuing corporation. That's why we might want to see what S&P and Moody's have to say about a particular issuer's full faith and credit. Regardless of the rating, if we buy a bond backed simply by the full faith and credit of an issuer, we are buying a debenture. Debenture holders are general creditors and have a claim that is junior to secured bondholders. Therefore, debentures pay a higher coupon than secured bonds, since they carry more risk of getting stiffed. Corporations typically establish a "sinking fund" to make sure they'll be able to repay the principal on the bonds. A sinking fund is an escrow account invested in safe, liquid securities, just like the escrow account homeowners use to pay taxes and insurance. The existence of a sinking fund is a positive sign to an investor.

"Sub" means "below," as in "submarine" for "below the water," or "subterranean" for "below the ground." Subordinated debentures are below debentures when it comes to liquidating a company and paying out money to the bondholders. Since these bonds are riskier, they pay a higher coupon than debentures.

If all the bondholders have been paid with the proceeds of the liquidation sale and there's still money left over, then we start talking about paying out some money to stockholders. Preferred stock gets preference, so we pay them first, and common stock is always last in line.

So, if a company goes belly up, investors make their claims on the company's assets in the following order of priority:

1. Secured creditors
2. Debentures/general creditors
3. Subordinated debentures
4. Preferred stock
5. Common stock

Convertible Bonds

Even though bonds are safer than common stock, they also aren't going to double or triple in value over the years the way that stocks often do. That's why some really smart people developed convertible bonds. Now, your bond goes up if the company's stock price rises, giving you some growth potential. So, your bond is now less sensitive to interest rates, and because you get some growth potential on the stock, the interest payment is lower. That's the deal—the issuer wants to borrow your money a little more cheaply, and you will let them in exchange for the chance that their stock price will rise and take the price of your bond along for the ride.

When a convertible bond is issued, it is given a conversion price. If the conversion price is $40, that means that the bond is convertible into the issuer's common stock at $40. In other words, the investor can use the par value of her bond towards the purchase of the company's common stock at a set price of $40. Bonds have a par value of $1,000, so if she applies that $1,000 toward the purchase of stock at $40 per share, how many shares would she be able to buy? 25 shares, right? $1,000 of par value divided by $40 per share of stock tells us that each bond can be converted into 25 shares of common stock. So, the two securities should trade at a 25:1 relationship, since the big one (bond) can be turned into 25 of the little ones (stock). The company sets the conversion price; they have no control over where their common stock trades on the open market, right? If the price of the common stock goes up, the value of the convertible bonds goes up. If the company's common stock rises to $50, the bond should be trading for 25 times $50, since it is worth 25 shares of common stock.

$$25 \times \$50 = \$1,250$$

And if the common stock went up to $60 a share, the bond would be worth 25 times that number, right?

$$25 \times \$60 = \$1,500$$

There is no need to convert the bond, either—its market price is being pushed up by the stock, so you could just sell the bond if you wanted to take a capital gain on the investment. When would somebody convert the bonds to the underlying stock? Only if there were an "arbitrage opportunity," which means that the bonds are cheaper than what the underlying shares are worth. In our example above, when the stock rises to $60, the bond should trade for at least $1,500. That means if it's trading for less than $1,500, investors could buy $1,500 worth of stock for less than $1,500 by purchasing the bonds and converting to the stock.

Credit Ratings

When shopping for a mortgage, what determines your interest rate?
- Current interest rate environment
- Length of time (term) on the loan
- Your credit score

As we have seen, interest rates continuously fluctuate, so timing is everything when taking out a mortgage. Also, if you're taking 30 years to pay back the lender, you will have to pay a higher rate than if you're taking just 15 years. Based on these variables, two people could be in exactly the same situation: Joann wants to take out a 30-year mortgage today, and so does her sorority sister, Sheila. So, they both pay the same rate of interest, right?

Not necessarily. The lender uses the credit scores on both borrowers issued by Experian, TransUnion, and Equifax. The higher the credit score, the lower the interest rate the borrower must pay. Joann has a credit score of 750. Sheila has a credit score of 585. In other words, it stinks to be Sheila. Sure hope she enjoyed all those seven-hundred-dollar purses back before they cut up her credit cards.

Consumers pay rates of interest based on the big three credit rating companies. Corporations and municipalities pay rates of interest based on their credit scores from the big three of S&P, Moody's, and Fitch. Let's use a table and understand that as the credit rating drops, so does the *market price* of the bond. As bond ratings and prices drop, their yields increase. So, a "high-yield bond" is simply a bond that has to offer a huge yield to entice anyone to touch it. In other words, a bond rated AA does not have to offer a high yield, just as Joann does not have to pay a high interest rate to get a mortgage. But, a bond rated BB is backed by a shaky issuer, so, like Sheila, the issuer has to offer a high interest rate to entice anyone to lend them money.

S&P	MOODY'S	FITCH	NOTES
AAA	Aaa	Same as S&P	HIGHEST RATING
AA	Aa	"	VERY SOLID
A	A	"	STILL SOLID
BBB	Baa	"	STILL INVESTMENT GRADE
BB	Ba	"	JUNK, BE CAREFUL
B	B	"	JUNKIER
CCC	Caa	"	Watch out!
CC	Ca		
C	C		
D			D = "in default"

As you might imagine, when a bond becomes a "junk" or "high-yield bond," many mutual funds and pension funds have to follow their policy statement and *immediately* sell the junk/high-yield bonds that do not belong in their portfolios. Guess what happens to bond prices when all these huge institutions go to sell at the same time? Right, they drop even further, pushing the yield up even more. So, as the prospectus for the bond fund sitting on my desk explains, there is a risk both of an actual default and of perceived credit risk—if the market suddenly perceives your bond as shaky, you're going down, baby. By which I mean the *price* is going down. By definition, the yield is going *up*.

Callable Bonds

Treasury bonds can be repurchased by the US Treasury during the last five years of maturity, so the 30-year T-bonds issued in 1984 were callable in 2009. Municipal bonds are usually callable, which allows states, cities, and school districts to refinance their debt at a lower rate, just like homeowners. Corporate bonds are often callable, too, which just means that after a certain period of time, the issuer can repurchase the bonds at a certain price already agreed upon. A bond might be callable starting in the year 2015 at 104, meaning that in the year 2015 the issuer can retire the debt by giving each bondholder a check for $1,040 plus any accrued interest.

When might they want to call a bond? Probably when interest rates have fallen, right? Isn't that when homeowners refinance their loans? Works the same way for bond issuers. When rates go down, they start to think maybe the outstanding debt could be replaced with brand-new, much cheaper debt. If interest rates fall to 6%, they reason, let's issue new debt at 6% and use the proceeds to retire the outstanding debt we're currently paying 8% on.

Pretty simple.

Replacing one bond issue with another is called "refunding." It tends to happen when interest rates fall. It allows the issuer to issue less-expensive debt used to retire more-expensive debt. It's not such a great deal for the bondholders, though. What can they do with the proceeds of the call? Reinvest. At what rate? A lower rate. And, what happens to bond prices as rates decline?

They go up. Only they stop going up when the bonds are called, meaning the bondholder doesn't get the full appreciation in price he would have otherwise gotten. Therefore, the bond indenture would tell investors the first legal call date, and the period from now until then is called "call protection" for obvious reasons. You can certainly buy non-callable bonds, but you'll be offered a lower interest rate, since you aren't giving the borrower an opportunity to refinance in that case. The exam might bring up terms such as "advance refunding," "pre-refunding," and "escrowed to maturity." In this case the issuing municipality issues new bonds at attractive interest rates, then parks the proceeds into an escrow account, where it waits until the first legal call date. If they deposit enough money, invested in Treasury and agency securities, to cover the principal and interest, the original bond issue is considered to be "advance refunded" or "escrowed to maturity." Since there are sufficient funds to cover all the debt service, the bonds would pretty well have to be rated AAA at this point and would have "improved liquidity," should the exam care to mention that fact.

Guaranteed Bonds

The word "guaranteed" is always a red flag when used in connection with an investment. What does the seller mean when he says your bond is "guaranteed"? When the US Treasury says their T-bills, T-notes, and T-bonds are guaranteed, they mean that they will do whatever is humanly possible to pay the interest on time and will return the principal. Since their track record is stellar, you have to assume that the only way to lose money on a Treasury security is to sell it before maturity and after interest rates have risen. If you can hold on until maturity, you will get the principal back on a Treasury security and the US Treasury will not miss an interest payment ever.

So, how can a *corporate* bond be "guaranteed"? What the word means in this context is that a third party, such as the parent company, has promised to pay if the issuer of the bond cannot. In other words, it's a co-signer on the loan. ABC Enterprises issues the bond, which is, fortunately, guaranteed by somebody we've actually heard of called General Electric, the parent company. Is it a "guarantee" that the investor can't lose money?

No. But, just like a banker who has the parent's signature on the loan to Junior, bondholders usually feel better knowing there is a second and usually stronger source of payment should things get funky. The exam may want you to say that a security can be guaranteed as to interest, principal, or dividends. Just remember that the "guarantee" is simply a promise from a party other than the issuer.

Quotes

Bonds are quoted either in terms of their price, or their yield. Since the coupon rate or nominal yield doesn't change, if you give me the price, I can figure the yield. And, if you give me the yield, I can figure the price. If we're talking about a bond's price, we're talking about bond points. A bond point is worth $10, so if a bond is selling at "98," that means it's selling for 98 bond points. With each point worth $10, a bond selling for 98 bond points is trading for $980. A bond trading at 102 would be selling for $1,020. Although fractions have been eliminated from stock and options pricing, they are still very much alive in the world of bond pricing. If a bond point is worth $10, how much is ½ a bond point worth? Five dollars, right? A quarter-point would be worth $2.50, right? An eighth is $1.25, and so on. Therefore, if you see a bond priced at 102 3/8, how much does the bond cost in dollars and cents? Well, "102" puts the price at $1,020, and 3/8 of $10 is $3.75. So, a bond trading at 102 3/8 costs $1,023.75.

$$102 [\$1,020] + 3/8 [\$3.75] = \$1,023.75$$

If we're talking about basis points, we're talking about a bond's yield. Yield to maturity, to be exact. If I say that a bond with an 8% coupon just traded on a 7.92 basis, I'm telling you that the price went up above par, pushing the yield to maturity down to 7.92%. "Trading at a basis of…" just means that the price pushed the yield to maturity to a particular percentage, or number of "basis points." A basis point is the smallest increment of change in a bond's yield. When the media talks about the Fed easing interest rates by fifty basis points, they're talking about ½ of 1 percent. We would write 1% as .01, right? Well, basis points use a 4-digit display system, so .01 is written as:

$$.0\ 1\ 0\ 0.$$

Then, we read that figure as "100 basis points." Two percent would be 200 basis points. One-half of one percent would be written as .0050 or "50 basis points." So, a bond trading at a 7.92 basis means that the yield to maturity is 7.92% or 792 basis points.

Bearer, Fully Registered, Book Entry

In the olden days, some bonds were issued as "bearer bonds," which meant that whoever "bore" or had possession of the bonds was presumed to be the owner. No owner name at all on the certificate; it just said "pay to the bearer," and then the principal amount. So, whoever presented the bond at maturity received the principal. Basically, bearer bonds are like the tens and twenties in your wallet. To whom do those bills belong—you?

Prove it.

Luckily, you don't have to prove it. You are "bearing" those unnamed tens and twenties in your wallet, so they are yours. Period. Just like the bearer bonds in your hands—the fact that you're holding them means that you own them.

In order to receive the interest, investors holding bearer bonds used to present coupons attached to the bond certificate every six months for payment. There was no name on the interest coupon, either, so the IRS had no way of tracking the principal or the interest income. And you know how much that irritates the IRS. So, bonds haven't been issued in bearer form since the early '80s—that doesn't mean they don't exist. A few are still floating out there on the market, so you may have to know about them for the test. Just remember: no name on certificate, no name on payment coupons.

Bonds also used to be registered as to principal only. That meant that we had a name on the bond certificate—the person who would receive the <u>principal</u> amount at maturity. But, again, with the silly little unnamed interest coupons. Therefore, only the principal was registered, thus the name "registered as to principal only."

Anyway, the bond market got smart in the early 1980s and started registering both pieces of the debt service. Now, the issuer has the name of the owner [principal] and automatically cuts a check every six months for the interest. Therefore, the IRS—who is here to help—can also help themselves to a bit of the interest income. We call these bonds fully registered, because both pieces of the debt service (interest, principal) are <u>registered</u>.

Book entry/journal entry bonds are still fully registered. It's just that it's done on computer, rather than on paper. The investor keeps the trade confirmation as proof of ownership, but we still have an owner name on computer, and we automatically cut interest checks to the registered owner.

Trade Confirmations

Broker-dealers send trade confirmations to customers. A confirmation for a bond purchase or sale would typically include the following information:
- Name, address, telephone # of the broker-dealer
- Name of the customer
- Purchase or Sale
- Capacity in which the firm acted: principal, agent
- Trade date and time of execution
- Par value of the bonds ($1,000, $5,000, etc.)
- Settlement date
- Yield and dollar price
- Final monies (total dollar amount of transaction, accrued interest, extended principal, any other fees)
- Name of issuer
- CUSIP number
- Maturity date
- Interest rate
- Features: callable, putable, escrowed to maturity, in default, etc.

EQUITY SECURITIES

The money that investors put into equity securities should be the money they won't need to spend any time soon. In fact, it should be the money they can afford to lose. As many have discovered, sometimes when you try to put your money to work for you, it ends up getting fired. Why put any of your money at risk? Because history has shown that stocks provide some very nice returns over the long haul. The ride is often a wild one, but over time common stock in solid companies can provide some impressive long-term returns through dividends and capital appreciation. Unlike a bond that is eventually worth just the par value, no one can tell you what the value of a particular common stock will be someday. Long-term returns of 1,000% are rare, but they do happen; 100% losses are also not uncommon. Therefore, since anything can happen over a three- or five-year period, the time horizon for equity securities investments should generally be longer than a few years. Stock investments are for the long haul.

COMMON STOCK

Remember that holders of common stock are part-owners of a public corporation. They didn't lend money to the corporation; they bought a piece of the profits. Common stockholders enjoy several important rights the exam might bring up. The first right is the right of common stockholders to vote for any major issue that could affect their status as a proportional owner of the corporation. Things like stock splits, mergers, acquisitions, board elections, and changes of business objectives all require shareholder approval.

Shareholders vote their shares. If you own 100 shares of common stock, you have 100 votes to cast. So, whenever you get fired up about a big issue at the company, here's you with your 100 votes and here's some pension fund with 800 million votes. This explains why a few large shareholders tend to control things at a public corporation. Beyond voting, common stockholders also have the right to inspect the list of shareholders and copies of the minutes from shareholder meetings. Shareholders have the right to receive stock certificates to show proof of ownership. A stock certificate would state the name of the issuing corporation, the owner's name, and the number of shares the stockholder owns. A shareholder can transfer his shares freely, by selling them, giving them away, donating them to charities, or leaving them to his heirs through a will or trust. The issuing company pays a bank or other firm to keep track of all these transfers of ownership, and guess what we call them?

The *transfer agent*. The transfer agent is a record keeper who has a list of all the shareholders. The transfer agent cancels old shares and issues new ones when they're lost, stolen, or destroyed.

The *registrar* is another outside firm that audits the transfer agent and makes sure the company doesn't accidentally issue more shares than their corporate charter authorizes.

Should a corporation go belly-up and have to be liquidated, common stockholders get in line for their piece of the proceeds. Unfortunately, they are last in line. They are behind all the creditors, including bondholders, and also behind preferred stockholders. But, at least they are in line, and if there are any *residuals* left, they get to make their claim on those assets. That's known as a "residual claim on assets," for obvious reasons.

Buying common stock is really all about owning a piece of the corporation's earnings or "net income." As the earnings increase, usually, so does the price of the common stock. The other way to get a return from your common stock is to receive a piece of those earnings or profits *now*, in the form of a dividend. Which would you vote for as a shareholder—dividends now, or have the company reinvest the profits back into the business?

Trick question—shareholders don't get to vote on dividends. That's right, if a corporation's board of directors doesn't declare a dividend, the dividend doesn't get paid. End of story. But, if the board *does* declare a dividend, here's how it works. The day that the Board declares the dividend is known as the declaration date. The board wonders who should receive this dividend—how about investors who actually own the stock as of a certain date? We call that the record date because an investor has to be the owner "of record" on or before that date if she wants to receive the dividend. The board decides when they'll pay the dividend, too, and we call that the payable date.

Now, since an investor has to be the owner of record on or before the Record Date to receive the dividend, there will come a day when it's too late for investors to buy the stock and also get the dividend.

Why?

Because stock transactions don't settle until the third business day following the trade date. To "settle" means that the buyer has become the new official owner of the stock. If a stock is sold on a Tuesday, the trade doesn't actually settle (ownership doesn't officially change) until Friday, the third business day after the trade. This is known as regular way settlement, T + 3.

So, if an investor has to be the owner of record on the record date, and it takes three business days for the buyer to become the new owner, wouldn't she have to buy the stock at least <u>three</u> business days prior to the record date?

So, if she buys it just <u>two</u> business days before the record date, her trade won't settle in time. We call that day the ex-date or "ex-dividend" date, because starting on that day investors who buy the stock will <u>not</u> receive the dividend. On the ex-date, it's too late. Why? Because the trades won't settle in time, and the purchasers won't be the owners of record (with the transfer agent) on or before the record date.

The regulators (FINRA) set the ex-date, as a function of "regular way" or "T + 3" settlement. The ex-date is two business days before the record date.

So, remember DERP. <u>D</u>eclaration, <u>E</u>x-Date, <u>R</u>ecord Date, <u>P</u>ayable Date. The board sets all of them except the Ex-Date, which is set by the regulators. Also remember that cash dividends are taxable for the year received—yes, the tax rate has become quite enjoyable, but cash dividends are still taxable. That's why it's a violation if a registered representative deceives a client by telling her to hurry up and purchase a stock or mutual fund simply because it is about to distribute a dividend. First, the value of the stock or mutual fund will drop by the amount of the dividend—so what's the hurry? And, second, the dividend is taxable, so what was the point in hurrying? The point in hurrying would be that the registered representative wanted to make a commission at the expense of the investor, hoping nobody notices. This violation is called "selling dividends," and it could easily show up in a test question.

Another way an investor could receive a "dividend" is by receiving more shares from the issuer. This is called a "stock dividend," and it's easy to get excited about getting new shares of stock, until you realize that all the shareholders are getting more shares. No value was created. Basically, the company decided to give everybody more slices of the earnings pie by cutting the slices much smaller and giving everybody more of them. So, if an investor had 100 shares of XYZ that she bought @50, what would happen if the company paid a 10% stock dividend? She would have 110 shares worth $45.45 each. The same $5,000 investment divided among more shares, in other words. Perhaps you recall that a stock dividend does not meet the definition of an offer or sale of securities. Perhaps it's easier to see why that's the case now. Or not. Either way, let's keep moving.

The exam might bring up the difference between authorized, issued, treasury, and outstanding shares. The corporation is "authorized" to issue a certain number of shares in their corporate charter. The amount they have issued at this point is called, not surprisingly, the "issued" shares. Companies often buy back shares and put them in "treasury," so to figure out how many shares are left "outstanding," just take the number of shares issued minus the number repurchased and placed in the treasury. For example, if the company has issued 1,000,000 shares and has 400,000 in treasury, there are 600,000 shares outstanding. Many companies like using cash to buy back shares, as it generally boosts the earnings per share and does not get taxed as a dividend to shareholders.

Assuming the net income was exactly the same year-over-year, reducing the number of outstanding shares would, by definition, increase the earnings per share. It also shows the markets that this company truly believes its stock is worth more than people realize.

RIGHTS AND WARRANTS

Another feature common stockholders enjoy is the right to maintain their proportionate ownership in the corporation. The corporation can sell more shares to the public, but they have to give the existing shareholders the right to buy their proportion of the new shares before the public gets to buy theirs. For every share owned, an investor receives what's known as a right. It's an equity security with a very short life span. It works like a coupon, allowing the current shareholders to purchase the stock below the market price over the course of a few weeks. If a stock is trading at $20, maybe the existing shareholders can take one subscription right plus $18 to buy a new share. Those rights act as coupons that give the current shareholders two dollars off the market price. So, the investors can use the rights themselves or sell them on the secondary market.

Another type of special security is called a warrant. It has nothing to do with shareholder rights; it's just easier to learn about warrants and rights together. A warrant is a long-term equity security. There are no dividends attached to a warrant. If you own a warrant, all you own is the opportunity to purchase a company's stock at a predetermined price. If you have a warrant that lets you buy XYZ for $30 per share, then you can buy a certain number of shares at that price whenever you feel it makes sense to do so, like when XYZ is trading for a lot more than $30 per share. When issued, the price stated on the warrant is above the current market price of the stock. It usually takes a long time for a stock's price to go above the price stated on the warrant. But, they're good for a long time, typically somewhere between two and ten years.

Warrants are often attached to a bond offering. Corporations pay interest to borrow money through bonds. If they attach warrants, they can "sweeten" the deal a little and maybe offer investors a lower interest payment.

PREFERRED STOCK

Another equity security that could show up on the exam is called preferred stock. This stock gets preferential treatment over common stock if the company has to be liquidated in bankruptcy, and receives dividends whether common stock receives a payment or not. The preferred dividend is printed right on the stock certificate. The par value for a preferred stock is often $100. The stated dividend is a percentage of that par value. Six-percent preferred stock would pay 6% of $100 per share, or $6 per share per year, then.

We hope.

See, dividends still have to be declared by the Board of Directors. Preferred stockholders aren't creditors. They're just owners who like to receive dividends. If the board doesn't declare a dividend, do you know how much an owner of a 6% preferred stock would receive?

Nothing.

However, if the investor owned cumulative preferred stock, that might be different. She wouldn't necessarily get the dividend now, but the company would have to make up the missed dividend in future years before it could pay dividends to any other preferred or common stockholders. If the company missed the six dollars this year and wanted to pay the full six dollars next year, cumulative preferred stockholders would have to get their $12 before anybody else got paid.

This 6% works more like a maximum than a minimum. If an investor wants the chance to earn <u>more</u> than the stated 6%, he'd have to buy participating preferred stock, which would allow him to share in dividends <u>above</u> that rate. Dividends paid on common stock are frequently increased over time, and participating preferred stockholders will also enjoy that increase.

Callable preferred stock may be repurchased by the issuer as of a certain date for a certain price. The "call" generally happens only if interest rates drop. When interest rates go down, the issuer might get tired of paying generous 6% dividends every year. If so, they can buy the preferred stock back and retire the shares. Or replace them with new preferred stock paying lower dividends that reflect the new lower interest rate environment. So, if the exam asks when preferred stock or bonds get called, tell it that it happens when rates are falling…the same time that homeowners refinance. Also, if you give the issuer this type of flexibility, they'll usually pay you a higher rate of return. So, callable preferred stock tends to pay the nicest rate of return. Most types of preferred stock have no maturity date and are, therefore, "perpetual." That's why callable preferred stock is unique. Since this type of preferred stock is callable, it can be repurchased and retired by the issuer instead of paying out preferred dividends indefinitely.

A truly wild type of preferred stock is called convertible preferred stock. As with convertible bonds, convertible preferred stock lets an investor exchange one share of preferred stock for a certain number of common shares whenever the investor wants to make the switch. Let's say the convertible preferred stock is convertible into 10 shares of common stock. Therefore, the convertible preferred stock is usually worth whatever 10 shares of common stock are worth. When the 10 shares are worth exactly the market price of the convertible preferred stock, the two securities trade at "parity," which means "equal." Just multiply the price of the common stock by the number of shares the investor could convert the preferred into. That gives you the preferred stock's parity price. In our example, if the common stock rises to $13, the parity price of the convertible preferred stock is 10 times $13 or $130.

If a security has a fixed payment, the market compares that fixed payment to current interest rates. Current interest rates represent what investors could receive if they bought newly issued fixed income securities. If fixed income securities are paying 4%, and your preferred stock pays you a fixed 6%, how do you feel about your preferred security? Pretty good, since it's paying a higher rate than current interest rates. If somebody wanted to buy it, they'd have to pay a higher price. But, if interest rates shoot up to 10%, suddenly your 6% preferred doesn't look so good, right? In that case the market price would go down. Not the par value—par value is etched in stone. It's the market price that fluctuates. Who cares about the market price? Well, if you have to sell when the market price is down, you take a loss, right? Many homeowners have recently felt the painful truth of this concept. When you plan to hold the stock, bond, or townhouse for a long while, its market value doesn't seem so important, but when you go to liquidate it (turn it into cash), suddenly the market price is supremely important.

AMERICAN DEPOSITORY RECEIPTS (ADRs)/ AMERICAN DEPOSITORY SHARES (ADS)

If you wanted to buy shares in Toyota, you would probably prefer to buy them in American dollars and be able to trade them while the American exchanges are open. To accommodate folks like you, ADRs have been created. ADRs make it easier for Americans to buy shares of foreign stocks. You no longer have to deal with a stock priced at, say, 1,167.59 yen, since the Toyota ADR is priced in American dollars and trades alongside any other stock on the NYSE. An ADR might pay a dividend, but the dividend has to be converted from the foreign currency into US currency, which is partly why ADR owners are subject to currency risk. If the US dollar is strong, the dividend won't be worth as much to an American. If the US dollar is weak, then the dividend will convert to *more* dollars. So, tell the exam that a weak dollar is actually beneficial to an American holding an ADR, while a strong dollar is not. Sounds almost backwards, right? And that's what makes it such a natural Series 63 question.

The exam might also mention that ADR holders have the right to exchange their receipts for the actual underlying foreign shares. And that they allow US investors to give their portfolios international exposure without having to utilize foreign markets. Finally, a sponsored ADR would typically give voting rights to the owner, while an unsponsored ADR would not.

REITs AND REAL ESTATE LIMITED PARTNERSHIPS

Investing in real estate has many advantages and disadvantages. The advantages are that property values usually go up and that real estate provides diversification to a portfolio. A disadvantage is that real estate ties up a lot of capital. And, it isn't liquid. It often takes months to get a house sold, or sold for a decent price, so the lack of liquidity keeps many investors from buying real estate, especially commercial real estate (shopping malls, skyscrapers, factories, etc.).

This is where REITs come in. A Real Estate Investment Trust (REIT) is a company that owns a portfolio of properties and sells shares in the operation to investors. You could buy into REITs that own apartment buildings, office buildings, shopping centers, hotels, convention centers, self-storage units, you name it. Now, if there were no REITs, it's safe to say that I would probably never be investing in shopping centers or office buildings. But through REITs, I can participate in big, commercial (or residential) real estate without having to be rich or putting up with the traditional liquidity problems. I can liquidate my REITs as fast as I can sell most any other stock.

Real Estate Limited Partnerships are different. First, they are extremely *illiquid*. Meaning, if you think you're going to want to sell, don't buy in. If you buy in as a limited partner (LP), you have limited liability. But, you don't get to sell your limited partnership interest. You're in for the long haul. Often, the folks who buy limited partnership interests are looking for tax write-offs. Since the partners take a share of the income and expenses, often a new partnership will generate losses for the first several years that can be used to offset passive income for the partners. But, these partnership losses can *only* be used to offset passive income—not earned income or portfolio income. Passive income is received from partnerships and any rental units an investor might own.

Not all partnerships are about showing a loss. Some provide new construction. Put up a new townhouse development, sell them all real quick, and walk away with a nice profit. That doesn't sound too bad. Some real estate partnerships are more into owning real estate and making money by renting it out. More income oriented, then, as opposed to new construction, which is more about capital gains. The partners may be able to shelter some income during the early years of operations, but eventually the partnership will likely hit the "crossover point," which is where income begins to exceed deductions.

A fairly likely point on an exam would be that real estate partnerships do pass through losses to the partners, while REITs do NOT pass through losses to the shareholders. REITs pass through income, but not losses. If the company had a loss, that would just push the stock price of the REIT down, like any other company. Also, there are no net worth requirements for REITs, which explains why a schmuck like me has owned them for so long. Finally, note that I've been explaining the REITs that own property and lease it out. There are also "mortgage REITs" that focus more on financing real estate projects, in case you don't already have enough to remember at this point.

INVESTMENT COMPANIES

Any one security in a portfolio is always subject to the risk that its price will plummet. That's why most investors spread this "non-systematic risk" among several stocks or bonds, often from several different industries. That way, if one security loses value, maybe another one will increase in value and offset the loss. While it makes good sense to use this practice of diversification, it also takes a lot of time and money to buy stocks and bonds from many different companies in many different industries, doing all your own research and sweating all the details yourself. So, instead of trying to assemble a large, diversified portfolio on your own, you can buy shares of a large, diversified portfolio managed by a professional. That's what a mutual fund is. It's a big diversified portfolio of many securities managed by a professional and packaged as a complete set to the investor. Think of a mutual fund as a big portfolio pie that can serve up as many slices as investors care to buy.

Investors send in money to buy slices of the big pie; the fund uses the money to buy ingredients, like IBM, MSFT, and GM. When an investor sends in money, the pie gets bigger, but it also gets cut up into more slices—however many she is buying. That way each slice stays the same size. The only way for the slices to get bigger is for the pie to get sweeter, which happens when securities in the fund go up in value, or when those securities kick in dividend or interest payments to the fund. Please understand that mutual funds do not rise in value because people are buying them. In fact, that's backwards.

See, the mutual fund adds up the value of the portfolio at the end of the trading day, which is simply the market price of all the stocks and bonds plus any cash those securities throw off in the form of dividends and interest payments. They divide that total value of cash and market value by the number of existing shares and call that the "net asset value" or "NAV" of the shares. *Now* they put new money in on behalf of the buyers at that NAV. Similarly, the NAV does not drop because there are sellers redeeming their shares to the fund. If we have more sellers than buyers, the pie gets smaller, but it also gets cut up into fewer slices. So, net assets of the fund go up and down due to customer purchases and sales, but the number of shares changes right along with the in-flow and out-flow of cash, leaving everything proportional.

NAV goes up and down each trading day the same way as my little SIMPLE IRA. When the stocks in my online account go up in value, I see a little plus sign and some positive numbers in beautiful, glowing green. When the stocks go down in value, I see a minus sign and some negative numbers in dark, depressing red. Whenever dividends are paid into my portfolio, that raises the value of the account. I mean, what else would it do? Abbott Labs cuts a check to my account for $750. If that doesn't raise the value of my account, what does? Only when Abbott Labs rises in market value. What else would do it?

Nothing. That's the whole story of investing. There is growth, there is income, and sometimes there is both growth *and* income. If you were looking for excitement, please tell me you didn't buy a mutual fund. Mutual funds are about as boring as it gets, and we intend to prove it. Just keep reading; you'll see.

Like any portfolio, when the stocks or bonds inside the mutual fund portfolio appreciate, so do the shares of the mutual fund owned by investors. I mean, if I decided to cut my little SIMPLE IRA into slices, the value of those slices would go up just as I explained above with the little green (positive) and red (negative) numbers. Mutual funds are gigantic portfolios cut up into bazillions of shares. Each share is worth the net asset value or NAV per share. If the fund has $10 million in assets and $500,000 in liabilities, that leaves net assets of $9.5 million. If the pie is worth $9.5 million on net, and there are 1 million slices (shares) of the pie, each slice is worth exactly $9.50. So the NAV of this fund would be $9.50. The net asset value fluctuates with market fluctuations and is re-figured every trading day. Mutual funds will repurchase or redeem their shares whenever an investor decides to sell them. The fund pays investors the NAV per share, which is computed the next time the fund computes it. This is known as forward pricing. If an investor has 1,000 shares to redeem, and the NAV is $9.50 when the fund next computes it, how much do you suppose the investor receives for redeeming her shares?

$9,500. If the fund has no front-end load, the buyers would also pay the NAV. If these are front-end-loaded or "A-shares," we simply add a sales charge on top of the NAV. So, if the NAV is $9.50 but we pay a POP (public offering price) of $10, that extra 50 cents is the sales charge that covers the costs of marketing and selling the fund and leaves a handsome profit for those who market and sell the fund to investors. And those people would be the FINRA member firms who distribute the shares and make money through sales charges and 12b-1 fees, which will be discussed later.

Investment companies are defined and regulated under the Investment Company Act of 1940. That act of Congress classifies investment companies into three types: face amount certificate companies, unit investment trusts, and management companies. We're mostly concerned with the management companies, which are either open-end funds or closed-end funds. Open-end funds issue new shares whenever investors feel like buying them. They will also buy back/redeem shares whenever investors feel like selling them.

OPEN- VS. CLOSED-END FUNDS

On the other hand, we have closed-end funds, which do a fixed offering of shares, and that's it. A fixed number of shares are sold, unlike an open-end fund that issues an unknown number on a continuous basis. Another major difference is that closed-end funds can use more leverage than their open-end counterparts, which is the phrase used for "borrowed money." Unlike open-end funds, closed-end funds also don't redeem their own shares. Investors buy and sell them, just like individual stocks. Therefore, unlike an open-end fund, whose shares are always worth the NAV per share, closed-end funds are worth whatever the market says they're worth. So, for the test, if you see that a fund has a net asset value of $9 per share and is currently trading for only $7.50, you know it's a closed-end fund. Doesn't mean that closed-end funds always trade below the NAV. It means that open-end funds do *not* do that, because open-end funds do not trade among investors—they are redeemed/sold back to the issuer. Closed-end funds trade on the secondary market among investors, so they can end up trading at their NAV, at a discount to the NAV, or at a *premium* to the NAV.

Why?

Supply and demand. If buyers really want the shares of your closed-end fund, they may pay you more than you ever thought possible. Or less. That's the deal with the closed-end fund; you have to trade it just like any other share of stock. By the way, Nuveen here in Chicago is a leader in closed-end funds—check out their website and you'll quickly see the real-world view of closed-end and open-end funds (www.nuveen.com).

OPEN-END	CLOSED-END
Continuous offering	Fixed initial offering only
Investors redeem shares to fund	Investors sell shares OTC/exchange
Investors may pay sales charge	Investors pay commissions
Priced by formula	Priced by supply/demand

SALES CHARGE, OPEN-END FUNDS

An open-end fund will redeem/buy back its shares at the NAV. If you want to buy shares in the fund, you often have to pay a little more than that. The "extra" that investors pay to buy the shares is called a sales charge or sales load. It covers the costs of printing up sales literature, running advertisements in magazines, newspapers, TV and radio, mailing out the prospectus, and paying sales people. It also leaves a profit for the distributors and the broker-dealers who market and sell the shares to investors.

If a fund has a net asset value per share of $9.50 and costs $10.00, how much is the sales charge? Fifty cents.

What is the sales charge as a percentage? Ask yourself how much of ten dollars is the sales charge? Fifty cents. Fifty cents divided by ten dollars equals 5%. The sales charge is 5% of the public offering price. That's how sales charges are expressed, as a percentage of the public offering price, or the "gross amount invested."

Now, if you get an exam question that gives you the NAV and the sales charge percentage, asking you to calculate the POP, remember that the sales charge is a percentage of the POP. If the test doesn't tell you the POP, how can you figure it? Just take the NAV—which the test has to give you—and divide it by the "complement of the sales charge." The "complement of the sales charge" just means to take 100% minus the sales charge and divide the NAV by that. For example, if the NAV is $9.60 and the sales charge is 4%, the POP would simply be $9.60 divided by .96 = $10.00

9.60 divided by .96 = $10.00

NAV divided by (100% – sales charge) = POP

We said that the fund figures the net asset value at the end of each trading day and *then* new money goes into the fund. So, if the fund has a front-end sales charge, different people will pay different charges depending on the amounts they invest into the fund. Therefore, the fund uses the formula above to figure out how much an investor paying the 3% sales charge pays per share and how much another investor paying the 5.5% sales charge pays per share. If an investor is at the 3% breakpoint level, the fund would take the NAV divided by .97. For the investor at the 5.5% level, the fund would take the NAV divided by .945. This type of calculation seems much more likely to show up on the Series 7 or 6 than the 63, but that is just a guess.

Reducing the Sales Charge

Ever noticed that the more you want to buy of something, the better the deal? Doesn't a small bottle of laundry detergent at the convenience store cost a lot more per ounce than a massive, industrial-sized container at Sam's Club®?

Breakpoints

Same with mutual funds. If you want to invest $1,000, you're going to pay a higher sales charge than if you want to invest $100,000. For mutual funds, investors are rewarded with breakpoints. Let's say that Cromwell Funds has the following sales charge schedule:

INVEST	SALES CHARGE
< $50,000	5%
$50,000 – $149,999	4%
$150,000 – $249,999	3%
$250,000 – $399,999	2%

That means that an investor who buys $200,000 worth of the fund will pay a much lower sales charge than an investor who invests $10,000. In other words, less of her money (as a %) will be deducted from her check when she invests $200,000 as opposed to, say, $10,000. A breakpoint means that at this *point* the fund will give you this *break*. A lower sales charge means that an investor's money ends up buying more shares. For mutual funds, we don't pick the number of shares we want; we send in a certain amount of money and see how many shares our money buys us. With a lower sales charge, our money will buy us more shares. Keep in mind that fractional shares are common. For example, $1,000 would buy 12.5 shares if the POP were $80.

Husband and wife get to combine their investments for the purpose of achieving reduced sales charges. A parent and minor child in a custodial arrangement also get to combine their purchases. So, if the mom puts in $25,000 and also puts in $25,000 for her minor child's UGMA account, that's a $50,000 investment in terms of achieving a breakpoint. The child cannot be an adult; he/she must be a minor. Corporations and other businesses qualify for breakpoints. About the only folks who *don't* qualify for breakpoints are investment clubs.

Another important consideration for breakpoints is that a sales rep can never encourage an investor to invest a lower amount of money in order to keep him from obtaining a lower sales charge offered at the next breakpoint. That's called **breakpoint selling** and is a major violation. Likewise, if a rep fails to point out to an investor that a few more dollars invested would qualify for a breakpoint, that's just as bad as actively encouraging him to stay below the next breakpoint. Remember, sales reps (broker-dealers) get part of the sales charge. It would definitely be to their advantage to get the higher sales charge. Unfortunately, they have to keep their clients' interests in mind, too. Yes, they take all the fun out of this business.

Letter or Statement of Intent

So, what if we didn't have the $250,000 needed to qualify for the lowest sales charge offered by Cromwell Funds? We could write a letter explaining our intent to invest $250,000 in the fund over the next 13 months. Now, as we send in our money, say, $25,000 at a time, the fund applies the lower 2% sales charge, as if we'd already invested the full amount. The lower sales charge means we end up buying more shares, right? So, the fund holds those extra shares in a safe place (escrow), just in case we fail to invest that $250,000 we intended to. If we don't live up to our letter of intent, no big deal. We just don't get those extra shares. In other words, the higher sales charge applies to the money actually invested.

Also, that letter of intent (LOI) could be backdated up to 90 calendar days in order to cover a previous purchase. If an investor bought $10,000 of the fund on March 10, he might decide in early June that he should write a letter of intent to invest $250,000 over 13 months. He could backdate the letter to March 10 to cover the previous investment and would then have 13 months from that date to invest the remaining $240,000.

Remember that this LOI covers new money only. Reinvested dividends/capital gains do not count toward this total, and neither does account value. Account value comes into play only if we're talking about the next item, rights of accumulation.

Rights of Accumulation

If an investor's fund shares appreciate up to a breakpoint, the investor will receive a lower sales charge on additional purchases. In other words, when an investor is trying to reach a breakpoint, new money and account accumulation are counted the same way. So, if an investor's shares have appreciated to, say $42,000 and the investor wanted to invest another $9,000, the entire purchase would qualify for the breakpoint that starts at $50,000. $42,000 of value plus an additional $9,000 would take the investor past the $50,000 needed to receive the breakpoint. This is known as rights of accumulation. Don't confuse rights of accumulation with a Letter of Intent, because they have nothing to do with each other. If you sign an LOI for $250,000, the fact that your account value later rises $50,000 has nothing to do with the $250,000 you intend to invest.

Concurrent Purchases

Most "funds" are part of a "family" of funds. Many of these fund families will let you combine your purchase in their Income Fund with, say, their Index or Growth Fund in order to figure a breakpoint. They call this, very cleverly, a combination privilege. So, if the individual invests $20,000 in the Income Fund and $30,000 in the Growth Fund, that's considered a $50,000 investment in the family of funds, and that's the number they'd use to figure the breakpoint.

Just trying to keep everybody in our happy family.

Conversion/Exchange Privileges

The fund might also offer a conversion/exchange privilege. This privilege allows investors to sell shares of, say, the Cromwell Growth Fund, in order to buy shares of the Cromwell Income Fund at the NAV, rather than the higher POP. If we didn't do that, the investor might get mad enough to leave our happy family, since there would be no immediate benefit to his staying with us. I mean, if he's going to be charged the POP, why not look for a new family with a growth fund that might actually, you know, *grow?* But remember that buying the new shares at the NAV is nice for the investor, but the IRS still considers the sale a taxable event. So if you get a test question on the tax treatment, tell the exam that all gains or losses are recognized on the date of the sale.

Distribution Expenses

What is this sales charge/sales load for, anyway?

Let's say that you and your friends want to start a mutual fund. How would you get the shares sold to investors? First, you'd have to pay someone to print the prospectus and a whole bunch of sales literature. Then, you'd have to line up some broker-dealers interested in selling the fund, and—guess what—broker-dealers expect to be paid for their trouble. You'll need to buy some advertising in magazines, newspapers, radio, and TV. And, when somebody sees the advertisement and calls the 800-number, you'll have to mail out the prospectus, which is another cost on top of the cost of printing the prospectus and running the advertisement.

Guess you and your friends won't be starting that fund, after all, huh?

But, wait, there is a FINRA member firm with a big, fat checkbook interested in sponsoring/ underwriting/distributing/wholesaling your fund for you. They're so nice, they're willing to bear all those costs we just mentioned, known as "distribution expenses." Why are they being so nice? Because they're going to charge customers a sales load to not just cover those expenses but also make a profit.

So, how much of an operating expense is the sales load?

Trick question—it isn't an operating expense. It's just an extra fee that the distributor takes from the customer's check. The underwriter/sponsor/distributor bears the distribution costs up front, then covers them (plus a profit) by tacking on a sales charge to the customer. The fund invests the customer's money at the NAV; the distributors take the amount above that (the load) and share it with the broker-dealers who sold the shares. Some distributors even cut out the middlemen and sell to the investors directly. And—as we'll see later—some funds cut out everybody and act as their own distributor. If they do that, they don't charge a "load" per se. They usually charge a 12b-1 fee, instead, which is the same thing only different and which will be explained later.

For now, just remember that a sales charge covers distribution expenses and is not an operating expense to the fund. It's a charge taken out of the investor's check. And it cannot cover management fees, which are operating expenses deducted from the fund's assets on an ongoing basis.

The ABCs

These sales loads/charges can be charged when a customer buys the shares or when the customer sells the shares. Again, the sales charge is taken out of the customer's check. A-shares charge a front-end load when the investor acquires them. A = "acquire." When the investor cuts a check for, say, $10,000, maybe 5% or $500 is taken right off the top to cover the distribution expenses plus a nice profit for the distributors and broker-dealers. B-shares don't charge a front-end load. Instead, B-shares charge a back-end load when the investor sells them. B = "back end." For a "B" share, the investor buys in at the NAV, but she will leave a percentage behind when she sells. For a test question on the proceeds of a B-share redemption, just take the NAV and deduct the appropriate percentage from the investor's proceeds. If the NAV is $10, the investor receives the $10, minus the percentage the fund keeps on the back end. So, if she sells 100 shares and there is a 2% back-end load, she gets $1,000 minus $20. The percentage usually starts to decline in the second year, and after several years (6 to 8), the back-end load goes away completely—effectively, the B-shares are converted to A-shares. That's why they associate B-shares with the phrase "contingent deferred sales charges." Break down those words. The sales charge is deferred until the investor sells, and the amount of the load is contingent upon when the investor sells. Often, the back-end load starts at 5% and gradually drops to 1% and then zero as the shares convert to A-shares, just to keep everything nice and simple. B-shares almost always have higher operating expenses than A-shares, so at some point, the load you avoid on the front end—and the back end after 6 to 8 years—could be outweighed by the higher expenses. In fact, unless you have a small amount of money to invest, an amount that would not help you achieve a breakpoint on the A-shares, it is seldom suitable to purchase B-shares. Most funds will not take an order for B-shares above $50,000. That's because that amount would be better invested in the A-shares, where we can knock down the sales charge and go forward with much lower operating expenses.

Just to make the decision harder, there are also C-shares, which are sometimes called "level load" because of a high and level 12b-1 fee. C-shares might charge a contingent deferred sales charge if the investor sells in less than 1 year or 1½ years, just to keep things nice and simple. But, really, if you can stay in the fund long enough for the back-end charge to go away, you will pay the high 12b-1 fee (usually 1%), but no front-end or back-end sales charges. That's why C-shares are suitable for a shorter-term investment. You wouldn't want to keep getting dinged on a 1% 12b-1 fee that never goes away for very long, but it's okay if you're in the fund for just a few years.

So, which share class should an investor buy? Usually, if the investor has at least $50,000 and a long time horizon, the A-shares will work out best. She'll knock down the front-end sales charge with a breakpoint and then go forward with lower operating expenses. The B-shares are for people who don't plan to invest enough to achieve the $50,000 breakpoint offered on A-shares. C-shares are for the shorter-term investor. Putting a long-term investor with lots of money to invest into C-shares would probably be a violation of suitability requirements. If an equal amount of money would have knocked down the sales charges on the A-shares, chances are the A-shares are what the investor should have been buying. And putting someone with $100,000 into A-shares when she's going to sell in 2 years or sooner would also probably be a bad idea, since the C-shares would have probably worked out better. Salespersons have suitability requirements and helping investors choose the right share class is part of that responsibility. FINRA has fined many member firms huge amounts of money for improper sales of A-, B-, and C-shares.

Share Class	Sales Charge	Operating Expenses	Suitability
A	Front-End, can be reduced	Lowest	Long-term investor with 50K +
B	Back-End, declining contingent deferred sales charges	High via 12b-1 fee	Investor with < 50K to invest, mid- or long-term holding period
C	Minimal if any	High via 12b-1 fee	Shorter-term investor with under ~ $500,000

Whether you buy A-, B-, or C-shares, there are different methods of making your purchases. Most funds have a minimum investment that might be different for a retirement plan as compared to a taxable account. Maybe it's $1,000 for an IRA and $3,000 for a taxable account.

Investors can choose to reinvest dividend and capital gains distributions (explained next), and if they do, they reinvest at the NAV, avoiding the sales charge. They get the effect of "compounding" that way, which is why most folks do this. They can certainly take the distributions in cash if they want, as we'll explain in a second. Some investors set up "voluntary accumulation plans," which means they let the fund automatically deduct a set amount of money each month from their bank account or paycheck. If they're putting in a set dollar amount each month, they are "dollar cost averaging."

TYPES OF FUNDS

We talked about diversification at the beginning of this discussion. Mutual funds can be as diversified as they want to, but if the fund wants to advertise itself as being diversified, it has to follow the 75-5-10 rule under the Investment Company Act of 1940. That means that at least 75% of the fund's assets have to be diversified so that no more than 5% of the fund's assets are invested in any one stock. The 10 means that the fund cannot own more than 10% of a company's outstanding shares.

Mutual funds have to clearly state their investment objectives. Sales representatives like you have to match your investor's objectives with those of a particular fund.

Equity Funds

Growth Funds

If your investor's objective is capital appreciation, you need to find a mutual fund that invests for capital appreciation, which is also called *growth* or "growth of capital." The stocks in this fund might pay dividends, but that's not the objective. This fund wants to buy stocks and hold them until they appreciate significantly in value. The prospectus I'm looking at says "dividend income, if any, is incidental to the objective of capital appreciation." The trouble with growth funds is that when stock prices are on the decline, there is nothing to smooth out the ride. By definition, you won't be receiving much income from this fund, so when the stocks in the portfolio drop, say, 20%, that's pretty much the end of the story. Therefore, investing for growth involves more volatility than investing for income. It also involves more patience, since there is, again, very little income being paid out to the investors.

Growth and Income Funds

As the name implies, these funds invest in stocks for both their growth potential and their propensity to pay nice dividends. Now, if the market price of the stocks drops, say, 2%, but you receive a 3% dividend yield, you don't feel so bad about things. Therefore, growth and income funds are less volatile than pure growth funds. To achieve the income component, most growth and income funds also invest in debt securities.

Equity Income Funds

Not surprisingly, equity income funds focus on equity securities that pay regular or increasing income. Now, if the focus has been placed purely on the dividend/income potential of particular stocks, chances are, the portfolio manager will end up owning some pretty stable, tried-and-true companies that consistently lead their industry, increase their sales, and pay either a consistent or ever-increasing dividend. For example, I read the other day about an insurance company that has paid a dividend every quarter for the past 136 years. That stock belongs in an equity income fund. Since consistent dividends are paid by established, stable companies, it's a pretty safe assumption that equity income funds will be less volatile than either growth-and-income or pure growth funds.

Notice that even though growth, growth-and-income, and equity income funds are all stock funds, they typically are less volatile as the focus shifts more toward the income component of investing. See, some people are so obsessed with buying stocks and hoping they "go up" that they forget how useful dividend income can be. It can be reinvested into more shares to achieve compounding. Or, it can be used to buy other mutual funds, stocks, bonds, etc. It also tends to reduce the volatility of an investment.

Sector Funds

A fund that concentrates its investments in a particular sector of the market is called a sector fund. The name of the fund usually implies that it's a sector fund. An "aggressive growth" fund just refers to a style of investing—it doesn't say which industry the companies are in. But, a "science and technology" fund or a "precious metals" fund implies that the fund is concentrating in a particular sector, right? The exam may want you to know that sector funds involve high risk-reward ratios. If you invested in any "Internet funds" back in the late '90s, or any "financial sector" funds recently, that concept should be pretty easy to remember. Also, if it happens to be the hot sector of the moment, I would expect management fees and sales charges to be on the high side.

International, Global Funds

International funds come in a few flavors. They might concentrate in a single country, or a particular region (Latin America, Pacific Rim, etc.). Usually the fund concentrates in companies outside the US. A global fund would invest all over the globe, including the US. International and global funds investing requires a higher risk tolerance than purely domestic funds, but it also offers potential returns an American investor would otherwise miss out on while allowing the investor to diversify away from the US economy.

Emerging Market Funds

A particularly volatile type of international fund would be an emerging market fund. As the name implies, these markets are emerging, just getting started. Lots of wild ups and downs in an immature economy. And if the insurgents take over…well, you get the idea. Basically, the economies are transforming from agricultural-based to industrial (Brazil, for example) or from socialist systems to free market systems (Russia, Eastern Europe, China). If there are lots of labor strikes, banking disasters, material shortages, etc., it's going to make stock prices mighty volatile. But, there are also huge potential growth opportunities, so if the investor is aggressive and seeks capital appreciation, put a percentage of his money into emerging market funds and hope for the best.

Growth, Value, Blend

A growth investor is willing to pay high P/E, price-to-book, and other valuation multiples, while a value investor tries to buy stocks on the cheap. Well, some portfolio managers are absolute mavericks who refuse to be tied down to a label such as "growth" or "value." That means they end up investing in both growth and value stocks. Well, the mutual fund industry insists on labels, so they just labeled these portfolios "blend funds" and kept moving.

Balanced Funds

Balanced funds provide us the perfect bridge from the scary stock market to the boring bond market. A balanced fund always maintains a percentage of assets in bonds and a percentage in stocks. It's not a rigid percentage and the prospectus usually only gives us a vague idea of the split between stocks and bonds. Basically, if it looks like a good year for bonds, the investment adviser switches the concentration to bonds, and vice versa when it looks like a bull market for stocks. Since the fund stays in the bond market, the volatility of the fund is generally much lower than a growth fund or any fund that is primarily invested in stock.

A subtle difference arises when the exam talks about asset allocation funds. These funds, as their name implies, allocate the assets according to the perfect mix of stocks, bonds, and "cash," or "money market securities." So the only real difference I see between "balanced" and "asset allocation" funds is that balanced funds have stocks and bonds, while asset allocation funds go one better by throwing in the "cash" or "money market" component. Also, the percentage mixture is probably more rigid in asset allocation funds. But, many companies would consider their balanced fund to also be an asset allocation fund, so one would hope the exam would focus on better topics.

Bond Funds

Remember that mutual funds are just massive investment pies that serve up slices to investors, so anything that was true of corporate bonds individually is true of a mutual fund that invests in corporate bonds. Like, for example, corporate bonds are nowhere near as safe as municipal bonds, and neither one is as safe as bonds issued by the United States Treasury. Corporate bonds are only as solid as the company who issued them. Investment-grade corporate bonds are obviously more solid than high-yield corporate bonds, but don't kid yourself into thinking that Moody's, S&P, or Fitch can always predict which bonds will end up in default.

Anyway, if the investor's objective is high current income, her risk tolerance will tell us whether to use investment-grade bond funds or high-yield bond funds. For maximum income, we'll recommend high-yield bond funds, as long as her risk tolerance is commensurate with the fact that some of these bonds could implode without warning. Of course, these bonds are commonly referred to as "junk bonds," but the mutual fund industry is too smart to roll out the new "Junk Fund of America." Call that thing the "High-Income Trust Series B," though, and now you'll get yourself some customers.

Income investors looking for tax advantages should buy municipal bond funds. Municipal bond funds receive income from interest payments on municipal bonds, which are generally exempt from *federal* taxation. So, if an investor wants some tax-free dividends, he will get that from a municipal bond fund. Remember that municipal bond funds might pay tax-free dividends, but capital gains are still taxable, just as they are on municipal bonds purchased a la carte. And your state could even tax the dividends you receive, depending on who issued the bonds inside the mutual fund portfolio. Because of this ugliness, fund families have rolled out tax-exempt bond funds specifically for residents of high-tax states including California, Virginia, and Maryland. Investors who live in those states can then purchase mutual funds that pay dividend income exempt from both federal and state taxes. But—as always—capital gains are another story.

And then there are US Treasury funds for people who want to preserve their capital and earn a rather low rate of interest in exchange for that safety. The only way to lose money on Treasuries is to have interest rates go up and you decide to sell anyway. But, the interest payments will always be there on time and you will receive the principal when the thing matures. So, the NAV of the US Treasury fund definitely drops when interest rates rise, but if you have no need to sell, you'll come out okay.

Money Market Funds

Not surprisingly, money market mutual funds invest in money market instruments. They are no-load and maintain a stable value of $1 per share. Actually they "strive to maintain the share price at $1," but that is not guaranteed—it is possible to lose money by investing in a money market mutual fund. Highly unlikely, but possible. Money market mutual funds are good for people who need monthly income or have a near-term goal such as purchasing a house. You don't know how long it will take to find the right house, let alone when the deal will close, so a money market mutual fund is even better than a T-bill. A T-bill matures on a particular day, and God help you if you want to sell it early. For a money market mutual fund, you can simply write a check for $250 or more without paying any fees. Money market mutual funds are good for short-term liquidity and reducing the volatility of your portfolio, but they don't provide much growth of capital, if any.

Also remember that there are tax-exempt money market funds. These funds buy short-term municipal obligations (BAN, TAN, RAN, TRAN), or municipal bonds that are set to mature in a year or less.

Index Funds

The ugly truth is that not many active portfolio managers can consistently beat a comparable index. If you can't beat the S&P 500 index, why not join it? An actively managed stock fund is going to deduct sales charges that can easily be 5% or more for small investments, plus there are annual operating expenses that usually exceed 1%. If you don't like paying sales charges and operating expenses in order to lose to an unmanaged index, why not just buy an unmanaged index fund? Typically, there is no sales charge, and the annual expenses are often about 1/10th of what you'd pay for actively managed stock funds. The exam may point out that if somebody abhors expenses and has no faith in active portfolio management, the index fund is probably appropriate. There are also ETFs, which are index funds that are organized as UITs (unit investment trusts) and traded just like shares of GE or MSFT among investors. Again, we have low operating expenses, but the ETF allows the investor to bet against the market by selling short, purchasing on margin, and taking advantage of the intra-day movements of the index.

WRAP-UP

Keep in mind that mutual funds are just packages made up of many individual securities. So, if there is preferred stock, you know there are preferred stock funds. They would be primarily for income investors. If there are GNMAs, then there are, of course, GNMA funds for income investors looking for higher income than that offered by Treasuries. Could there be a convertible bond fund?

Absolutely. Whatever an investor could buy a la carte, she could buy as a complete dinner package through a mutual fund. She pays for the expenses of the fund plus sales charges in many cases, but she gets immediate diversification and professional management in return.

So, if you review the different styles of investing, and throw in the market caps, you see why we could really come up with a variety of fund types. For example:

Equity

Growth Funds
- Aggressive Growth
- Conservative Growth
- Small Cap Growth
- Mid Cap Growth
- Large Cap Growth
- International Growth
- New Economy Growth
- EuroPacific Growth

Value Funds
- Small Cap Value
- Mid Cap Value
- Large Cap Value

Other Equity Funds
- Growth & Income Funds
- Equity Income Funds
- Balanced Funds
- Sector/Specialized
- Index (S&P 500, Russell 2000, etc.)

Fixed Income
- Investment Grade
- High Yield
- Tax-Exempt (municipal bonds)
- Short-Term Treasury
- Short-Term Tax-Exempt (muni)
- Short-Term Corporate
- Intermediate-Term (treasury, muni, corporate)
- Long-Term (treasury, muni, corporate)

Money Market
- US Government/Treasury
- Tax-Exempt (muni notes, near-term bonds)

STRUCTURE OF THE FUND COMPANY

A mutual fund operation is divided among several important players: board of directors, investment adviser, custodian, transfer agent, sponsor.

Board of Directors

A mutual fund has a board of directors that oversees operations of the fund or family of funds. The board's responsibilities include the following:
- Establish investment policy
- Select and oversee the investment adviser, transfer agent, custodian
- Establish dividends and capital gains policy
- Approve 12b-1 plans

Remember, the board of directors does not manage the portfolio; they manage the company. The shareholders of the fund elect and re-elect the board members. Shareholders also vote their shares to approve the investment adviser's contract and 12b-1 fees. Those with enough moxie to open the proxy do, anyway.

Investment Adviser

Yes, we're still talking about investment advisers, the folks who need the Series 65/66. Each fund has an investment adviser, whose job is to manage the fund's investments according to its stated objectives. Shareholders and the board vote to hire/retain investment advisers, who are paid a percentage of the fund's net assets. That's why they try so hard. The more valuable the fund, the more they get paid. Their fee is typically the largest expense to a mutual fund. Investment advisers have to advise the fund (select the investments) in keeping with federal securities and tax law. They must also base their investment decisions on careful research of economic/financial trends.

Custodian

The fund also keeps its assets in a safe place at the custodian bank. Under very strict rules, some funds do this themselves, but most still let a bank take custody, since banks have vaults and security guards and stuff. The custodian receives the dividends and interest payments made by the stocks and bonds in the fund's portfolio. The custodian is also responsible for the payable/receivable functions involved when the portfolio buys and sells securities.

Transfer Agent

The transfer agent is incredibly busy. This is the bank or other company that issues new shares to buyers and cancels the shares that sellers redeem. Most of these "shares" are simply electronic files (book entry), but it still takes a lot of work to "issue" and "redeem" them. While the custodian receives dividends and interest payments from the portfolio securities, it is the transfer agent that distributes income to the investors. The transfer agent acts as a customer service rep for the fund and often sends out those semi-annual reports that investors have to receive. Finally, the transfer agent handles name changes. So if Joann Williams gets married and becomes Joann Williams-Davis, or if Calvin Broadus starts a music career and becomes Snoop Doggy Dogg, the transfer agent can change the names on the mutual fund shares accordingly.

Distributors

As we saw, some funds are sponsored by underwriters, who bear the costs of distributing the fund up front and then get compensated by the sales charge that they either earn themselves or split with the broker-dealers who make the sales. Underwriters (AKA "wholesalers," "distributors," or "sponsors") also prepare sales literature for the fund, since they're the ones who will be selling the shares, either directly to the public or through a network of broker-dealers.

If a fund wants to distribute itself, it can charge 12b-1 fees to cover the costs connected to landing new customers: printing and mailing the prospectus to new customers, paying sales reps, and buying advertising. In other words, mutual funds charge their customers for marketing costs. They either charge sales loads on the front or back end, or they charge little quarterly deductions called "12b-1 fees."

In fact, many charge *both*. As long as it keeps the 12b-1 fees to .25% of average net assets, the fund can call itself "no load."

There are many conveniences and services offered to owners of mutual funds:

- Investment decisions made by a professional portfolio manager
- Ease of diversification
- Ability to invest fixed amounts in full and fractional shares
- Ability to liquidate a portion of the investment without losing diversification
- Fund shares provide collateral for a loan (after 30 days)
- Simplified tax information (1099s make tax prep easier)
- Simplified record keeping (rather than getting 50 annual reports from 50 companies, you get two semi-annual reports from one mutual fund)
- Ease of purchase and redemption of securities
- Automatic reinvestments of capital gains and income distributions at NAV
- Safekeeping of portfolio securities
- Ease of account inquiry
- Mutual fund shareholders also have the right to:
  o Vote their shares by proxy on:
    › Board of director positions
    › Investment adviser's contract
    › Changes in investment objectives/policy
    › Changes in policy involving real estate or commodities transactions, borrowing/lending money, underwriting other issuer's securities
  o Receive a semi-annual report and an audited annual report (both have an income statement and a balance sheet)

The disadvantages of investing in mutual funds would be that the individual gives up the ability to pick individual securities and that funds have expenses including 12b-1 fees and/or sales charges.

PROSPECTUS

The prospectus is how the mutual fund provides full disclosure to prospective investors. See the connection? We send a prospect-us to a prospect-ive investor. First thing you'll find in the prospectus is a statement about risk/reward. This is generally the first page of information where they describe the investment objectives of the growth, income, bond, or whatever fund. In case the first few paragraphs don't sufficiently scare the bejeezus out of you, they often end up making statements that are as clear as the warnings from the Surgeon General. The prospectus I'm looking at (you should be looking at a few, too) says:

> Your investment in the fund is not a bank deposit and is not insured or guaranteed by the FDIC or any other government agency, entity, or person.

And, in case that didn't hit home, they follow up with a bold-letter warning:

> **You may lose money by investing in the fund. The likelihood of loss is greater if you invest for a shorter period of time.**

In the prospectus, we'll find the fund's 1-year, 5-year, and 10-year returns. If the fund hasn't been around for 5 or 10 years, they report their returns over the life of the fund. The investment adviser(s) is/are named and discussed. The portfolio's allocation is laid out as a pie chart showing which percentage is in, say, retail or pharmaceutical companies, or how much of the bond fund is generally devoted to BBB- versus AAA-rated issuers. The top 10 stock holdings are usually shown for equity funds; we don't get the actual holdings of the portfolio, because those can change every day, but we do get a pretty good idea of how this portfolio is laid out. The prospectus is really the "summary prospectus." Few folks actually read it, although everybody should, especially everybody sitting for a regulatory exam like the 6, 7, 63, or 65/66.

Yes—that includes *you*.

If someone is really curious, he can request the Statement of Additional Information (SAI), which provides pretty much what it sounds like. These are filed with the SEC and are available at the SEC's and the fund company's websites. Remember that corporations have to provide a prospectus when they do their IPO. Well, mutual fund companies are in a continuous state of IPO, which is why they have to provide full disclosure to investors in a prospectus. And, on the back of that prospectus, the prospect can also find a link to the SAI and even the fund's semiannual and annual reports to shareholders.

ETFs/EXCHANGE-TRADED FUNDS

Most investors probably associate the phrase "ETF" with index funds, which is a good place to start. Examples of exchange-traded index funds include the Spiders™ or Diamonds™ that track the major S&P indexes and the Dow Jones Industrial Average. There were already traditional open-end versions of those index funds, but those have to be redeemed, and all investors received the same price on an open-end fund—the closing NAV. With the ETF, investors buy and sell shares back and forth just as they trade shares of Microsoft, GE, and Starbucks throughout the day. As we mentioned, since they trade like shares of stock, they can be sold short to protect against market or systematic risk.

HEDGE FUNDS

Since the mutual fund is open to the average Joe and Joann, they can't focus on extremely risky investment strategies. It would be sort of rude to take the average Joe and Joann's retirement nest egg and lose it all on a couple of ill-placed foreign currency bets or poorly timed short sales. But, when the investors are all rich folks and institutions, the regulators can relax a little bit.

This is where hedge funds come in. In general, hedge funds are only open to institutions and to individuals called "accredited investors." An accredited investor includes any individual with over $1 million in net worth or who makes > $200,000 per year. If it's a married couple, the assets held jointly count toward that $1 million figure, and the annual income needs to be > $300,000. Now, that's *exactly* the kind of number that could change without warning and make a book look dated. First, the exam doesn't let you off that easy, anyway—you don't get to spit back a bunch of memorized numbers. The exam makes you think and analyze in either a very stimulating or painful manner depending on your experience. So, please, don't make the mistake that many test-takers do and start obsessing over numbers such as retirement plan maximums or the annual gift tax exclusion—that stuff can change quickly without warning. The test writers know this. You think *they* want to constantly have to rewrite all their questions just because the SEC changed a rule?

Anyway, we still have to give you the numbers, because they are "testable." Just don't put the *focus* of your studies on all the numbers. Learn the concepts well enough to get test questions right and keep moving.

So, why does the hedge fund investor need to be rich? Because these hedge funds use some very high-risk strategies including short selling, currency bets, risky options plays, etc. If you're an average Joe and Joann, it generally wouldn't be cool to let you risk your money on such high-risk investing. On the other hand, if you're a rich individual or big institution, chances are your hedge fund investment is just a percentage of the capital you invest. So, if you lose $1 million, chances are you have several more where that one came from. Also, hedge funds generally tie up your money for two years or more—there is, basically, no way to sell or liquidate your investment, so this had better not be your only investment. People do have financial emergencies, so a hedge fund is only for money you can afford to risk and don't need to touch any time soon. It is a "highly illiquid and speculative" investment, in other words.

The hedge fund escapes having to register under the Investment Company Act of 1940 because they have 100 or fewer investors and do not offer their securities generally to the public, or because their investors are all "qualified" high-net-worth individuals or institutions. If the exam mentions a "3(c)(7) fund," it is talking about the particular section of the Investment Company Act of 1940 that says an investment company does not include an issuer whose investors are qualified purchasers and who is not making a general public offering.

Now, just to keep everything nice and simple, although a non-accredited investor cannot invest directly in a hedge fund, there are mutual funds called "funds of hedge funds," which she can invest in. As the name implies, these mutual funds would have investments in several different hedge funds. In most cases, the investor would not be able to redeem her investment, since hedge funds are illiquid (they don't trade among investors). Also, these investments would involve high expenses, since there would be the usual expenses of the mutual fund, on top of the high expenses of the hedge funds the mutual fund invests in.

So, while some hedge funds have been known to make extremely high returns, even in bear markets, the regulators also want us to remember that they are expensive, very risky, and make it really tough for the investor to liquidate her position. The main testable points on hedge funds would seem to be:

- Open to sophisticated, accredited investors with high net worth
- Illiquid—usually can't be sold for two years

- Employ riskier, more diverse strategies
- Charge high management fees and usually 20% of all gains
- Non-accredited investors can buy mutual funds that invest in hedge funds

Glossary

12b-1 fee: an operating expense charged by a mutual fund to cover distribution/selling expenses. Charged in lieu of, or in addition to, any front- or back-end sales charges. Paid to sales representatives making sales of fund shares to customers.

401(k) Plan: a retirement plan in which matching contributions from the employer are usually offered.

403(b) Plan: retirement plan for non-profit organizations such as schools and hospitals.

457 Plan: a retirement plan for state and municipal workers.

529 Savings Plan: tax-deferred educational savings plan run by the various states and allowing for tax-exempt withdrawals for qualified education expenses. Compared to the "Coverdell," the 529 Plan allows for much larger contributions and remains the property of the account owner (not the beneficiaries).

1035 Exchange: a tax-free exchange among annuities or life insurance contracts.

1099-DIV: a form sent to investors showing dividends and capital gains received by a mutual fund for purposes of tax reporting.

A

A-shares: open-end mutual fund shares purchased with a front-end load but lower annual operating expenses than those charged on B- and C-shares.

Accredited Investors: large institutional investors, and individuals meeting certain income or net worth requirements allowing them to participate in, for example, a private placement under Reg D of the Securities Act of 1933, or hedge funds.

Adjustable Rate Preferred Stock: preferred stock whose dividend is tied to another rate, often the rate paid on T-bills.

ADR/ADS: American Depository Receipt/Share. A foreign stock on a domestic market. Toyota and Nokia are two examples of foreign companies whose ADRs trade on American stock markets denominated in dollars. Carry all the risks of owning stocks, plus "currency exchange risk."

Administrative Order: an order of the securities Administrator including punitive orders (deny, suspend, revoke) and non-punitive (withdraw, cancel) orders.

Administrator: official or agency designated by statute to enforce the securities laws and regulations of a particular state. Or, the person named by a probate court to oversee the estate of a deceased person who died without a valid will in place.

Adviser: see "investment adviser."

Affidavit of Loss: a written statement by the owner of a security declaring that the certificate has been stolen, lost, or destroyed.

Affiliated Person: anyone in a position to influence decisions at a public corporation, including board members (directors), officers (CEO, CFO), and large shareholders (Warren Buffett at Coca-Cola or Wells Fargo).

Agency Cross Transaction: recommending or using discretion to buy or sell a security for an advisory client where the transaction occurs between the advisory client and a client of the firm's broker-dealer. Requires disclosure of the potential conflict of interest that gives the adviser incentive to recommend or perform the transaction.

Agency Issue (Agency Bond): a debt security issued by an agency authorized by the federal government but not directly backed by the federal government.

Agent: an individual (natural person) who represents either an issuer or a broker-dealer in effecting transactions in securities.

AIR: Assumed Interest Rate. Determined by an actuary, representing his best estimate of the monthly annualized rate of return from the separate account. Used to determine value of annuity units for annuities and death benefit for variable life contracts.

All or None: a type of underwriting in which the syndicate will cancel the offering if a sufficient dollar amount is not raised as opposed to being responsible for the unsold shares (as in a "firm commitment").

Alternative Minimum Tax: or "AMT," a calculation that adds certain tax preference items back into adjusted gross income to make sure that April is, indeed, the cruelest month for those who make a good income. Tax preference items include accelerated depreciation taken in a partnership, and municipal bond interest paid on private purpose bonds.

American Stock Exchange (AMEX): a private, not-for-profit corporation that handles roughly 20% of all securities trades in the US. One of the big secondary markets, along with NYSE, and the various NASDAQ markets.

AMT: see Alternative Minimum Tax.

Annualized Rate of Return: an investment's increase or decrease measured in annual increments. For periods of less than 1 year, multiply the return by the appropriate number, e.g., a 6-month return is doubled; a 3-month return is multiplied by 4. For periods of more than 1 year, divide the return by the number of years.

Annual Report: a disclosure document filed by a public company with the SEC and also delivered to shareholders in which the company discusses operations, provides financial reports, and discloses current and potential risks that could have a negative impact on the market value of the stock.

Annual Updating Amendment: an update of all responses to Form ADV Part 1, submitted within 90 days after the end of the investment adviser's fiscal year.

Annuitant: the person who receives an annuity contract's distribution.

Annuitization Phase: the period when the annuitant starts to receive payments from the annuity.

Annuity Units: what the annuitant owns during the annuity period of the contract, which is the period during which withdrawals are made.

Anticipation Notes: short-term debt obligations issued by municipalities to be repaid in anticipation of some future revenue source…taxes, toll way revenues, bond issue, etc.

Arbitrage: exploiting a disparity between the prices of two things that should, theoretically, be the same. For example, if an investor can buy a convertible bond for $1,050 when that bond converts to stock currently worth $1,060, there is an arbitrage opportunity of $10 per bond. He can buy the bond for less than the underlying stock is worth. Or, if a trader could buy a stock on the Midwest Stock Exchange for 5 cents less than it's trading on the NYSE, he could perform an arbitrage trade where he buys the stock on the Midwest exchange while also selling it on NYSE.

Ask or Asked: what the customer pays a dealer to purchase a security; the dealer's "asking price."

Assessable Stock: a type of stock issued primarily in the olden days in which the issuing corporation could assess or charge investors more money in the future.

Asset: a "plus" to an individual's or business's account, e.g., cash, inventory, equipment. Something that can be pledged as collateral for a loan.

Asset Class: a class of investments with similar characteristics. Strictly, the three asset classes are stock, bond, and money market instruments, but some would argue that real estate and commodities are also asset classes.

Asset Allocation: an investment style that focuses on a mix of equity, bond, and money market exposure, e.g., 50% equity, 45% bonds, 5% money market.

Asset Allocation Fund: a mutual fund that focuses on allocating assets to minimize risk and achieve a total return in line with a lower-risk investment approach.

Assignment (of an options contract): the act of forcing the seller/writer of an option to honor his obligation to the buyer of the contract. For example, if an MSFT May 50 call is exercised by the buyer, the contract is assigned to a seller, who must deliver 100 shares of MSFT for $50 a share to the buyer, regardless of how high the market price actually is.

Assignment (of an advisory contract): selling or transferring a client's advisory account to another party. Also includes a transfer or pledging/hypothecation of a controlling block of the adviser's outstanding voting securities. Not allowed without written consent of client.

Associated Person: a registered representative or principal of a FINRA member firm.

Assumed Interest Rate (AIR): an actuarial determination affecting the payout to a variable annuitant. Annuity payments are determined each month by comparing the separate account returns to AIR.

Auction Market: the NYSE, for example, where buyers and sellers simultaneously enter competitive prices. Sometimes called a "double auction" market because buying and selling occur at the same time, as opposed to Sotheby's, where only buyers are competing.

Authorized Stock: number of shares a company is authorized to issue by its corporate charter. Can be changed by a majority vote of the outstanding shares.

Automatic Reinvestment: a feature offered by mutual funds allowing investors to automatically reinvest dividend and capital gains distributions into more shares of the fund, without paying a sales charge.

B

B-shares: open-end mutual fund shares purchased without a front-end load but carrying a back-end load or "contingent deferred sales charge" that gradually declines until the shares eventually convert to A-shares. These shares charge higher annual operating expenses than A-shares and are suitable for investors with smaller amounts to invest.

Backdating: pre-dating a letter of intent (LOI) for a mutual fund in order to include a prior purchase in the total amount stated in the letter of intent. LOIs may be backdated up to 90 calendar days.

Back-end Load: a commission/sales fee charged when mutual fund or variable contracts are redeemed. The back-end load declines gradually, as described in the prospectus. Associated with "B-shares" and, occasionally, "C-shares."

Backing Away: a violation in which a market maker fails to honor a published firm quote to buy or sell a security.

Backup Withholding: a tax that is levied on investment income, usually because the investor failed to provide a proper Taxpayer Identification Number. As investment income is withdrawn by the investor, the required percentage is remitted to the IRS.

Balanced Fund: a fund that maintains a mix of stocks and bonds at all times. Asset allocation funds are a type of balanced fund (or so darned close that they should be).

Balance Sheet: a statement of financial condition prepared by both individuals and businesses showing assets and liabilities, where the difference between assets and liabilities equals "net worth" for individuals and "stockholders' equity" for businesses.

Balance Sheet Equation: Assets − Liabilities = Shareholders' Equity, or Assets = Liabilities + Shareholders' Equity.

Banker's Acceptance (BA): money-market security that facilitates importing/exporting. Issued at a discount from face-value. A secured loan.

Bank Holding Company: a company whose assets hold banks. For example, First Midwest Bancorp, Inc., or Bancorp South. Both examples are public companies whose stock must be registered with the SEC. A "bank " does not have to be registered with the SEC because it is regulated by bank regulators.

Bank Secrecy Act: legislation that prevents financial institutions from being used as tools by criminals to hide or launder money earned through illegal activities. Financial institutions such as banks and broker-dealers must report currency transactions over $10,000 and must report suspicious activity to the Department of Treasury's Financial Crimes Enforcement Network or "FinCEN."

Bar: the most severe sanction that FINRA can impose on an individual, effectively ending his/her career.

Basis Point: 1/100th of 1%, a measurement of a bond's yield. 100 basis points = 1%. 50 basis points = ½ of 1%.

Basis Quote: the price at which a debt security can be bought or sold, based on the yield. A bond purchased at a "5.50 basis" is trading at a price that makes the yield 5.5%.

Bearish, Bear: an investor who takes a position based on the belief that the market or a particular security will fall. Short sellers and buyers of puts are "bearish." They profit when stocks go down. Seriously.

Bear Market: a market for stock or bonds in which prices are falling and/or expected to fall.

Benchmark Portfolio: the index that a portfolio manager is trying to beat. For example, a large-cap fund manager would be trying to beat the DJIA. A small-cap manager would be trying to beat the benchmark of the Russell small-cap Index (Russell 2000).

Beneficiary: the one who benefits. An insurance policy pays a benefit to the named beneficiary. IRAs and other retirement plans, including annuities, allow the owner to name a beneficiary who will receive the account value when the owner dies. A 529 plan names a beneficiary, who will use the money for educational expenses someday.

Best Efforts: a type of underwriting leaving the syndicate at no risk for unsold shares, and allowing them to keep the proceeds on the shares that were sold/subscribed to. Underwriters act as "agents," not principals, in a best efforts underwriting.

Beta: the volatility of an individual stock or portfolio compared to the overall market (S&P 500). A beta of "1" means the stock moves in lock-step with the overall market. A beta of more than 1 means the stock is more volatile than the overall market; a beta of less than 1 means the stock is less volatile.

Bid: the amount a customer can receive from a dealer when selling a security; what a market maker will pay to a seller.

Blend Fund: a fund that can't decide if it wants to be a growth fund or a value fund.

Blue Chip: stock in a well-established company with proven ability to pay dividends in good economic times and bad. Lower risk/reward ratio than other common stock.

Blue Sky: state securities law, tested on the Series 63, 65, and 66 exams.

Board of Directors: the group elected by shareholders to run a mutual fund or a public company and establish corporate management policies.

Bond: a debt security issued by a corporation or governmental entity that promises to repay principal and pay interest either regularly or at maturity.

Bond Anticipation Note (BAN): a short-term municipal debt security backed by the proceeds of an upcoming bond issue.

Bond Fund: a mutual fund with an objective of providing income while minimizing capital risk through a portfolio of bonds.

Bond Point: $10. A quote of "96" means 96 bond points or $960.

Bond Rating: an evaluation of a bond issue's chance of default published by companies such as Moody's, S&P, and Fitch.

Book Entry: a security maintained as a computer record rather than a physical certificate. All US Treasuries and many mutual funds are issued in this manner.

Books and Records: records that broker-dealers and investment advisers must keep, subject to inspection by representatives of the Administrator. For example, correspondence between the firm and clients, accounts over which the firm maintains discretion, financial records of the firm, etc.

Book Value (per share): theoretically, what a share of stock would be worth if the corporation was sold at auction today, with the proceeds used to pay off the creditors and the excess paid out to shareholders. Value investors like to buy stocks near or below book value.

Bottom-Up Analysis: using fundamental analysis at the company-specific level as opposed to focusing on overall economic conditions.

Brady Bonds: bonds issued by the governments of emerging markets, frequently Latin America.

Breakeven: a term used in connection to options meaning that the underlying security has moved by the amount of the premium paid or received on the option. For example, an ABC Apr 50 call @2 has a "breakeven" of $52 for either the buyer or seller of that option.

Breakpoint: a discounted sales charge or "volume discount" on mutual fund purchases offered on A-shares at various levels of investment.

Breakpoint Selling: preventing an investor from achieving a breakpoint. A violation.

Broad-based Index: an index such as the S&P 500 or the Value Line Composite Index that represents companies from many industries.

Brochure Rule: rule under the Investment Advisers Act of 1940 requiring advisers to provide prospects with a disclosure document detailing the services to be performed, the fees charged and the method for computing them, whether the adviser has discretion, and any conflicts of interest. Disclosure is provided either with a copy of Form ADV Part 2 or a brochure that contains at least that much information. Advisers would also disclose any legal/disciplinary actions in the last 10 years, and any financial conditions that could impair their ability to meet client commitments.

Broker: an individual or firm that charges a commission to execute securities buy and sell orders submitted by another individual or firm.

Broker-Dealer: any person effecting transactions in securities for the accounts of others (broker) or its own account (dealer).

Business Cycle: a progression of expansions, peaks, contractions, troughs, and recoveries for the overall (macro) economy.

Business Risk: the risk that the company whose stock or bond you own will not be successful as a business. Competition, poor management, obsolete products/services are all examples of business risk.

Buy and Hold: investment style noted for low transaction costs.

C

C-shares: open-end fund shares with no front-end load and a level 1% 12b-1 fee and, therefore, higher annual operating expenses than A-shares. Suitable for shorter-term investments in which paying a front-end load on A-shares would not be prudent.

Call: "to buy."

Call (Call Option): An option to purchase something at a fixed/set price known as the exercise price or strike price.

Callable: a security that may be purchased/called by the issuer as of a certain date, e.g., callable preferred, callable bonds. Generally pays a higher rate of return than non-callable securities, as it gives the issuer flexibility in financing.

Call Date: the date on which the issuer can redeem a bond before its maturity date. Bonds are typically called when interest rates have fallen.

Call Premium: the price paid and received on a call option. Or, the amount above the par value paid by the issuer to call/retire a bond.

Call Protection: the period during which a security may not be called or bought by the issuer, usually lasting five years or more.

Call Provision: agreement between the issuer and the bondholders or preferred stockholders that gives the issuer the ability to repurchase the bonds or preferred stock on a specified date or dates before maturity.

Call Risk: the risk that interest rates will drop, prompting issuers to call (buy back) their bonds or preferred stock.

Cancel/Cancellation: a non-punitive order issued by the Administrator when a registrant has died or cannot be located.

Capital Appreciation: an increase in the value of an investment. The investment objective of a growth investor.

Capital Gain: the profit made when selling a security for more than you bought it.

Capital Gains Distribution: distribution from fund to investor based on net capital gains realized by the fund portfolio. Holding period determined by the fund and assumed to be long-term.

Capital Loss: loss incurred when selling an asset for less than the purchase price. Capital losses offset an investor's capital gains and can offset ordinary income to a certain amount.

Capital Structure: the make-up of a corporation's financing through equity (stock) and debt (bonds) securities.

Cash Account: an investment account in which the investor must pay for all purchases no later than two business days following regular way settlement. Not a margin account.

Cash Dividend: money paid to shareholders from a corporation's current earnings or accumulated profits.

Cash Equivalent: a security that can readily be converted to cash, e.g., T-bills, CDs, and money market funds.

Cash Flow: the amount of cash being generated by a company. Found either on the separate cash flow statement or by taking net income from the income statement and adding back non-cash charges (depreciation, amortization).

Cash Settlement: same-day settlement of a trade requiring prior broker-dealer approval. Not the "regular way" of doing things.

Cash Value: the value of an insurance policy that may be "tapped" by the policyholder through a loan or a surrender.

C-Corporation: a traditional corporation that elects to be taxed as a corporation as opposed to passing income and expenses directly to the owners. Triggers double taxation of dividends.

Cease and Desist: an Administrative order thanking you in advance for agreeing not to violate the securities laws of the state.

CEO: chief executive officer. Individual ultimately responsible for a corporation's results.

CFO: chief financial officer. Individual in charge of a corporation's financial activities.

Chinese Wall: the separation that is supposed to exist between the investment banking department and the traders and registered representatives in order to prevent insider trading violations.

Civil Liabilities: a legal responsibility or obligation to follow a civil court's decision to, for example, return an investor's money, plus interest, after selling him unregistered securities without proper disclosure of material facts.

Closed-end Fund: an investment company under the Investment Company Act of 1940, sub-classified as a management company whose shares are not redeemable.

Code of Ethics: investment adviser's policy to ensure that employees adhere to all federal and state securities regulations and requiring "access persons" to disclose all investing activity to prevent insider trading, frontrunning, etc.

Collateralized Mortgage Obligation (CMO): a mortgage-backed security that creates different pools of pass-through rates for different "tranches" with different maturities.

Collateral Trust Certificate: a secured corporate bond backed by a portfolio of securities.

Commercial Paper: a short-term unsecured loan to a corporation. Issued at a discount from the face value. See "money market securities."

Common Stock: a basic form of equity/ownership in a business that provides voting rights to the owner and a claim on earnings/dividends.

Compensation: any form of economic benefit, including money, material goods, even soft-dollar compensation (research services, software, clearing services, etc.).

Confirmation: document stating the trade date, settlement date, and money due/owed for a securities purchase or sale. Delivered on or before the settlement date.

Conflict of Interest: anything that could make an investment adviser's advice less than objective, e.g., receiving extra compensation if the client accepts the advice.

Consent to Service of Process: a form filed by an issuer, agent, broker-dealer, IA, or IAR which gives the Administrator the authority to receive service of process (court papers) on behalf of the party filing the consent with the same force as if served on the suddenly-hard-to-locate party.

Consolidated Tape: reporting system for all NYSE-listed securities transactions.

Constant Dollar Risk: the risk that inflation/rising prices will erode the value of a fixed-income payment. A 6% coupon payment on a bond won't provide much purchasing power if consumer prices are rising faster than 6%.

Consumer Price Index (CPI): a measure of the prices for consumer goods and services.

Contempt of Court: failing to comply with a court order, subject to monetary penalties and jail time.

Contraction: phase of the business cycle associated with general economic decline, recession or depression.

Contumacy: disobeying or ignoring an Administrative order.

Conversion/Exchange Privilege: feature offered by some mutual funds in which the sales charge is waived when an investor sells shares of one fund to buy another one within the mutual fund family.

Convertible Securities: bonds and preferred stock that allow the holder to use the par value toward the purchase of the issuer's common stock at a set price.

Corporate Bonds: bonds issued by corporations.

Cost Basis: the money that has already been taxed and gone into an investment. The amount above this cost basis is usually taxable as a capital gain when realized.

Coupon Rate: the rate of interest paid by a bond. Aka "nominal yield."

Covered Call: a position in which an investor generates premium income by selling the right to buy stock the investor already owns, and at a set price.

Coverdell Education Savings Account: tax-deferred education savings account allowing for tax-exempt withdrawals for qualified education expenses incurred by schoolchildren at any grade level. Compared to the 529 Plan, offers smaller contributions and becomes the property of the beneficiary upon reaching the age of adulthood.

Credit Risk: the risk of losing principal or the promised rate of return on a debt security due to the issuer's inability to meet interest and/or principal payments as they come due. Aka "default risk."

Cumulative Preferred Stock: preferred stock where missed dividends go into arrears and must be paid before the issuer may pay dividends to other preferred stock and/or common stock.

Cumulative Voting: method of voting whereby the shareholder may take the total votes and split them up any way he chooses. Said to benefit minority over majority shareholders. Total votes are found by multiplying the number of shares owned by the number of seats up for election to the Board of Directors.

Currency Exchange Risk: the risk presented to the holder of an ADR or an investor in international or global mutual funds that fluctuations in currency exchange rates will have a negative impact on the value of their investment. Aka "foreign exchange risk."

Currency Transaction Report: a report filed by banks and broker-dealers with the US Treasury when customers perform transactions larger than $10,000 cash money.

Current Assets: a balance sheet account in which the company lists assets reasonably expected to be converted to cash in the short run, e.g., inventory or accounts receivable.

Current Liabilities: a balance sheet account in which the company lists obligations to be paid out in the short run, e.g., accounts payable.

Current Ratio: taken from the balance sheet, the current assets divided by the current liabilities. The higher the number, the stronger the financial condition.

Current Yield: annual interest compared to/divided by market price. An 8% coupon bond bought at $800 has a current yield of 10%. The nominal yield is 8%, but compared to the $800 paid for the bond, the bond is currently yielding 10%.

CUSIP Number: an identification number assigned to stocks and registered bonds. The acronym stands for the Committee on Uniform Securities Identification Procedures.

Custody: possession/control of securities and/or cash. Or, the ability to appropriate (gain control of) client assets without the client's knowledge or consent.

Custodian: the party that maintains custody of a mutual fund's securities and cash. Performs payable/receivable functions for portfolio purchases and sales. In an UGMA or UTMA account, the custodian is the adult named on the account who is responsible for the investment decisions and tax reporting.

Cyclical: an industry highly dependent on the business cycle, susceptible to recession. For example, steel and auto manufacturing are highly cyclical industries that do well during expansions and get crushed during recessions/depressions.

D

Death Benefit: the amount on a life insurance policy, annuity, or a pension payable to the beneficiary upon death of the contract holder.

Debenture: a bond backed by the issuer's "full faith and credit" or ability to pay. No specific assets are pledged as collateral to secure the loan.

Debt Ratio: a measurement of a company's long-term financial strength. The formula is simply total debt divided by total assets, where the lower the number, the better.

Debt Security: a security representing a loan from an investor to an issuer. Offers a particular interest rate in return for the loan, not an ownership position.

Debt Service: the schedule for repayment of interest and principal on a debt security.

Declaration Date: the date the Board declares a dividend.

Default: the failure of an issuer to pay interest and/or principal when it comes due.

Default Risk: the risk of getting stiffed by the issuer of a bond.

Defensive: an industry that is not highly susceptible to economic downturns, e.g., food, alcohol, cigarettes.

Deferred Annuity: an annuity that delays payments of income, installments, or a lump sum until the investor elects to receive it. Usually subject to surrender charges during the deferral period.

Defined Benefit Plan: employer-sponsored pension plan promising a defined benefit to retirees, e.g., 70% of the employee's average salary over the final five years of service.

Defined Contribution Plan: employer-sponsored retirement plan passing investment risks to the participants. For example, 401(k), profit-sharing.

Deflation: falling prices due to low demand relative to supply.

Deferred Compensation Plan: a non-qualified business plan that defers some of the employee's compensation until retirement.

Deficiency Letter: SEC notification of additions or corrections that an issuer must make to a registration statement before the offering can be cleared for distribution.

Denial/Deny: an Administrative enforcement order denying a registration of a security or an agent, broker-dealer, investment adviser, or investment adviser representative.

Depression: 6 quarters/18 months or more of economic downturn.

Developed Market: an international market whose economic and financial systems are more mature than in emerging markets. For example, Japan and Singapore are developed markets while India and Brazil are still (we hope) emerging.

Diluted Earnings: the earnings per share that would result after the conversion of all convertible preferred, convertible bonds, and warrants into common stock. Same earnings pie cut into more (smaller) equity slices.

Disclosure Brochure: typically a copy of Form ADV Part 2, on which the investment adviser provides important information to advisory prospects, including disclosures of potential conflicts of interest and—if applicable—any criminal, civil, and regulatory problems occurring in the previous 10 years.

Discount Rate: the rate of interest that the FRB charges member banks. Or, the rate of return used to calculate the present value of future dividends in the "dividend discount model."

Discretion (Discretionary Account): the ability of an investment adviser or broker-dealer to make trading decisions for clients without first talking to them.

Distribution: the money you take out of a retirement plan.

Distribution Expenses: the cost of distributing/marketing a mutual fund, including selling, printing prospectuses and sales literature, advertising, and mailing prospectuses to new/ potential clients. Covered by sales charges/12b-1fees.

Distribution Stage: the period during which an individual receives payments from an annuity.

Distributor: the sponsor of a mutual fund responsible for marketing the shares, usually through a network of broker-dealers. Receives the sales charge in exchange for underwriting distribution expenses such as printing, mailing, selling, and advertising.

Diversifiable Risk: aka systematic risk/market risk, which cannot be avoided through diversification but, rather, must be hedged.

Diversification: purchasing securities from many different issuers, or industries, or geographic regions, to reduce "nonsystematic risk."

Diversified Mutual Fund: complies with an SEC rule so that no more than 5% of assets are invested in a particular stock or bond and so that the fund does not own more than 10% of any issuer's outstanding stock. Often called the "75-5-10 rule," where the 75 means that only 75% of the assets have to be diversified this way.

Dividend: a payment from a corporation's profits to an equity holder that must first be declared by the board of directors.

Dividend Payout Ratio: the annual dividends divided by the earnings per share, showing what percentage of earnings are paid out as dividends.

Dollar Cost Averaging: investing fixed dollar amounts regularly, regardless of share price. Usually results in a lower average cost compared to average of share prices, as investors' dollars buy majority of shares at lower prices.

Donation: a tax-deductible gift to a charitable organization where the donator deducts the fair market value of the security from income for purposes of reducing taxes paid.

Dow Jones Industrial Average: a price-weighted index or "basket" or 30 large-cap stocks.

DRIPs: dividend reinvestment programs in which investors automatically reinvest dividends into more shares (and fractional shares) of stock.

Dual-Purpose Fund: a closed-end fund with two classes of stock: income shares and capital shares. The income shares receive dividends and interest, while the capital shares receive capital gains distributions.

Due Diligence Meeting: the process in which the underwriters, issuer, attorneys, accountants, etc., review the final prospectus they are about to put out for accuracy and completeness. Remember that the SEC does not verify accuracy or adequacy of the information in the prospectus; this is the responsibility of the parties bringing the security to the primary market.

Durable Power of Attorney (Healthcare Power of Attorney): the authorization granted by an individual to a third party to make financial and/or healthcare decisions for the individual even after the individual is incapacitated.

Duration: a measure of a bond's price volatility. A duration of "10" means that for every 1% change in interest rates the bond's price will go up or down 10%.

E

Earned Income: income derived from active participation in a business, including wages, salary, tips, commissions, and bonuses. Alimony received is also considered earned income. Earned income can be used toward an IRA contribution.

Earnings Available to Common: the amount of earnings/net income left after any preferred stock dividends are paid. When divided by the number of outstanding shares, we arrive at the EPS/earnings per share.

Earnings per Share: the amount of net income/profit the company makes per share of common stock. Net income minus preferred dividends divided by the number of outstanding common shares. Or, "earnings available to common divided by outstanding shares."

Economic Indicator: economic data used by investors to interpret current or future investment possibilities and judge the overall health of an economy.

Education IRA: another name for the Coverdell Education Savings Account in which after-tax contributions may be made to pay qualified education expenses for the beneficiary.

Effective Date: the date declared by the SEC or state securities Administrator on which a new issue can be sold to investors.

Eligibility: a section of ERISA that outlines who is/is not eligible to participate in a qualified plan. Those 21 years old who have worked "full time" for one year (1,000 hours or more) are eligible to participate in the plan.

Emerging Market: the financial markets of a developing country. Generally, a small market with a short operating history, not as efficient or stable as developed markets. For example, Brazil, China, India.

Emerging Market Fund: a mutual fund investing in stocks and/or bonds issued and trading in emerging (undeveloped) markets.

Employment Indicator: economic indicators focused on employment, e.g., weekly claims for unemployment insurance, unemployment rate, and the employment cost index.

Equipment Trust Certificate: a corporate bond secured by a pledge of equipment, e.g., airplanes, railroad cars.

Equity: ownership, e.g., common and preferred stock in a public company. A type of fund focusing on equity securities.

Equity Securities: securities representing ownership of a corporation, i.e., common and preferred stock.

Equity Income Fund: a mutual fund that purchases common stocks whose issuers pay consistent and, perhaps, increasing dividends. The fund has less volatility than an equity fund with "growth" as an objective.

Equity Indexed Annuity (indexed annuity): a fixed annuity providing for limited participation in the gains of an index, usually the S&P 500.

Equity Style Box: a diagram by Morningstar showing where a mutual funds along the large cap value–to–small cap growth continuum.

ERISA: the Employee Retirement Income Security Act of 1974 that governs the operation of most corporate pension and benefit plans.

Estate: the assets owned by the deceased at the time of death.

Eurodollar Bonds: bonds issued and traded outside the US but denominated in US dollars. Not registered with the SEC (unlike "Yankee Bonds").

Exchanges: any electronic or physical marketplace where investors can buy and sell securities. For example, NASDAQ, NYSE, AMEX.

Exchange-listed Security: a security that has met listing requirements to trade on a particular exchange such as NYSE, AMEX, or NASDAQ.

Exchange Privilege: see "Conversion Privilege."

Exchange Traded Fund: called an "ETF," generally an index fund that trades among investors. Not a redeemable security except into something called a "creation unit." Associated with low management and other operating expenses, but is bought and sold like any other stock, with commissions added. Organized as a Unit Investment Trust (UIT) under the Investment Company Act of 1940.

Exclusion: excluded by definition. For example, a bank is excluded from the definition of "investment adviser."

Exclusion Ratio: the portion of a non-qualified annuity payment that is tax-exempt, representing a return of the investor's cost basis.

Ex-Dividend Date (Ex-Date): the date on which an upcoming dividend will not be received by a buyer in a regular way transaction. Two business days before the Record Date.

Executor: person named in the will charged with distributing assets to the beneficiaries of the estate.

Exemption: excused from registration requirements. A Treasury bond is a security, but it is excused from having to register. Therefore, it is an exempt security.

Exempt Security: a security not subject to registration requirements, e.g., a Treasury bond.

Exempt Transaction: a transaction done in a specific way to avoid registration requirements of otherwise non-exempt securities, e.g., a private placement.

Exercise Price: see "Strike Price."

Expansion: phase of the business cycle associated with increasing gross domestic product for at least two financial quarters.

Expected Return: the possible returns on an investment weighted by the probability of the outcomes.

Expense Ratio: a fund's expenses divided by/compared to average net assets. Represents operating efficiency of a mutual fund, where the lower the number the more efficient the fund.

F

Face-Amount Certificate: a debt security bought in a lump-sum or through installments that promises to pay out the stated face amount, which is higher than the investor's purchase price.

Face-Amount Certificate Company: one of the three types of investment company under the Investment Company Act of 1940. Issues face-amount certificates. Not a UIT of "management company."

Farm Credit System: organization of privately owned banks providing credit to farmers and mortgages on farm property.

FDIC (Federal Deposit Insurance Corporation): federal government agency that provides deposit insurance for member banks and prevents bank and "thrift" failures. Bank deposits are currently insured up to $250,000, a number that could have changed by the time you read this definition. A trip to your local bank will give you the updated number, assuming they're still open.

Federal Covered: covered exclusively at the federal level, SEC-registered. For example, a federal covered investment adviser or a federal covered security are not subject to state registration requirements. However, they are subject to filing a consent to service of process and the state's anti-fraud authorities.

Federal Reserve Board: a seven-member board directing the operations of the Federal Reserve System.

Federal Reserve System: the central bank system of the United States, with a primary responsibility to manage the flow of money and credit in this country.

Fed Funds Rate: overnight lending rate between/among banks.

FEIN: federal employer identification number. A tax identification number given to estates, corporations, and other entities.

FHLMC: the Federal Home Loan Mortgage Corporation, the smaller "cousin" of FNMA (Fannie Mae). Aka "Freddie Mac." A government-sponsored enterprise that purchase mortgages from lenders and issues various securities to investors that are not directly backed by the US Government.

Fiduciary: party who makes investment decisions for another party, putting the other party's interests first and foremost.

Final Prospectus: document delivered with final confirmation of a new issue of securities detailing the price, delivery date, and underwriting spread.

Financial Planner: a person who receives compensation for constructing financial plans that are generally all-encompassing, including retirement strategies, educational savings, tax-reduction strategies, wealth transfer, etc.

FINRA: the new securities regulator formed through a merger of NASD and NYSE regulators. A self-regulatory organization that licenses and regulates broker-dealers and their associated persons.

Firm Commitment: an underwriting in which the underwriters agree to purchase all securities from an issuer, even the ones they failed to sell to investors. Involves acting in a "principal" capacity, unlike in "best efforts," "all or none," and "mini-max" offerings.

First-In-First-Out (FIFO): an accounting method used to value a company's inventory or to determine capital gains/losses on an investor's securities transactions.

Fixed Assets: property with a long useful life that generally is depreciated gradually as a subtraction on the income statement. Equipment, factories, delivery vans, computers, and office furniture are all examples of fixed assets.

Fixed-Income: debt securities and preferred stock. A type of fund focusing on securities producing a stream of income.

FNMA: the Federal National Mortgage Association, a government-sponsored enterprise and shareholder-owned corporation that buys mortgages from lenders and issues various securities to investors that are not directly backed by the US Treasury.

Footnotes: explanatory notes included in a corporation's quarterly and annual reports providing details to help analysts interpret financial reports contained therein.

Foreign Exchange Risk: see "currency exchange risk."

Form ADV: registration form filed by Investment Advisers. Has a Part 1 and a Part 2—Part 2 can be used as the IA's disclosure brochure to customers.

Form ADV Part 2: an investment adviser's disclosure brochure that must be delivered to all prospects and offered to all existing customers (annually, upon written request).

Form ADV-W: a form used by an investment adviser to withdraw from either state or federal registration.

Form BD: registration form used by broker-dealers.

Form 8-K: a form used by a public company to announce an unusual material development that cannot wait until the next quarterly or annual report.

Form 144: a form filed with the SEC when an executive officer, director, or affiliate of the company is going to sell shares of that company's stock.

Form 1099-DIV: a tax-reporting form sent to mutual fund investors showing the dividends and capital gains paid out by the fund over the tax year.

Form U4: registration form for agents/representatives of broker-dealers, issuers, or investment advisers. Used when the agent/IAR associates with the firm.

Form U5: form used to terminate an agent's association with a broker-dealer, issuer, or investment adviser.

Fourth Market, INSTINET: an ECN (electronic communications network) used by institutional investors, bypassing the services of a traditional broker. Institutional = INSTINET.

Forward Pricing: the method of pricing redemption and purchase orders for open-end mutual funds, based on the NAV as next calculated by the fund.

Fraud: manipulation, deceit, trickery, etc., used for wrongful financial gain.

Free Credit Balance: the cash in a customer account that can be withdrawn.

Front-end Load: an open-end mutual fund share purchased with a sales charge added to the Net Asset Value. An A-share.

Frontrunning: a violation in which a firm or employee takes advantage of a large customer order to buy securities by first buying for themselves and then placing the customer order that will take the market price in the desired direction.

Frozen Account: an account in which purchase orders will be accepted only if the cash is in the account due to the customer's failure to comply with Reg T.

Fundamental Analysis: analyzing financial statements in order to uncover investment opportunities. Concerned with earnings per share, price-to-earnings ratio, profit margins, etc.

G

GDP: gross domestic product. Basically, it's the sum total of the economy's output, the total value of all goods and services being provided by the economy currently.

General Account: where an insurance company invests net premiums in order to fund guaranteed, fixed payouts.

General Obligation Bond: bond issued by a municipality and backed by the full faith and credit or full taxing authority of the issuer.

General Partnership: form of business ownership in which the owners agree to own the business jointly and with unlimited liability. Offers flow-through of income and expenses to the partners.

General Securities Representative: an agent who passed the Series 7 and may sell virtually any security, unlike a Series 6 holder, who sells mutual funds and variable contracts only.

Generic Advertising: communications with the public that promote securities as investments but not particular securities.

Gift: transferring property to someone else and expecting nothing in return, or selling something to someone for far less than its fair market value. Taxable to the giver if it exceeds the annual gift tax exclusion, most recently $13,000.

Gift Splitting: method of avoiding gift tax liability in which a married couple claims that a gift above the annual exclusion is half from one spouse and half from the other.

Ginnie Mae/GNMA: Government National Mortgage Association, an entity of the federal government that guarantees the timely payment of FHA, VA, and Rural Housing Authority mortgages. Financial institutions create pass-through securities based on pools of these guaranteed mortgages, paying investors interest and principal from the pool.

Global Fund: a mutual fund investing in companies located and doing business all across the globe, including the US.

Government Sponsored Enterprise: a privately held corporation that provides a public purpose and carries the implicit backing of the US Government—though not the explicit guarantee that comes with the "full faith and credit of the US Government." Examples include Freddie Mac and the Federal Farm Credit Bank. Without the explicit "direct obligation of the US Government" guarantee, these securities generally offer a higher yield than Treasury securities.

Grantor: the party who moves assets into a trust.

Growth Fund: a mutual fund investing with the objective of capital appreciation, not income.

Growth Investing: purchasing stocks in companies whose earnings are expected to grow faster than other companies' or faster than the overall market. Since much speculation is built into the stock's price, growth investors often pay high multiples, e.g., P/E or price-to-book.

Growth & Income: a fund that purchases stocks for growth potential and also for dividend income. Less volatile than pure growth funds due to the income that calms investors down when the ride becomes turbulent.

Growth Stock: common stock trading at high multiples and expected to grow faster than competitors and/or the overall market.

Guaranteed Bond: bond that is issued with a promise by a party other than the issuer to maintain payments of interest and principal if the issuer cannot. Bonds can be guaranteed as to payment of interest, principal, or dividends.

Guardian: a fiduciary who manages the financial affairs of a minor or a person declared mentally incompetent by a court of law.

H

Head-and-Shoulders: a chart pattern indicating the imminent reversal of a trend.

Hedge: to use options, futures, and various investment strategies designed to protect against an adverse movement in a particular stock or a particular index. To protect against systematic/market risk, investors can buy puts on broad-based indexes or sell ETFs short. To protect against un-systematic risk, investors can diversify and also buy puts/sell calls on particular securities.

Hedge Funds: private investment partnerships for people and institutions who can afford to lose more money than most people will ever see in a lifetime. Do not meet the definition of an "investment company" under the Investment Company Act of 1940 due to their lack of liquidity and accredited-investor requirements.

High-Yield: an investment whose income stream is very high relative to its low market price. A high-yield bond is either issued by a shaky company or municipal government forced to offer high nominal yields, or it begins to trade at lower and lower prices on the secondary market as the credit quality or perceived credit strength of the issuer deteriorates.

Holding Company: a company organized to invest in other corporations, e.g., Berkshire-Hathaway, which holds large stakes in other companies such as Coca-Cola, See's Candy, Dairy Queen, and Wells Fargo.

Holding Period: the length of time that an investor held a security for purposes of tax reporting. Starts the day after the trade date and ends with/includes the date of sale.

Holding Period Return: the return an investment provides irrespective of time frame. A 10% return over a 5-year-holding period is simply a holding period return of 10%.

Howey Decision: a US Supreme Court decision that defined an "investment contract" as "an investment of money in a common enterprise where the investor will profit solely through the efforts of others."

Hypothecation: using a security as collateral to secure a margin loan.

I

IARD: electronic registration system for investment advisers and IARs.

Immediate Annuity: an insurance contract purchased with a single premium that starts to pay the annuitant immediately. Purchased by individuals who are afraid of outliving their retirement savings.

Income Statement: financial statement showing the results of a company's operations over a particular time period, such as a financial quarter or fiscal year.

Income: investment objective that seeks current income, found by investing in fixed-income securities, e.g., bonds, money market, preferred stock. An equity income fund buys stocks that pay dividends; less volatile than a growth & income fund or a pure growth fund.

Income Bond: a bond that will pay interest only if the issuer earns sufficient income and the board of directors declares the payment.

Income Statement: a financial statement showing a corporation's results of operations over the quarter or year. Shows revenue, all expenses/costs, and the profit or loss the company showed over the period. Found in the annual shareholder report among other places.

Index: a theoretical grouping of stocks, bonds, etc., that aids analysts who want to track something. The Consumer Price Index is a theoretical grouping or "basket" of things that consumers buy, used to track inflation. The Dow Jones Industrial Average is a theoretical grouping of 30 large-company stocks that analysts use to track the stock market.

Index Fund: a mutual fund or exchange-traded fund that simply mimics an index, with no active portfolio management.

Indication of Interest: an investor's expression of interest in purchasing a new issue of securities after reading the preliminary prospectus; not a commitment to buy.

Individual Retirement Account (IRA): also called an "individual retirement arrangement" to make sure it has at least two names. A tax-deferred account that generally allows any individual with earned income to contribute 100% of earned income up to the current maximum contribution allowed on a pre-tax basis that reduces the current tax liability and allows investment returns to compound.

Inflation: rising prices resulting from high demand relative to supply.

Inflation-adjusted Return: another name for "real rate of return," the investor's return minus the rate of inflation.

Initial Public Offering (IPO): a corporation's first sale of stock to public investors. By definition, a primary market transaction in which the issuer receives the proceeds.

Injunction: a court order that orders a party to do or refrain from doing something. Also called "restraining orders."

Inside Information: material information about a corporation that has not yet been released to the public and would likely affect the price of the corporation's stock and/or bonds. Inside information may not be "disseminated" or acted upon.

Insider: for purpose of insider trading rules, an "insider" is anyone who has or has access to material non-public information. Officers, CEO, CFO, members of the board of directors, and investors owning > 10% of the company's outstanding shares are assumed to possess and have access to inside information. As fiduciaries to the shareholders, insiders may not use inside information to their benefit.

Insider Trading and Securities Fraud Enforcement Act (ITSFEA) of 1988: an Act of Congress that addresses insider trading and lists the penalties for violations of the Act. Insider traders may be penalized up to three times the amount of their profit or their loss avoided by using inside information.

Insurance: protection against loss of income due to death, disability, long-term care needs, etc.

Institutional Investor: not an individual. An institution is, for example, a pension fund, insurance company, or mutual fund. The large institutions are "accredited investors" who get to do things that retail (individual) investors often do not get to do.

Intangible Asset: property owned by the company that cannot be seen or touched but which allows the company to generate revenue. Patents, trademarks, and goodwill are examples of intangible assets.

Interest Rate Risk: the risk that interest rates will rise, pushing the market value of a fixed-income security down. Long-term bonds most susceptible.

Interest Rates: the cost of a commodity called money. In order to borrow money, borrowers pay a rate called an interest rate on top of the principal they will return at the end of the term. A one-year loan of $1,000 at 5% interest would have the borrower pay $50 on top of the $1,000 that will be returned at the end of the year.

Internal Revenue Code (IRC): tax laws for the US that define, for example, maximum IRA contributions, or the "conduit tax theory" that mutual funds use when distributing 90% of net income to shareholders, etc.

Internal Revenue Service (IRS): an agency for the federal government that no one seems to like very much. Responsible for collecting federal taxes for the US Treasury and for administering tax rules and regulations.

International Fund: a mutual fund investing in companies established outside the US.

Inter-positioning: a violation in which a specialist or broker-dealer inserts himself between a buyer and seller to pocket an improper/unnecessary commission.

Interstate Offering: an offering of securities in several states, requiring registration with the SEC.

Intestate: to die without a will.

In-the-Money: options that offer an inherent advantage to the owner by letting him buy lower (call option) or sell higher (put option) than the actual market value.

Intrastate Offering: an offering of securities made only in one state and subject to that state's regulatory authority, not the SEC's.

Intrinsic Value: (options) the amount that the market price exceeds the strike price of a call option, or the amount that the strike price exceeds the market price for a put option. Value investors also estimate intrinsic value of a stock to see if it can be purchased for less on the open market.

Inventory: finished goods that have yet to be sold and/or delivered to buyers.

Inverse Relationship: as one goes up, the other goes down and vice versa. There is an inverse relationship between bond prices and interest rates.

Inverted Yield Curve: interest rate environment in which short-term debt securities yield more than intermediate and long-term debt securities. Aka "negative yield curve."

Investment Adviser: any person who receives compensation for providing advice on investing in securities.

Investment Adviser Representative: individual who represents an investment adviser by selling the services of the firm, making or determining recommendations, managing accounts, or supervising those who perform such activities.

Investment Banker: a broker-dealer that advises and/or assists corporations and governments in raising capital.

Investment Company: a company engaged in the business of pooling investors' money and trading in securities on their behalf. Examples include unit investment trusts (UITs), face-amount certificate companies, and management companies.

Investment Company Act of 1940: federal legislation that classified investment companies (management, UIT, face-amount) and set rules for registration and operation.

Investment Contract: named as an example of a security in federal and state law and defined through the Howey Decision as "an investment of money in a common enterprise where the investor benefits solely through the efforts of others."

Investment Counsel: a title used by certain investment advisers. The Investment Advisers Act of 1940 stipulates that to use this title, the primary activity of the person must be providing investment advice, with a substantial part of that advice meeting the definition of "supervisory services."

Investment Grade: a bond rated at least BBB by S&P or Baa by Moody's. The bond does not have severe default risk, so it is said to be appropriate for investors, as opposed to the speculators who buy non-investment grade bonds.

Investment Objective: any goal that an investor has including current income, capital appreciation (growth), capital preservation (safety), or speculation.

Investment Policy Statement: documents that govern how a pension fund or other trust, for example, will and will not invest its assets.

Investment Style: an approach to investing, such as active, passive, or buy-and-hold.

Irrevocable Trust: a trust that may not be altered or revoked/canceled by the grantor. Because the trust is irrevocable, the grantor is no longer responsible for paying taxes on the income generated by the trust, and the assets do not count as part of the grantor's estate when he dies.

Issued Shares/Issued Stock: the number of shares of common stock that have been sold by a corporation to investors. Often a lower number than the number of shares authorized. Found by taking Issued − Treasury shares.

Issuer: any individual or entity who issues or proposes to issue any security. For example, the issuer of Google common stock is Google.

Issuing Securities: raising capital by offering securities to investors on the primary market.

J

Joint Account: investment account owned by more than one individual. Account owners sign a joint account agreement that stipulates which % of the assets is owned by each individual. Joint accounts are either "tenants in common" or "tenants with rights of survivorship."

JTWROS: Joint Tenants with Rights of Survivorship, a type of investment account usually shared by a husband and wife, where the assets of the deceased pass directly to the survivor…thus the "rights of survivorship" part of the title.

JTIC: Joint Tenants in Common, a type of investment account shared by two or more persons where the assets of the deceased pass to the deceased's estate, not the surviving account owners.

Junk Bond: a bond backed by a shaky issuer. It was either issued by an entity with shaky credit, or is now trading at a frightfully low price on the secondary market because the issuer's credit has suddenly or recently been downgraded. Since the price is low, given the low quality of the debt, the yield is high. High-yield and junk are synonymous.

K

K-1: a tax form filed by the owner of a pass-through entity such as a limited partnership or S-corporation.

Keogh: a qualified retirement plan available to sole proprietors with self-employment income. Not available to corporations. Pre-tax contributions, taxable distributions. Must cover all eligible employees.

L

Lagging Indicator: an economic factor that changes after the economy has already begun to follow a particular trend/pattern. For example, inventory levels or corporate profits.

Large Cap: a stock where the total value of the outstanding shares is large, generally greater than $10 billion. For example, GE, MSFT, IBM.

Last-In-First-Out (LIFO): an accounting method used for random withdrawals from an annuity. The IRS assumes that all withdrawals represent part of the taxable "excess over cost basis" first. Also an accounting method for valuing inventory.

Leading Indicator: an economic factor that changes before the economy begins to follow a particular trend. Leading indicators are used to predict changes in the economy, but are not always accurate. For example, the average hours worked by manufacturing workers, new claims for unemployment, building permits.

Legal Person: an entity such as a corporation, trust, or estate.

Legislative Risk: the risk that legislation will have a negative impact on the value of securities. For example, if investors lose favorable tax treatment for municipal bond interest or cash dividends on stock, the market price of those investments might plummet. Aka "regulatory risk."

Letter of Intent (LOI): an agreement to invest a certain amount of new dollars into a mutual fund in order to achieve breakpoint pricing without having to invest the entire amount as a lump sum. If the amount is not invested, shares held in escrow are taken back, but no penalties are assessed.

Level Load: an ongoing asset-based sales charge (12b-1 fee) associated with mutual fund C-shares. Appropriate for short-term investments only.

Leverage: using borrowed money to increase returns. Debt securities and margin accounts are associated with "leverage."

Liability: a minus to your account, something you have to pay out, e.g., accounts payable. One of the three categories on a balance sheet: assets, liabilities, net worth (shareholders' equity).

Life Settlement: an investment that pays out when somebody dies. If a 60-year-old policyholder sells her insurance policy with a $1 million death benefit to an investor for $700,000, the sooner the insured dies the better the investor's return and vice versa. Also known as a "viatical settlement."

Life Only/Life Annuity: a payout option whereby the insurance/annuity company promises to make payments only for the rest of the annuitant's life.

Life With Joint and Last Survivor: a payout option whereby the insurance/annuity company promises to make payments to the annuitant for the rest of his life, then to the survivor for the rest of her life.

Life With Period Certain: a payout option whereby the insurance/annuity company promises to make payments to the annuitant for the rest of his life or a certain period of time, whichever is greater.

Life With Unit Refund: a payout option whereby the insurance/annuity company promises to make at least a certain number of payments to the annuitant or beneficiary.

Limited Liability: an investor's ability to limit losses to no more than the amount invested. Holders of common stock and limited partnership interests enjoy "limited liability," which means they can only lose 100% of what they invest.

Limited Liability Company (LLC): form of business ownership in which the owners have limited liability for the company's actions. Provides flow-through of income and expenses to the owners, called "members."

Limited Partnership: form of business ownership with at least one general partner and at least one limited partner whereby the limited partners have limited liability and receive a direct flow-through of income and expenses.

Limited Trading Authorization: an authorization for someone other than the account owner to enter purchase and sale orders but make no withdrawals of cash or securities.

Limit Order: an order to buy or sell a security at a set price or better.

Liquidation Priority: the priority of claims on a bankrupt entity's assets that places creditors (bondholders) ahead of stockholders and preferred stockholders ahead of common stockholders.

Liquidity: ability to quickly convert an investment to cash and get a fair price. A home is not a liquid investment—100 shares of GE are extremely liquid. Mutual funds are very liquid, since the issuer has to pay the NAV promptly. The most liquid investment is the money market mutual fund.

Liquidity Risk: aka "Marketability Risk," the risk that an investor will not be able to turn a financial asset into cash either at all, or at a fair price.

Liquid Net Worth: an investor's net worth excluding assets that are difficult to sell quickly at a fair price (e.g., house, commercial properties, limited partnerships).

Long: to buy or own.

Long-Term Gain: a profit realized when selling stock held for at least 12 months plus 1 day. Subject to lower capital gains tax rates than short-term gains.

Long-Term Liability: an obligation listed on the balance sheet representing amounts to be paid out over the long-term, e.g., the principal value on bonds maturing in 10 years.

Long-Term Loss: a loss realized when selling stock held for at least 12 months plus 1 day. Used to offset long-term capital gains.

Lump Sum Payment: a settlement/payout option for annuities or insurance where the annuitant or beneficiary receives a lump sum payment. Go figure.

M

Management Company: one of the three types of Investment Companies, including both open-end and closed-end funds.

Management Fee: the % of assets charged to a mutual fund portfolio or other investing client to cover the cost of portfolio management.

Manager's Fee: typically the smallest piece of the spread, paid to the managing underwriter for every share sold by the syndicate.

Margin: amount of equity contributed by a customer as a percentage of the current market value of the securities held in a margin account.

Margin Account: a higher-risk account in which the broker-dealer extends loans to customers with the securities purchased serving as collateral.

Markdown: the difference between the highest bid price for a security and the price that a particular dealer pays an investor for her security.

Market Capitalization: the total current market value of an issuer's outstanding shares, found by multiplying the closing price of the stock times the shares outstanding.

Market Letter: a publication of a broker-dealer sent to clients or the public and discussing investing, financial markets, economic conditions, etc. Can be considered correspondence if sent to a limited number of clients; otherwise, considered sales literature and subject to pre-approval.

Market Maker: a dealer in the OTC market maintaining an inventory of a particular security and a firm Bid and Ask price good for a minimum of 100 shares. Acts as a "principal" on transactions, buying and selling for its/their own account.

Market Order: an order to buy or sell a security at the best available market price.

Market Risk: also called "systematic risk," the risk inherent to the entire market rather than a specific security. The risk that the stock market may suffer violent upheavals due to unpredictable events including: natural disaster, war, disease, famine, credit crises, etc. Market risk can be reduced by hedging with options or ETFs.

Marketability: the ease or difficulty an investor has when trying to sell a security for cash. Thinly traded securities have poor marketability.

Markup: the difference between the lowest ask/offer price for a security and the price that a particular dealer charges.

Material Information: any fact that could reasonably affect an investor's decision to buy, sell, or hold a security. For example, profits and losses at the company, product liability lawsuits, the loss of key clients, etc.

Maturity: the date that a bond pays out the principal, and interest payments cease. Also called "redemption."

Minimum Death Benefit: the minimum death benefit payable to the insured, regardless of how low the separate account returns are in a variable policy.

Minimum Net Capital: a specified minimum net worth required of broker-dealers or advisers who maintain custody of or exercise discretion over client assets.

Modern Portfolio Theory: A theory on how risk-averse investors can construct portfolios to optimize expected return based on a given level of market risk.

Monetary Policy: fighting inflation and stimulating the economy by manipulating short-term interest rates. Enacted by the FRB/FOMC.

Money Market Securities: short-term (one year or less) debt securities. Examples include commercial paper, banker's acceptance, T-bills.

Money Market Mutual Fund: a highly liquid mutual fund used to hold cash. Sometimes called "stable value" funds, as the share price is generally maintained at $1. The mutual funds invest in—surprisingly—money market securities.

Money Purchase: a retirement plan in which the employer must contribute a set percentage of the employee's salary, regardless of profitability.

Monte Carlo Simulation: a technique used to approximate the probability of certain outcomes by running various simulations that use random variables. Often used to determine a safe withdrawal rate from a retirement account given various possibilities for inflation, market returns, interest rates, etc.

Moody's Investors Service: one of the top three credit rating agencies for corporate and municipal bonds as well as stocks.

Mortality Guarantee: a promise from an insurance company to pay an annuitant no matter how long he lives, or to pay an insurance policyholder no matter how soon he dies.

Mortgage Bond: a corporate bond secured by a pledge of real estate as collateral.

Mortgage-backed Securities: debt securities created from the interest and principal payments made from a pool of mortgages.

Moving Average: the average closing price of a stock or index on a rolling basis. The 200-day moving average shows the average closing price of a stock or an index over the previous 200 days. Helps technical analysts spot up and down trends.

MSRB (Municipal Securities Rulemaking Board): the self-regulatory organization overseeing municipal securities dealers.

Municipal Bond Fund: a mutual fund that invests in municipal bonds with an objective to maximize federally tax-exempt income.

Municipal Note: a short-term obligation of a city, state, school district, etc., backed by the anticipation of funds from revenues, taxes, or upcoming bond issues.

Municipal Security/Municipal Bond: a security issued by a municipality borrowing money to construct roads, sewers, schools, stadiums, etc. Usually pays federally tax-free interest.

Mutual Fund: an investment company offering equity stakes in a portfolio that is usually managed actively and that always charges management fees and other expenses.

N

Naked Call: a call written by a seller who does not yet own the underlying shares he is obligated to sell at the strike price. Unlimited risk potential.

NASD: the National Association of Securities Dealers, a self-regulatory organization that licenses and regulates member firms and their associated persons. Now merged with the NYSE to form FINRA. Whatever we call them, investment advisers are not subject to their regulations—they regulate broker-dealers, not advisers.

NASDAQ: National Association of Securities Dealers Automated Quotation System.

Over-the-counter stocks with enough interest among traders to make it worth quoting prices all throughout the day. 4-letter symbols such as MSFT, ORCL, and INTC are NASDAQ stocks.

NASAA: North American Securities Administrators Association, a group of state and Canadian provincial regulators that attempts to standardize state/provincial securities regulations and help investors avoid being scammed.

Natural Event Risk: the risk that a natural disaster such as a hurricane or tsunami will disrupt securities markets and, therefore, the value of an investor's holdings.

Natural Person: an individual human being.

Negotiable: the characteristic of a security that allows an investor to sell or transfer ownership to another party. For example, savings bonds are not negotiable, while Treasury Bills are negotiable (able to be traded).

Negotiated Market: the over-the-counter market in which dealers negotiate prices among themselves as opposed to an auction market in which participants indicate competitive bids and offers on the floor of an exchange.

Net Asset Value (NAV): the current value of one share of a mutual fund portfolio. Calculated by taking net assets of the fund divided by the outstanding shares.

Net Income: or "net income after tax," the bottom line of the income statement; what's left after all subtractions from revenue have been made.

Net Investment Income: the source of an investment company's dividend distributions to shareholders. It is calculated by taking the fund's dividends and interest collected on portfolio securities, minus the operating expenses. Funds using the "conduit tax theory" distribute at least 90% of net investment income to avoid paying taxes on the amount distributed to shareholders.

Net Margin: or "net profit margin," a company's profit expressed as a percentage of revenue. The bottom line of the income statement divided by the top line; a company with $100 million in revenue and $10 million in net income has a 10% net margin.

Net Worth: the difference between what is owned and what is owed (assets − liabilities).

New Issue Market: the primary market, where securities are issued to investors with the proceeds going to the issuer of the securities. Initial public offerings (IPOs), for example, take place on the "new issue market."

Nominal Yield: the stated interest rate paid to the holder of a bond or other debt security.

Non-accredited Investor: an investor who does not meet various SEC net worth and/or income requirements. For a Reg D private placement, accredited investors may participate, but only a limited number of non-accredited investors may purchase the issue.

Non-cumulative Preferred Stock: a type of preferred stock that does not have to pay missed dividends (dividends in arrears).

Non-diversified Fund: a fund that doesn't care to meet the 75-5-10 rule, preferring to concentrate more heavily in certain issues.

Non-farm Payroll: a monthly figure showing the size of the workforce excluding farm workers and government employees. Also called "payroll employment."

Non-recourse Debt: a loan secured by collateral, but if the borrower defaults and the collateral is insufficient, the lender has no recourse to come after the borrower personally.

Non-systematic Risk: the risk that any one security could lose value. Reduced through diversification.

Normal Yield Curve: aka "positive yield curve," the usual situation in which longer-term bonds yield more than short-term debt securities of similar credit quality.

Note: a short-term debt security.

Notice Filing: a copy of the paperwork filed with the SEC that is sent to state regulators and accompanied by a notice filing fee and a U4 for each of the federal covered adviser's investment adviser representatives. Under NSMIA certain investment company shares also perform a notice filing with the state regulators.

NSMIA: National Securities Markets Improvement Act, 1996. Legislation that created "federal covered" status for certain investment advisers and certain securities. Seeks to clarify confusion and eliminate red tape created by redundancies and discrepancies between federal and state securities laws.

NYSE: New York Stock Exchange. An "auction market" for listed securities such as GE and IBM.

O

Obsolescence Risk: the risk that the company's products or service will become obsolete, e.g., 8-track tapes, printed encyclopedias, etc.

Odd Lot: a trade for less than the typical unit of stocks or bonds. For most common stock, an odd lot is a trade for fewer than 100 shares; 10 shares for preferred stock.

Odd Lot Theory: the theory that anyone too poor to buy or sell at least 100 shares of stock at a time is a loser who is so consistently wrong that the bigger, smarter traders can see what the odd lot losers are doing and win big by doing the opposite.

Offer: (1) the price at which a security may be purchased from a willing seller, (2) any attempt or offer to dispose of a security or an interest in a security for value—or the solicitation of an offer to buy a security (or interest in a security).

Omitting Prospectus: an advertisement for a mutual fund that typically shows performance figures without providing (omitting) the full disclosure contained in the prospectus. Therefore, it must present caveats and encourage readers to read the prospectus and consider all the risks before investing in the fund.

Open-End Fund: an investment company under the Investment Company Act of 1940 sub-classified as a management company whose shares are redeemable.

Operating Expenses: expenses that a mutual fund deducts from the assets of the fund, including board of director salaries, custodial and transfer agent services, management fees, 12b-1 fees, etc. Or, the operating expenses at any company that are not "cost of goods sold" or depreciation, amortization, interest, or taxes.

Opportunity Cost: the return on the security you could have bought but didn't.

Option: a derivative giving the holder the right to buy or sell something for a stated price up to expiration of the contract. Puts and calls.

Ordinary Dividends: dividends subject to the investor's ordinary income tax rate.

OTC/Over-the-Counter: called a "negotiated market." Securities traded among dealers rather than on exchanges. Includes NASDAQ and also Bulletin Board and Pink Sheet stocks, plus government, corporate, and municipal bonds.

OTC Bulletin Board: the over-the-counter stocks not welcome on NASDAQ. Many thinly traded stocks with very wide "spreads," which is another way of saying "liquidity risk."

Out-of-the-Money: an option offering no inherent advantage to the holder. An out-of-the-money call carries a strike price even higher than the current market price. If the stock trades for $50, the Jun 55 and Jun 60 calls are out-of-the-money.

Outstanding Shares: the number of shares that investors currently own. Found by taking Issued shares minus Treasury stock.

P

Par Value: the amount that a bond pays out at maturity.

Parity: equal, i.e., when the price of a convertible bond is exactly the same as the market price for the underlying stock it converts to.

Partial Surrender: when a life insurance policyholder cashes in part of the cash value. Excess over premiums is taxable.

Participating Preferred Stock: preferred stock whose dividend is often raised above the stated rate.

Participation: provision of ERISA requiring that all employees in a qualified retirement plan be covered within a reasonable length of time after being hired.

Passive Income: income derived from rental property, limited partnerships or other enterprises in which the investor is not actively involved.

Passive Loss: a loss from rental property, limited partnership or other enterprise in which the investor is not actively involved. Can only be used to offset passive (not ordinary or portfolio) income for tax purposes.

Passive Management: exclusive use of index funds rather than actively selecting securities. Linked heavily with "Random Walk Theory" and "Efficient Market Theory."

Pass-Through Certificate: a debt security based on a pool of mortgages paying investors part of the interest and principal being returned by the homeowners every month. GNMA, for example. Like a bond, except it repays principal gradually, rather than at maturity-only.

Payable Date: the date on which the dividend is paid to all shareholders of record.

Person: a legal entity including trusts, estates, broker-dealers, investment advisers and anything that is not dead, mentally incompetent, or a minor child.

Pink Sheets: thinly traded over-the-counter stocks associated with wide "spreads" or "liquidity risk."

Political Risk: the risk that a country's government will radically change policies or that the political climate will become hostile or counterproductive to business and financial markets.

Pooled Investment: sometimes called a "packaged product," includes open- and closed-end investment companies, unit investment trusts (UITs), REITs, and exchange-traded funds (ETFs). In all cases, a portfolio of securities or real estate is either overseen or managed by professionals and investors own units of that portfolio.

POP: public offering price. For an IPO, this includes the spread to the underwriters. For a mutual fund, this includes any sales loads that go to the underwriter/distributor.

Portfolio: a collection of stocks, bonds, money market securities, or any combination thereof that an investor owns.

Portfolio Income: income received from investments, including dividends, interest, capital gains, and royalties.

Pre-emptive Right: the right of common stockholders to maintain their proportional ownership if the company offers more shares of stock.

Preferred Stock: a fixed-income equity security with a stated rate of return, which makes it very sensitive to interest rates.

Premium: the price that the buyer pays and the seller receives for a call or put option. Also, the amount paid on an insurance contract to keep the policy in force.

Premium Bond: a bond purchased for more than the par value, usually due to a drop in interest rates.

Prepayment Risk: the risk that the mortgages underlying a mortgage-backed security/pass-through will be paid off sooner than expected due to a drop in interest rates. Investors reinvest the principal at a lower rate going forward.

Preservation of Capital: an investment objective that places the emphasis on making sure the principal is not lost. Also called "safety."

Price-to-Book Ratio: the market price of the stock compared to its book value.

Price-to-Earnings Ratio: the price of the stock compared to/divided by the earnings each share represents. If the EPS (earnings per share) equals $1, and the stock costs $20, the P/E is 20.

Primary Market: where issuers raise capital by selling/issuing securities to investors. As opposed to the secondary market, where securities are traded among investors.

Prime Rate: interest rate paid by creditworthy corporations for unsecured loans.

Principal: A) a firm that has capital at risk in a transaction. B) the amount of money to be repaid on a bond at maturity. C) the supervisor at a broker-dealer responsible for sales activities, advertising, compliance, etc.

Private Placement: an exempt transaction under Reg D (Rule 506) of the Securities Act of 1933, allowing issuers to sell securities without registration to accredited investors, who agree to hold them fully paid a certain time period before then selling them through Rule 144.

Private Securities Transaction: offering an investment opportunity not sponsored by the employing broker-dealer. Requires permission from the firm and any disclosure demanded; otherwise, a violation called "selling away."

Probate: the process of resolving all claims against the estate of a deceased person and redistributing assets according to a valid will.

Profit Sharing: a defined contribution plan whereby the company shares any profits with employees in the form of contributions to a retirement account.

Progressive Tax: a tax where the rate increases as the amount of the thing being taxed increases, e.g., income, estate, and gift taxes.

Prospectus: document used to give prospects full disclosure of important information about the security being offered and the issuing corporation itself.

Proxy: a form granting the power to vote according to a shareholder's instructions when the shareholder will not attend the meeting.

Public Appearance: addressing an audience on topics related to securities. Before speaking at a local Chamber of Commerce function, for example, registered representatives need prior principal approval.

Purchasing Power Risk: inflation or "constant dollar risk." Also, the risk that a fixed income payment will lose value due to inflation.

Put: an option to sell something at a set price.

Q

Qualified Client: an individual client of an investment adviser who can pay for performance because he/she meets net worth requirements or because he/she has sufficient assets under management and understands the risks involved with the program.

Qualified Dividends: dividends qualifying for a lower tax rate than most investors would pay for ordinary income.

Qualified Plan: a plan offered by an employer that must follow the rules of ERISA. Contributions are made with pre-tax dollars, leaving participants with no cost basis; therefore, all distributions are taxable at the ordinary income rate.

Qualified Purchaser: an investor that meets certain SEC criteria based on the amount of assets available. Certain securities are eligible for exemptions and advisers may charge performance-based compensation based on the "qualified purchaser" status of the investors.

R

Random Walk Theory: investment theory stating that a random selection of stocks is likely to perform as well or better than an actively managed portfolio.

Real GDP: Gross Domestic Product adjusted for inflation.

Real Estate Limited Partnership: a limited partnership formed to buy raw land, construct new housing, or buy existing properties. Unlike REITs, these investments require investors to verify net worth and do pass through a share of losses for tax shelter (especially in the initial phase of operations).

Real Rate of Return: an investor's return adjusted for inflation.

Rebalancing: a portfolio management style that seeks to maintain a particular mix of asset classes by periodically selling some securities and buying others to bring the portfolio back to the ideal mix.

Recession: economic decline lasting from two to six financial quarters.

Record Date: the date determined by the Board of Directors upon which the investor must be the holder "of record" in order to receive the upcoming dividend. Settlement of a trade must occur by the record date for the buyer to receive the dividend.

Redeemable Security: a security that may be redeemed or presented to the issuer for payment, e.g., open-end (but not closed-end) funds and UITs.

Redemption: an investor's sale of investment company shares back to an open-end fund or Unit Investment Trust. Or, when the issuer of a bond pays the final interest payment and returns the principal to retire the bonds at maturity.

Redemption Fee: a fee charged by a mutual fund when investors redeem shares before a certain time period, often one year. Discourages short-term trading of mutual funds.

Refunding: what a bond issuer does when calling an outstanding of bonds prior to maturity by issuing new bonds, usually at a lower nominal rate of interest.

Registrar: company hired by an issuer of common stock to audit the transfer agent.

Regressive Tax: any flat tax, such as sales, gasoline, or excise.

Reg A: a laid-back and predictable form of island music. Also, an exempt transaction under the Securities Act of 1933 for small offerings of securities ($5 million issued in a 12-month period).

Reg D: an exempt transaction under the Securities Act of 1933 for private placements.

Reg SHO: rules governing short sales requiring broker-dealers to first locate securities to be borrowed.

Reg T: established by the FRB as the amount of credit a broker-dealer may extend to a customer pledging a security as collateral for a margin loan. In a margin account, customers must put down ½ of the security's value, or at least $2,000.

Reg U: established by the FRB as the amount of credit a bank may extend to a broker-dealer or public customer pledging a security as collateral.

Registration by Coordination: used for interstate IPOs where the issuer registers with the SEC and then coordinates the process with the state regulators. Effective concurrent with federal release date provided certain conditions are met.

Registration by Filing (Notification): used for additional offerings of established issuers in solid financial condition.

Registration by Qualification: used for intra-state offerings where issuer is not filing with the SEC. Effective date established by Administrator.

Registration Statement: the legal document disclosing material information concerning an offering of a security and its issuer. Submitted to SEC under Securities Act of 1933.

Regular Way Settlement: T + 3, trade date plus three business days. T + 1 for Treasury securities.

Regulated Investment Company: an investment company using the conduit tax theory by distributing 90% or more of net investment income to shareholders.

Regulatory Risk: see "legislative risk."

Reinstatement Privilege: a feature of some mutual funds allowing investors to make withdrawals and then reinstate the money without paying another sales charge.

REIT: Real Estate Investment Trust. An equity security that usually pays the owner high dividend yields and allows him/her to participate in real estate without the traditional problems of liquidity and prohibitively large capital commitments.

Reinvestment Risk: the risk that interest and/or principal payments from debt securities will not be reinvested at attractive rates. Eliminated with zero coupons, such as STRIPS.

Release Date: date established by the SEC as to when the underwriters may sell new securities to the buyers; aka "effective date."

Repurchase Agreement (Repo): an agreement in which one party sells securities to the other and agrees to repurchase them for a higher price over the short-term, often next-day. The other party of the transaction is engaging in a "reverse repurchase agreement."

Required Minimum Distribution: the minimum amount that the owner of an IRA or other plan must withdraw by a certain age. For the Traditional IRA, the owner must begin making withdrawals/distributions by age 70½.

Rescission: the act of rescinding or un-doing a transaction done in violation of securities law.

Resistance: the upper limit of a stock's closing price over a certain time period, the price at which sellers step in to depress the price of the stock.

Respondent: the party named in an Administrative proceeding to deny, suspend, or revoke a registration/license.

Revenue: the top line of the income statement, aka "sales."

Revenue Anticipation Note (RAN): short-term debt obligation issued by a municipality and backed by future receipts of revenue … from user fees, tolls, etc.

Revenue Bond: municipal bond backed by the revenues generated by the facility being built with the bond proceeds, e.g., a bond issued to build a toll way and backed by the tolls collected.

Revocable Trust: a trust in which the provisions can be altered or canceled by the grantor.

Revocation/Revoke: an Administrative enforcement order that permanently nullifies the registration of an agent, broker-dealer, investment adviser, or investment adviser representative.

RIA: Registered Investment Adviser. Not a credential, just a statement of fact.

Rights: short-term equity securities that allow the holder to buy new shares below the current market price. Aka "subscription rights."

Rights Offering: additional offer of stock accompanied by the opportunity for each shareholder to maintain his/her proportionate ownership in the company.

Rights of Accumulation: for mutual fund A-shares, the right of the investor to have the current value of the account used to compute a breakpoint on future purchases.

Risk-Averse: an investor not able or willing to tolerate wide fluctuations in her investment account values.

Riskless Rate of Return: the rate on 3-month (90-day) T-bills. Used as a comparison in the Sharpe ratio to show if an investment with real risk did significantly better than the worry-free return on short-term T-bills. If not, why take that risk?

Risk Premium: the extra yield or return demanded by investors taking on extra risk. For example, investors generally demand higher yields on long-term bonds as a risk premium to compensate them for taking on higher price volatility.

Risk Tolerance: an investor's ability to withstand wide fluctuations in returns and/or principal values.

Rollover: moving retirement funds from a 401(k) to an IRA, or from one IRA to another. In a "60-day rollover," the check is cut to the individual, who must then send a check to the new custodian within 60 days to avoid early distribution penalties.

Roth IRA: individual retirement account funded with non-deductible (after-tax) contributions. All distributions are tax-free provided the individual is 59½ and has had the account at least five years.

Round Lot: the usual or normal unit of trading. 100 shares for common stock.

Rule (and Form) 144: regulates the sale of "control stock" by requiring board members, officers, and large shareholders to report sales of their corporation's stock and to adhere to volume limits. The form is filed as often as quarterly and no later than concurrently with the sale.

Rule 144a: rule that allows restricted securities to be re-sold to institutional investors including banks, insurance companies, broker-dealers, investment advisers, pension plans, and investment companies without violating holding period requirements.

Rule 145: rule that requires corporations in a proposed merger/acquisition to solicit the vote of the shareholders of both the purchasing and the acquired corporation.

S

S-Corporation (S-Corp): "corporations that elect to pass corporate income, losses, deductions and credit through to their shareholders for federal tax purposes. Shareholders of S-corporations report the flow-through of income and losses on their personal tax returns and are assessed tax at their individual income tax rates. This allows S-corporations to avoid double taxation on the corporate income."— *www.irs.gov*

Safety: an investment objective that seeks to avoid loss of principal first and foremost. Bank CDs, Treasury securities, and fixed annuities are generally suitable.

Sale/sell: (from the Uniform Securities Act) every contract of sale of, contract to sell, or disposition of, a security or interest in a security for value.

Sales Charge, Sales Load: a deduction from an investor's check that goes to the distributors/sellers of the fund. Deducted from investor's check, either when she buys (A-shares) or sells (B-shares).

Sales Literature: communications of a member broker-dealer delivered to a targeted, controlled audience, e.g., brochures, research reports, cold calling scripts.

Savings Bond: a US Government debt security that is not "negotiable," meaning it can't be traded or pledged as collateral for a loan. Includes EE and HH series bonds.

Scheduled Premium: life insurance with established, scheduled premium payments, e.g., whole life, variable life. As opposed to "universal" insurance, which is "flexible premium."

Secondary Offering/Distribution: a distribution of securities owned by major stockholders—not the issuer of the securities.

Secondary Market: where investors trade securities among themselves and proceeds do not go to the issuer.

Section 457 Plan: retirement plan for state and municipal workers, e.g., police and fire workers.

Secured Bond: a corporate bond backed by a pledge of specific assets as collateral, i.e., an "equipment trust certificate."

Sector Fund: a fund that concentrates heavily in a particular industry, e.g., a "Science & Technology Fund." Higher risk/reward than funds invested in many industries.

Secured Bond: a corporate bond secured by collateral, e.g., mortgage bond, collateral trust certificate, equipment trust certificate.

Securities Act of 1933: aka "Paper Act," regulates the new-issue or primary market, requiring non-exempt issuers to register securities and provide full disclosure to investors.

Securities and Exchange Commission: SEC, empowered by passage of Securities Exchange Act of 1934. A government body, the ultimate securities regulator.

Securities Exchange Act of 1934: prevents fraud in the securities markets. No person and no person exempt from anti-fraud regulations. Created/empowered the SEC. Requires broker-dealers, exchanges and securities associations to register with SEC. Requires public companies to report quarterly and annually to SEC.

Security: an investment of money subject to fluctuation in value and negotiable/marketable to other investors. Other than an insurance policy or fixed annuity, a security is any piece of securitized "paper" that can be traded for value.

Self-dealing: a breach of fiduciary duty in which an investment adviser uses client assets in a way that benefits the adviser, with no disclosure provided. For example, if an investment adviser uses client funds to invest in various other business ventures controlled/owned by the adviser and no disclosure is provided, the adviser is engaging in "self-dealing."

Self-Regulatory Organization: SRO, e.g., FINRA. An organization given the power to regulate its members. Not government bodies like the SEC, which oversees the SROs.

Selling Away: a violation that occurs when a registered representative offers investment opportunities not sponsored by the firm.

Selling Concession: typically, the largest piece of the underwriting spread going to the firm credited with making the sale.

Selling Dividends: a violation where an investor is deceived into thinking that she needs to purchase a stock in order to receive an upcoming dividend.

Selling Group: certain broker-dealers with an agreement to act as selling agents for the syndicate (underwriters) with no capital at risk.

Semi-Annual: twice per year, or "at the half year," literally. Note that "bi-annually" is an ambiguous term, which can mean "every two years" or "twice per year." Bond interest is paid semi-annually. Mutual funds report to their shareholders semi-annually and annually.

Senior Security: a security that grants the holder a higher claim on the issuer's assets in the event of a liquidation/bankruptcy.

Separate Account: an account maintained by an insurance/annuity company that is separate from the company's general account. Used to invest clients' money for variable annuities and variable insurance contracts. Registered as an investment company under Investment Company Act of 1940.

SEP-IRA: pre-tax retirement plan available to small businesses. Favors high-income employees (compared to SIMPLE). Only employ-er contributes.

Series I Bond: a savings bond issued by the US Treasury that protects investors from inflation or purchasing power risk.

Settlement: final completion of a securities transaction wherein payment has been made by the buyer and delivery has been made by the seller.

Settlement Options: payout options on annuities and life insurance including life-only, life with period certain, and joint and last survivorship.

Share Identification: a method of calculating capital gains and losses by which the investor identifies which shares were sold, as opposed to using FIFO or average cost.

Sharpe Ratio: a method of measuring returns adjusted for risk in which only portfolio returns above the "riskless rate of return" are counted, and then divided by standard deviation. The higher the Sharpe Ratio the better the investor is being compensated for risk.

Short: to initiate a position by selling.

Short Sale: method of attempting to profit from a security whose price is expected to fall. Trader borrows certificates through a broker-dealer and sells them, with the obligation to replace them at a later date, hopefully at a lower price. Bearish position.

Short-Term Capital Gain: a profit realized on a security held for 12 months or less.

Short-Term Capital Loss: a loss realized on a security held for 12 months or less, deductible against Short-Term Capital Gains.

SIMPLE IRA: a retirement plan for businesses with no more than 100 employees that have no other retirement plan in place. Pre-tax contributions, fully taxable distributions. Both employer and employees may contribute.

Simple Trust: a trust that accumulates income and distributes it to the beneficiaries annually.

Simplified Arbitration: a method of resolving disputes involving a small amount of money.

Single-Payment Deferred Annuity: annuity purchased with a single payment wherein the individual defers the payout or "annuity" phase of the contract.

Single-Payment Immediate Annuity: annuity purchased with a single payment wherein the individual goes immediately into the payout or "annuity" phase of the contract.

Sinking Fund: an account established by an issuing corporation or municipality to provide funds required to redeem a bond issue.

SIPC: Securities Investor Protection Corporation, a non-profit, non-government, industry-funded insurance corporation protecting investors against broker-dealer failure.

SMA (Special Memorandum Account): a line of credit in a margin account.

Small Cap: a stock where the total value of all outstanding shares is considered "small," typically between $50 million and $2 billion.

Sole Proprietor: someone who owns an unincorporated business by him or herself.

Solicit: to entice or attempt to interest someone in what you're selling.

Solicitor: any person who, directly or indirectly, solicits any client for, or refers any client to, an investment adviser.

Solvency: the ability of a corporation or municipality to meet its obligations as they come due.

Specialist: NYSE member that maintains a fair and orderly market in a particular exchange-listed security.

Specialized Fund: a mutual fund that specializes in a particular approach, e.g., covered-call writing, sector funds

Spousal Account: an IRA established for a non-working spouse.

Spread: generally, the difference between a dealer's purchase price and selling price, both for new offerings (underwriting spread) and secondary market quotes. For underwritings the spread is the difference between the proceeds to the issuer and the POP.

Spread Load: sales charges for a mutual fund contractual plan that permits a maximum charge of 20% in any one year and 9% over the life of the plan.

Stabilizing/Stabilization: the surprising practice by which an underwriting syndicate bids up the price of an IPO whose price is dropping in the secondary market.

Standard Deviation: the degree to which an investment's returns deviate from the average return. A measure of volatility.

Standby Underwriting: a commitment by an underwriter to purchase any shares that are not subscribed to in a rights offering.

Statute of Limitations: a time limit that, once reached, prevents criminal or civil action from being filed.

Statutory Disqualification: prohibiting a person from associating with an SRO due to disciplinary or criminal actions within the past 10 years, or due to filing a false or misleading application or report with a regulator.

Statutory Voting: method of voting whereby the shareholder may cast no more than the number of shares owned per candidate/item.

Stock: an ownership or equity position in a public company whose value is tied to the company's profits (if any) and dividend payouts (if any).

Stock Dividend: payment of a dividend in the form of more shares of stock; not a taxable event.

Stockholders' Equity: another name for the "net worth" of a company, found on the balance sheet by subtracting liabilities from assets.

Stock Market Data: information about the stock market used by technical analysts, including volume, 200-day moving average, etc.

Stock Split: a change in the number of outstanding shares designed to change the price-per-share; not a taxable event.

Straddle: buying a call and a put on the same underlying instrument with the same strike price and expiration…or selling a call and a put on the same underlying instrument with the same strike price and expiration. For example, an investor who buys an ABC Aug 50 call and buys an ABC Aug 50 put is establishing a "long straddle."

Straight Life Annuity: a settlement option in which the annuity company pays the annuitant only as long as he or she is alive. Also called "straight life" or "life only."

Straight Preferred: a preferred stock whose missed dividends do not go into arrears, aka "non-cumulative preferred."

Strike Price: the price at which the underlying security of an option can be bought or sold, regardless of the actual market price. Aka "exercise price."

STRIPS: Separate Trading of Registered Interest and Principal of Securities. A zero coupon bond issued by the US Treasury in which all interest income is received at maturity in the form of a higher (accreted) principal value. Avoids "reinvestment risk." Aka "Treasury STRIPS."

Subaccount: investment option available within the separate account for variable contract holders. Basically, a mutual fund that grows tax-deferred.

Subchapter M: section of the Internal Revenue Code providing the "conduit tax treatment" used by REITs and mutual funds distributing 90% or more of net income to shareholders. A mutual fund using this method is technically a Regulated Investment Company under IRC Subchapter M.

Subordinated Debenture: corporate bond with a claim that is subordinated or "junior" to a debenture and/or general creditor.

Suitability: a determination by a registered representative that a security matches a customer's stated objectives and financial situation.

Summarily Suspend (verb) or Summary Suspension (noun): a rare order issued by the securities Administrator when a situation appears so dangerous and out-of-control that the respondents must be stopped even without prior notice and even before a hearing has been granted/held.

Supervision: a system implemented by a broker-dealer to ensure that its employees and associated persons comply with federal and state securities law, and the rules and regulations of the SEC, exchanges, and SROs.

Support: the price at which investors continue to step in and bid the stock's price back up.

Surety Bond: form of insurance required under the Uniform Securities Act for investment advisers, broker-dealers, and agents with custody or discretion over client assets.

Surrender: to cash out an annuity or life insurance policy for its surrender value.

Surrender Charge: the penalty to the annuitant from the insurance/annuity company charged on withdrawals during the surrender period.

Surrender Period: the period during which surrender charges apply to withdrawals on an annuity contract.

Syndicate: a group of underwriters bringing a new issue to the primary market.

Systematic Risk: another name for "market risk," or the risk that an investment's value could plummet due to an overall market panic or collapse.

T

T-bill (Treasury bill): short-term direct obligation of the US Treasury issued at a discount, maturing at the face value. Maturities are one year or shorter, with 3-month and 6-month the most common maturities.

T-note (Treasury note): interest-paying direct obligation of the US Treasury with a 2- to 10-year maturity.

T-bond (Treasury bond): interest-paying direct obligation of the US Treasury with a 10- to 30-year maturity.

Tactical Asset Allocation: changing the allocation of a portfolio based on anticipated market developments. Related to "market timing" as opposed to "strategic asset allocation."

Tax Anticipation Note (TAN): a short-term debt obligation issued by a municipality and backed by future tax receipts.

Tax and Revenue Anticipation Note (TRAN): a short-term debt obligation issued by a municipality and backed by future receipt of taxes and revenues.

Tax Credit: an amount that can be subtracted from the amount of taxes owed.

Tax Deduction: a subtraction from income that reduces taxable income and, therefore, taxes owed. For example, a Traditional IRA contribution.

Tax Deferral: putting off the payment of taxes until the investor takes constructive receipt—either by taking distributions from a retirement plan or selling securities for capital gains.

Tax-Deferred: an account where all earnings remain untaxed until "constructive receipt."

Tax-Equivalent Yield: the rate of return that a taxable bond must offer to equal the tax-exempt yield on a municipal bond. To calculate, take the municipal yield and divide that by (100% − investor's tax bracket).

Tax-Exempt Bonds: municipal bonds whose interest is not subject to taxation by the federal government.

Tax-Exempt Money Market Mutual Fund: a money market fund that receives tax-exempt interest by purchasing short-term municipal debt obligations.

Tax Preference Item: certain items that must be added back to an investor's income for purposes of AMT, including interest on certain municipal bonds.

Tax-Sheltered Annuity (TSA): an annuity funded with pre-tax (tax-deductible) contributions. Available to employees of non-profit organizations such as schools, hospitals, and church organizations. The investment vehicle used for 403b plans.

Technical Analysis: using market data (price, volume, moving averages, etc.) to evaluate stocks and the overall markets.

Term Life Insurance: insurance policy that provides only for a death benefit and no cash value. When each term expires, the policy must be renewed at a higher rate. Suitable for young parents who need to protect their children but have limited financial resources.

Third Market: exchange-listed stock traded OTC primarily by institutional investors.

Third-Party Account: account managed on behalf of a third party, e.g., trust or UGMA.

Time Horizon: an investor's anticipated holding period for an investment.

Timing Risk: the risk of purchasing an investment at a peak price not likely to be sustained or seen again. Timing risk can be reduced through dollar cost averaging, rather than investing in a stock with one purchase.

Tippee: the guy who listened to the insider information.

Tipper: the guy who told him.

TIPS (Treasury Inflation Protected Securities): a direct obligation of the US Government, and a negotiable security, that protects the holder from inflation by increasing the amount of principal the coupon rate is applied to due to increases in the Consumer Price Index.

Tombstone: an advertisement allowed during the cooling-off period to announce an offer of securities, listing the issuer, the type of security, the underwriters, and directions for obtaining a prospectus.

Top-down Analysis: using fundamental analysis that starts with the overall economy and then moves down to industries and particular companies within industries.

Total Return: yield plus capital appreciation, compared to original investment. For a stock or bond, total return represents the income paid as dividends or interest and the amount the security has advanced or declined in value.

Trading Authorization: a form granting another party the authority to make trading decisions for the investor. Aka "power of attorney."

Traditional IRA: individual retirement arrangement/account offering tax-deductible contributions and tax-deferred earnings. Income is subject to ordinary income tax when withdrawn and withdrawals must begin by age 70½.

Trade Confirmation: a document containing details of a securities transaction, e.g., price of the security, commissions, stock symbol, number of shares, registered rep code, trade date and settlement date, etc.

Trade Date: the date that a trade is executed.

Trading Authorization: a form granting another individual the authority to trade on behalf of the account owner. Either "limited" (buy/sell orders only) or "full" (buy/sell orders plus requests for checks/securities) authorization may be granted. Sometimes referred to as "power of attorney."

Tranche: a class of CMO. Principal is returned to one tranche at a time in a CMO.

Transfer Agent: a firm hired by an issuer to maintain records of shareholders. Transfer agents: issue and redeem certificates, handle name changes, validate mutilated certificates, distribute dividends, gains, and shareholder reports to mutual fund investors.

Transfer on Death: individual account with a named beneficiary—assets transferred directly to the named beneficiary upon death of the account holder.

Treasury Receipt: a zero coupon bond backed by US Treasury securities, but not a direct obligation of the US Treasury. Created by a financial institution.

Treasury Security: a debt security issued and guaranteed by the US Treasury. For example: T-bill, T-note, T-bond, STRIPS. Aka "government securities."

Treasury Stock: shares that have been issued and repurchased by the corporation. Has nothing to do with the US Treasury.

Treasury STRIPS: see "STRIPS."

Trough: phase of the business cycle marking the end of a contraction, just before the next expansion/recovery.

Trust: a legal entity holding assets to be used according to trust documents.

Trustee: a person legally appointed to act on a beneficiary's behalf.

Trust Indenture: a written agreement between an issuer and creditors wherein the terms of a debt security issue are set forth, e.g., interest rate, means of payment, maturity date, name of the trustee, etc.

Trust Indenture Act of 1939: corporate bond issues in excess of $5 million with maturities greater than one year must be issued with an indenture.

U

U4: a form used to register an agent or an investment adviser representative as an associated person of a firm or an issuer.

U5: a form used to terminate the association of an agent or investment adviser representative.

UGMA: Uniform Gifts to Minors Act, a custodial account established for the benefit of a minor—currently used in only two states.

UIT: Unit Investment Trust. A type of investment company where investments are selected, not traded/managed. No management fee is charged. Shares are redeemable.

UTMA: Uniform Transfers to Minors Act, a custodial account established for the benefit of a minor.

Unearned Income: income derived from investments and other sources not related to employment, e.g., savings account interest, dividends from stock, capital gains, and rental income.

Uniform Securities Act: a model act that state securities laws are based on. Designed to prevent fraud and maintain faith in capital markets through registration of securities, agents, broker-dealers, and investment advisers. Main purpose is to provide necessary protection to investors.

Unit of Beneficial Interest: what an investor in a Unit Investment Trust (UIT) owns.

Universal Life Insurance: a form of permanent insurance that offers flexibility in death benefit and both the amount of, and method of paying, premiums.

Unrealized Gain: the increase in the value of a security that has not yet been sold. Unrealized gains are not taxable.

Unsecured Bond: a debenture, or bond issued without specific collateral.

Un-systematic Risk: the risk that any one investment could lose value. Reduced through diversification.

V

Valuation Ratio: a comparison of a stock's market price to the company's cash flow, sales, earnings, or book value per-share.

Value: as in "value investing" or a "value fund," the practice of purchasing stock in companies whose share price is currently depressed. The value investor feels that the stock is trading below its "estimated intrinsic value" and, therefore, sees an opportunity to buy a good company for less than it's really worth. Like a "fixer-upper" house in need of a little "TLC." With a few quick improvements, this property is going to be worth a lot more than people realize.

Value Stock: common stock currently out-of-favor with investors and trading at low multiples to earnings, book value, etc.

Variable Annuity: an annuity whose payment varies. Investments allocated to separate account as instructed by annuitant. Similar to investing in mutual funds, except that annuities offer tax deferral. No taxation until excess over cost basis is withdrawn.

Variable Life Insurance: form of insurance where death benefit and cash value fluctuate according to fluctuations of the separate account.

Variable Universal Life Insurance: flexible-premium insurance with cash value and death benefit tied to the performance of the separate account.

Vesting: a schedule for determining at what point the employer's contributions become the property of the employee.

Viatical Settlement: aka "life settlement," the sale and purchase of a life insurance policy wherein the investor buys the death benefit at a discount and profits as soon as the insured dies.

Volatility: the up and down movements of an investment that make investors dizzy and occasionally nauseated.

Volume: the number of shares traded.

W

Warrants: long-term equity securities giving the owner the right to purchase stock at a set price. Often attached as a "sweetener" that makes the other security more attractive.

Wash Sale Rule: the rule requiring an investor selling a security at a loss to stay out of that security for a full 30 days before and after the sale.

Whole Life Insurance: insurance policy that pays a guaranteed death benefit and builds cash value that can be borrowed or withdrawn by the policy owner. The premium is fixed over the life of the policy and may actually be reduced over time due to a payment of dividends by the insurance company.

Willful Violation: a violation of securities law in which the defendant knew what he was doing. As the notes to the Uniform Securities Act explains, "As the federal courts and the SEC have construed the term 'willfully' ... all that is required is proof that the person acted intentionally in the sense that he was aware of what he was doing. Proof of evil motive or intent to violate the law, or knowledge that the law was being violated, is not required."

Withdrawal: a non-punitive administrative order in which the registrant notifies a securities regulator that they will no longer register with that regulator. For example, a federal covered adviser whose assets fall below $100 million would withdraw its registration with the SEC by filing a form ADV-W and would then register with the state or states where they maintain a place of business or have more than 5 non-institutional clients.

Working Capital: Current Assets minus Current Liabilities. A short-term measure of liquidity for a company.

Wrap Fee/Program: charging an advisory client one fee for all services rendered—advice, execution, billing, etc.

Y

Yankee Bond: bonds issued by foreign issuers, denominated in US Dollars, and registered with the SEC.

Yield: the income that a security produces. Bond interest, for example, or dividends paid on stock.

Yield Curve: the different yields currently available on debt securities of similar credit quality according to their term-to-maturity. A positive yield curve shows yields on long-term securities higher than short-term. An inverted yield curve shows the yields on short-term securities higher than on long-term. A "flat yield curve" reveals similar yields across all maturities.

Yield Spread: the difference between the yields on high-quality bonds and low-quality bonds. The greater the spread, the less confident investors are about the financial strength of bond issuers.

Yield to Call: a calculation that factors in all the coupon payments received plus/minus what the investor in a debt security makes/loses if the bond is called at the earliest call date.

Yield to Maturity: a calculation that factors in all the coupon payments received plus/minus what the investor in a debt security makes/loses at maturity.

Z

Zero Coupon Bond: a bond that does not distribute interest payments per se. Rather, the par value goes up over time, and the difference between the purchase price and the par value is treated as interest income. Eliminates "reinvestment risk."

Index